W9-BCT-961

9-5-61   57-8884   Powell

The South
in Northern Eyes
1831 to 1861

917.5
F

The South
in Northern Eyes
1831 to 1861

By HOWARD R. FLOAN

Austin : University of Texas Press

Wingate College Library

Library of Congress Catalog Card No. 57–8824
© 1958, by the University of Texas Press

Manufactured in the United States of America
by the Printing Division of the University of Texas

To
Maxine

16218

Preface

ALTHOUGH we have given much attention to the events leading to the Civil War and to the question of its "irrepressibility," one of the most haunting aspects of the struggle, the psychological conditioning for civil war, has been left comparatively untouched. To explore this aspect meaningfully, one must re-create a point of view that was current with the steadily mounting tensions between North and South during the middle third of the nineteenth century. My purpose in writing this book has been to present to the reader attitudes held toward the South by the major Northern men of letters who were actively writing during this period and, wherever possible, to identify an ante bellum image of the South. How relentlessly the sense of cultural difference prepared Northern minds for the grim logic of the battlefield can be significantly revealed by tracing the picture of the South through some of the best minds of the age. (Indeed, I need hardly note that the greatest crisis this nation has ever faced coincided with our greatest generation of writers.) What is more, as antagonisms grew, these men of letters became inescapably involved in the question of the conflicting demands of art and controversy. Their varying response to this question, as well as their place in the range of Northern opinion of the South, tells us much about these writers, while at the same time it gives us an added awareness of the debilitating effects of propaganda upon the processes of literary creation.

In order to view this subject in relation to the larger picture of Northern opinion, I have also considered some representative New England and New York periodicals, and, at the same time, I have dealt briefly with certain writers who either antedated this group of

major men of letters or were less prominent than they as literary figures. Since my presentation extends from those writers of least sympathy to those of most sympathy, the result is a spectrum that shows
the shadings of regional differences; for, in general, I have found the
enmity among the New England writers, the sympathy among the
New York writers. I have used a descriptive approach to the subject
matter, believing that such a presentation—when read from the relative detachment of the mid-twentieth century—best reveals American character under stress and that it does so with cumulative force.

The reader may reasonably ask what the South was actually like on
the eve of the Civil War. There were few Americans of the time who
knew. Reliable news coverage of the national scene was as yet unknown. In a day when travel was both slow and arduous, only a small
number of Northerners had been in the South. The Southerner, on
the other hand, tended to judge the entire South on the basis of his
immediate region, and thus he often failed to appreciate the variety
of the South. The importance of the Southern frontier, never accurately or completely assessed, was almost totally disregarded before
the Civil War by Northerners and by many Southerners. Moreover,
the eyes of both were well adjusted to the distorting haze of proslavery and antislavery propaganda. It has been left to our present
generation of historical scholars to pursue the systematic and disinterested answer to the question of what the ante bellum South was
actually like.

There has been a tendency, stubbornly persistent even in our time,
to mistake the planter aristocracy for the entire South, to envision the
Southerner simply as the slaveholder. It is therefore important to
point out that if one could identify an average Southerner of the
eighteen fifties, statistics would demand that he be, at least by plu-
rality of numbers, a nonslaveholding white farmer who cultivated a
few acres with the help of his wife and children. Of eight million
whites, less than four hundred thousand owned slaves, about half of
whom owned as many as ten. A small nucleus, about 4 per cent of all
slaveholders, held one hundred or more slaves. Yet it was the large
slaveholder, fictionalized by partisan pens, that has constituted popular portraits of the South.

Moreover, a sense of history was conspicuously lacking in ante bellum Northern views of the South. It is not inappropriate here to recall that the beginnings of slavery coincide with the first English settlements in America. During the seventeenth century slave-traders of many nations joined in establishing in America, North and South, an institution which was not to become "peculiar" in anyone's eyes for nearly two centuries. No generation was alone responsible for the enslavement of men; but no generation could escape the mounting social tensions and moral complexities that accompanied its growth. By the time prevailing ideologies of the world had become expressly opposed to slavery, most Southerners had come to consider it indispensable to either their economic or their social well-being. Viewing the South from a historical perspective, one must sooner or later come to regard slavery less as the crime and more as the calamity of the South, particularly of its Civil War generation. To understand the tragedy of the South is to realize that it is inescapably America's tragedy.

I wish to express my gratitude to the Graduate English Faculty of Columbia University, under whose direction this work was originally done, to Professor Lionel Trilling for suggesting to me the subject of this study, to Professor Elliott Van Kirk Dobbie for many helpful suggestions, to Professor Dumas Malone, of the Department of History, for valuable criticism. I especially wish to express my indebtedness to Professor Lewis Leary for his discerning and inspirational guidance. I would like also to acknowledge the generous help of my wife, whose patience, understanding, and candid criticisms have been invaluable.

For permission to quote from material under copyright, I am indebted to Professor Odell Shepard, Professor Ralph Leslie Rusk, Mr. Edward W. Forbes, President of the Emerson Memorial Association, to Houghton Mifflin Company, Random House, Inc., G. P. Putnam's Sons, Harcourt, Brace and Company, Inc., Columbia University Press, Harvard University Press, and the Bald Eagle Press. Portions of Chapter 9 have appeared in the *American Quarterly*, VIII, Fall, 1956, under the title "The New York *Evening Post* and the Ante-bellum South."

HOWARD R. FLOAN

Bronxville, New York, 1957

Contents

Part I

New England

· 1 ·

Garrison and Phillips

DURING the middle third of the nineteenth century the New Englander became highly conscious of social wrongs, and, imbibing "the new wine of idealism," he developed a passion for reform. In 1844 Ralph Waldo Emerson observed sardonically: "What a fertility of projects for the salvation of the world!"[1] In the preface to *Uncle Tom's Cabin*, Harriet Beecher Stowe exclaimed that a new day had dawned in America: "The hand of benevolence is everywhere stretched out, searching into abuses, righting wrongs, alleviating distresses, and bringing to the knowledge and sympathies of the world the lowly, oppressed, and the forgotten." More and more the artists of the land were tuning their hearts to "the great master chord of Christianity, good-will to man." This was 1852. For over twenty years a small though steadily growing number of people had striven to build up an atmosphere if not of benevolence then at least of moral fervor. William Lloyd Garrison's determination to make himself heard, which he so tersely expressed in the first issue of the *Liberator* (January 1, 1831), had been realized. He and his followers had fanned the coals of New England idealism and prepared it for the stoking which Mrs. Stowe so effectively administered with the picture of life among the lowly.

[1] Ralph Waldo Emerson, "New England Reformers," *The Complete Works of Ralph Waldo Emerson* (Houghton Mifflin Co., Boston, 1883–93), III, 240. Hereafter cited as Emerson, *Works*.

The times were propitious for the growth of dissension between North and South. Political and economic policies that were necessary concomitants to the plantation system inevitably conflicted with Northern interests. Such issues as the tariff, internal improvements, and subsidies to transatlantic shipping continually stirred up strife. As the nation expanded toward the West the question of how to govern the new territories necessarily became insistent. Lands acquired from Mexico during the latter half of the eighteen forties accentuated intersectional antipathies and nearly brought about Southern secession. As tensions increased, there was a growing tendency among New Englanders to transfer their hostility toward slavery to the South itself, thus merging two separate but related subjects. After the Compromise of 1850, the Fugitive Slave Law furnished more fuel for the abolitionist agitators in New England. Aroused by the attempt in 1854 to open Kansas and Nebraska to slavery, irate New Englanders sent rifles and recruits to Kansas, which became known as "the bloody ground." To many Northerners, President Buchanan's attitude toward the Kansas issue appeared to lend credence to abolitionist charges that the federal government was under the control of the South. Growing dissension reached a high point in the Senate when, in 1856, Charles Sumner, the antislavery senator from Massachusetts, was assaulted by Preston Brooks, of South Carolina. In the following year the Supreme Court handed down the Dred Scott decision with the famous extrajudicial opinion that Congress had no constitutional power to prohibit slavery in the territories. To many, the spirit of compromise which had prevailed in 1820 and again in 1850 seemed dead. In 1859 the earlier violence in Kansas was brought closer to the nation's heart by John Brown's attempt to incite a slave insurrection in Virginia. With the success of the newly formed Republican party in 1860, economic and political antagonisms had nearly completed their regional alignment.

Although it is necessary to keep in mind the background of political events leading to the Civil War, one must realize that in determining the attitudes of New England literary men toward the South a consideration of their political affiliations is not of primary importance. Their attitudes, deriving from a hatred of slavery, first were based on moral grounds and then gradually extended to the political. The nature of John Greenleaf Whittier's political activities was determined by his abolitionism; James Russell Lowell's political position was dictated by his humanitarianism; and Henry Wadsworth Longfellow's support of Charles Sumner was an expression of his antislavery opinions. Ralph Waldo Emerson and Henry David Thoreau were not men to echo the sentiments of a political party. But these writers shared the conviction prevailing in New England that slavery was contrary both to the teachings of Christ and to the expressed principles of natural rights upon which American society was based. These elements in the New England cultural soil made it possible for abolitionism to grow. Because New England literary figures expressed the spirit of abolitionism in their writings, it is important to consider what was being said by the most severe exponents of the abolition movement in New England, William Lloyd Garrison and Wendell Phillips.[2]

When, in the first issue of the *Liberator,* Garrison swore that he would be "as harsh as truth," he was in earnest.[3] Agitation in the United States has never known a more dedicated practitioner. His zeal, however, was more productive of harshness than of truth, for one sees the distorting power of abolition rhetoric and notes the facility with which Garrison and his colleagues fell into the habit of fictionalizing a way of life that was out of harmony with their own. Garrison's hatred of slavery became hatred of the slaveholder, and the slaveholder became indistinguishable from the Southerner. Any Southerner, by virtue of his association with slavery, was guilty of all the crimes which Garrison identified with slavery, and, for that mat-

---

[2] The precedence of the moral consideration over the political among the abolitionists, especially those in New England, has often been pointed out by historians. See, for example, Albert Bushnell Hart, *Slavery and Abolition, 1831–1841* (Harper & Brothers, New York, 1906), pp. 174–75, 188–89, 196–97, 316; Allan Nevins, *The Ordeal of the Union* (Charles Scribner's Sons, New York, 1947), I, 143. The importance of Garrison in the larger antislavery movement has long been exaggerated, as Hart, Nevins, and others have shown; nevertheless, for the purposes of this study, the familiarity of many New England writers with Garrison makes him of basic importance.

[3] In this and subsequent paragraphs the references are to William Lloyd Garrison, *Selections from the Writings and Speeches of William Lloyd Garrison* (R. E. Wallcut, Boston, 1852), pp. 63, 138–39, 144, 178, 180–81, 307, 334, 358. Hereafter cited as Garrison, *Selections.*

ter, with human nature itself. For co-operating with Southerners, Senator Peleg Sprague, of Maine, was denounced by Garrison:

You are in amicable companionship and popular repute with thieves and adulterers; with slave-holders, slave-breeders, slave-dealers, slave-destroyers; with those who trample law and order beneath their feet; with the plunderers of the public mail; with ruffians who insult, pollute and lacerate helpless women; and with conspirators against the lives and liberties of New England citizens.

This passage is typical of Garrison's method of cataloguing evil, ascribing it to Southern society, and then suggesting its threat to New England welfare. It was a compilation of "undeniable facts," he insisted to Sprague, adding that none of his Southern associates could be exonerated from the charges: "None are honorable, who throw the weight of their influence into the scale of oppression." Reviling those who counseled prudence and circumspection in respect to slavery, Garrison declared that he was "for digging under its foundations, and springing a mine that shall not leave one stone upon another." If, in the explosion, party, church, state, or the American Union was destroyed, the price, he assumed, would be worth paying.

Garrison's single-mindedness can be accounted for partly by his assumption that the abolition of slavery would somehow usher in the millennium. Just as the South of the present was to him an image of evil, the South of the future, under the blessings of free labor, was a utopian dream. Pointing to the example of the West Indian emancipation, Garrison urged the slaveholders of the South to free their slaves.

Instead of darkness, you shall have light; instead of tribulation, joy; instead of adversity, prosperity. For barrenness, you shall have fertility; for wasteful, indolent and revengeful serfs, provident, industrious and grateful laborers; for liability to servile insurrections, perfect exemption from danger. The execrations of your victims shall be turned into blessings; their wailings into shouts of joy; the judgments of God into mercies. Your peace shall flow like a river, for there shall be none to molest or make afraid.

One has only to recall the working conditions in the Northern mills at the time to realize how complete was Garrison's divorce from reality. But these blessings were sure, Garrison added. "For the mouth of the Lord hath spoken it." Like much antislavery writing, however, this appeal for liberty was addressed not to the slaveholder but to the Northerner, for whose palates Garrison added the ideals of thrift, industry, and rectitude, with the usual dash of Scripture.

Though no picture of the South as a social or geographical entity emerged from his writings and speeches, Garrison painted vivid portraits of the Negro and the white, presenting each as composite and representative.[4] His Negro was well meaning, hard working. He longed for the life of rectitude and family responsibility. But he was always in chains, hungry, bruised, and cut from whippings. He was treated licentiously, kept in heathenish ignorance, treated only as a marketable commodity, as beast or chattel. Negro infants were always torn from the arms of frantic mothers, heartbroken wives from weeping husbands. One of the few distinctions which Garrison made in his account of the Negro was that in Maryland and Virginia Negro life was depicted as a process of "fattening for the shambles," while in Alabama and Louisiana it was " a wasting, as with a pestilent disease, on cotton and sugar plantations." Garrison preferred the concrete image. It was not only more evocative but was also more suitable to his indignation. In his occasional sally into the less colorful realm of abstractions, he was less forceful though equally arbitrary and partial: "A slave is one who must have no other God than his master—no higher law than the will of him who claims him as his property; whose intellect must not be developed; whose conscience is not to be governed by moral considerations; whose soul may lay no claim to immortality."

At the same time, Garrison's Southerner was an irresponsible tyrant, a hypocrite, and a robber of God's poor—guilty of fraud, of atrocious impiety, of unequaled baseness and meanness. With wolflike ferocity he multiplied stripes on the bodies of his victims. He reveled in their blood. He drove women into the fields, stole infants, trafficked

---

[4] The characterization of the Negro and the white in this and the following paragraph is essentially an arrangement of Garrison's own statements as found in "The American Union," "Declaration of Sentiments of the American Anti-Slavery Convention," "Harsh Language—Retarding the Cause," "The Great Apostate," "Extracts from a Fourth of July Oration," and "No Compromise with Slavery." Quotations are from Garrison, *Selections*, pp. 188, 202.

in human flesh, dishonored the marriage institution, licensed incest and adultery. He refused to teach the Bible to the Negro. Beneath his cruelty and licentiousness lay fear, for he lived in daily terror of revolt.[5] Nevertheless, his power in national affairs was to be feared, Garrison repeatedly affirmed. The slaveholder controlled church and government, using both for his own ends. He had corrupted the clergy, who, in justifying slavery, justified robbery, adultery, barbarity, manstealing, and murder. With the agitator's instinct for effect, Garrison avoided those aspects of Southern life that would provide pleasing, domestic overtones. Only the Negroes seemed to have families, and these were constantly dispersed by the oppressor. "In slavery, all human ties are abrogated. The parent has no child, the child no parent; there is neither father nor mother, neither husband nor wife, neither brother nor sister." Garrison willingly acknowledged that his language was harsh, but he refused to admit that he or any abolitionist exaggerated.[6]

It is important to realize how closely the antislavery feeling was related to the sense of sin. Many New Englanders joined with Garrison in regarding slavery as a sin and resolving that it must be cast off immediately and unconditionally. Immediate abolition, Garrison asserted, was "the mandate of Heaven." Yvor Winters has pointed out that to the Puritans a particular sin could signify complete corruption and that therefore human behavior often took on for them symbolic value.[7] The residue of this Puritanism in the New England of Garrison's day no doubt contributed to the force of abolitionist propaganda. The antipathy between freedom and slavery was in a sense an aspect of the eternal opposition between good and evil. The

[5] *Ibid.*, pp. 193–94, 358.   [6] *Ibid.*, pp. 137–38, 180–81.

[7] Yvor Winters, *Maule's Curse: Seven Studies in the History of American Obscurantism* (New Directions, Norfolk, 1938), pp. 4–6. For an excellent discussion of the place of Evangelical Protestantism in the antislavery movement, see Gilbert Hobbes Barnes, *The Antislavery Impulse, 1830–1844* (D. Appleton-Century Co., Inc., New York, 1933). For the place of the clergy in the slavery question, see Chester Forrester Dunham, *The Attitude of the Northern Clergy toward the South, 1860–1865* (The Gray Co., Toledo, Ohio, 1942). The early chapters of this book deal with the ante bellum period. See also Henry Steele Commager, *Theodore Parker* (Little, Brown & Co., Boston, 1947), especially Chap. X, "Slavery and the Higher Law"; Carl Russell Fish, *The Rise of the Common Man, 1830–1850* (The Macmillan Co., New York,

struggle between Northerner and Southerner was the struggle between God's elect and damned. "Let it be premised," Garrison wrote, "that the slave-system is one of the strongholds of the devil—perhaps the strongest."[8]

Garrison's contentions were given further, and more immediate, enforcement in the growing competition between North and South as they elbowed each other for new territory in the West. As distrust and hostility mounted, his charges became increasingly acceptable to the North. After nearly a quarter of a century of puffing such blackness into the air, New England eyes were hardly able to penetrate the subtler but nonetheless distorting haze which hung over Mrs. Stowe's picture of life in the South. Like that of Garrison and Phillips, Mrs. Stowe's firsthand knowledge of the South was extremely limited. Her husband and brother once helped a slave to escape through the Underground Railroad, and Mrs. Stowe no doubt heard many tales from the Negro women who helped her with the housework in Cincinnati. But her only direct, personal acquaintance with the South was a visit of a few hours to a Kentucky plantation. To many, her picture seemed accurate if only because, compared with abolitionist rhetoric, it was mild. The pertinence of her theme of bondage has been aptly pointed out by Constance Rourke. It was in a sense a projection of Mrs. Stowe's own particular kind of bondage just as Uncle Tom's pathos was her own. There was unintentional irony in the comment of Mrs. Shelby, when she learned that her husband had been forced to sell Tom: "Abolitionists! if they knew all I know about slavery they *might* talk!"[9]

Revolt from bondage was a theme which appealed to a generation still close to the religious and political rebellion of its forefathers, one which was involved, moreover, in a revolt of its own against certain social and moral restraints long imposed by the tyranny of Puritan custom. Legree's plantation was closer to the Gothic romance than to the real South, George and Eliza Harris to the enterprising and

---

1927), pp. 278 ff.; William Warren Sweet, *The Story of Religion in America* (Harper & Brothers, New York, 1950), pp. 285–311.

[8] Garrison, *Selections,* p. 130.

[9] Harriet Beecher Stowe, *Uncle Tom's Cabin; or Life among the Lowly* (Riverside ed. n.d.), p. 38; Constance Mayfield Rourke, *Trumpets of Jubilee* (Harcourt, Brace and Co., Inc., New York, 1927), pp. 101–102, 108–109.

competent Yankee than to the flesh-and-blood Negro in a real situation. Nevertheless, the book had vitality and power. In its pages the New Englander lived vicariously an experience which purged his emotions and pleased his religious and social preconceptions. Tom's descent from Kentucky to Louisiana may well have typified for the New Englander the fate of a society which was selling itself down the river for the lucre of slavery. The succession of planters to which Tom was attached in his epical journey—the Shelbys, the St. Clares, and, finally, Simon Legree—presented a downward gradation in sensibility and moral response which seemed to reinforce the abolitionist's claim that slavery inevitably brutalizes.

Late in the fifties, Garrison combed the papers, Northern and Southern, for incidents of Southern violence. He found the examples which he sought: beatings, arrests, tar-and-feather treatments, mail seizures, public burnings of papers and books, and expulsions of citizens unsympathetic to slavery. He gathered this sensationalism into a book entitled *The Reign of Terror*.[10] Although presenting the traditional abolitionist view of the South, it had the added force of documentation. *The Reign of Terror* was vivid, dramatic, and well calculated to feed Northern hatred and fear. John Brown had been captured at Harper's Ferry, and fear was doing its work in the Southern mind, too. But Garrison's picture excluded this third dimension. To him, the Southerner was simply the heartless villain.

In the job of molding public opinion, Garrison needed help. His own most effective work was done with the pen; but he was living in an age of oratory, and abolitionism needed the atmosphere of the town meeting to flourish. During the middle years of the nineteenth century, the lecture platform functioned as a kind of theater, church, and school combined. At the meetinghouse the community purged away accumulated emotions and gave expression to its humanitarianism and piety. The sincere reformers were joined by those who looked for relief from boredom and by the inevitable contingent of eccentrics who together imparted a flavor to the meetings that often

[10] William Lloyd Garrison, *The New "Reign of Terror" in the Slaveholding States, for 1859–1860* (New York, American Anti-Slavery Society, 1860).

made them appear to be dramatics collectively performed rather than gatherings of serious-minded citizens facing real life situations.[11] Nevertheless, these meetings made attitudes contagious. The persistence of the more dedicated gradually made itself felt. The New England intellectual climate became increasingly favorable to the agitator.

The need of a platform personality to carry the cause directly to the people was answered, unsolicited, by Wendell Phillips. At a meeting in 1837, young Phillips rose from the audience, denounced the murderers of Elijah Lovejoy, the antislavery editor, of Alton, Illinois, and upheld the tradition of free speech in an unrehearsed oration that has been compared in its effectiveness with the greatest speeches in American history. Phillips combined the ardent idealism of his era with a persuasive power probably unexcelled in America. Significantly, it was Phillips the orator rather than Garrison the journalist who became increasingly influential in the abolition movement. Phillips captured the podium for the cause, a decisive victory in an era of oratory.

Phillips trained himself for his role as abolitionist by developing his powers of oratory and his platform technique, not by studying slavery in its context of day-to-day living. Thomas Wentworth Higginson noted that although Phillips was surpassed by Garrison "in grave moral logic," by Theodore Parker "in grasp of facts," by Charles Sumner "in copiousness of illustration," he was nevertheless a greater orator than these men and, in the post-Revolution era, was rivaled only by Daniel Webster. Logic and facts are important ingredients in an address, unless it is judged solely on the basis of emotional appeal. Higginson has given testimony that "many a respectable lawyer or divine felt his blood run cold, the next day, when he found that the fascinating orator whom he had applauded to the echo had really made the assassination of an emperor seem as trivial as the doom of a mosquito."[12] A Bostonian once reported that during a Phillips speech he had heard a man in the audience applauding,

---

[11] For Emerson's personal reactions to some of the New England town meetings, see Edward Waldo Emerson and Waldo Emerson Forbes (eds.), *The Journals of Ralph Waldo Emerson* (Houghton Mifflin Co., Boston, 1911–13), III, 504; IV, 360; VII, 96, 178.

[12] Thomas Wentworth Higginson, *Wendell Phillips* (Lee and Shepard, Boston, 1884), pp. xii, xv.

stamping his feet, and exclaiming enthusiastically, "The damned old liar! The damned old liar!"[13] In speaking of Phillips' preparation, the author of an early biographical sketch made this comment: "In the trial of cases at the bar, he was training his eloquence; and before juries he was modulating that sweet voice which was so soon to thrill humanity with its melody of freedom. He was, indeed, learning the gamut of the harp of hearts." How well he learned to play on human hearts can be measured by the constant demand for his platform performances. Emerson said that Phillips was "such a perfect artist that he ought to be walking all the galleries of Europe."[14]

In 1837, long before William Henry Seward spoke of the irrepressible conflict or Abraham Lincoln of a house divided, Phillips insisted that the spirit of freedom and the spirit of slavery were contending for mastery. "They cannot live together." The South, he said, could not fall and the North stand, the South be corrupt and the North sound. He strove to foster a public opinion hostile to slaveholding, believing that if such an opinion did not arise, slavery would finally "overshadow and mildew our free institutions."[15] Phillips' battleground was the Northern mind. His eye was on the North, though his shots appeared to be aimed at the South. The North, he thought, must be aroused from its supineness, must be made to realize both its complicity in and its danger from slavery. To arouse Northern awareness of danger, Phillips emphasized the political threat of the South by pointing to its wealth and its continued success in Washington. To emphasize the moral danger he maintained that Northerners were

[13] Ralph Korngold, *Two Friends of Man: The Story of William Lloyd Garrison and Wendell Phillips and Their Relationship with Abraham Lincoln* (Little, Brown & Co., Boston, 1950), p. 178. For the importance of Phillips in the abolition movement, see Gilbert Hobbes Barnes, *The Antislavery Impulse, 1830–1844,* and Richard Hofstadter, *The American Political Tradition: And the Men Who Made It* (Alfred A. Knopf, Inc., New York, 1948).

[14] Wendell Phillips, *Speeches, Lectures, and Letters* (Lee and Shepard, Boston, 1884), p. iii; George Lowell Austin, *The Life and Times of Wendell Phillips* (B. B. Russell, Boston, 1888), p. 244; Frank Preston Stearns, *Sketches from Concord and Appledore* (G. P. Putnam's Sons, New York, 1895), p. 203.

[15] Phillips, "The Right of Petition" (speech delivered at Lynn [Mass.], Mar. 28, 1837), *Speeches, Lectures, and Letters* (Lee and Shepard, Boston, 1892), pp. 4-5.

dangerously exposed to a pernicious disease that had struck their Southern neighbors.

The disease motif, however, implied a distinction between slavery and the South, disease and victim, which was not congenial to Phillips' larger intention. The general bearing of his orations was toward an identification of slavery with the South. For all practical purposes, Phillips said, the slave power was the South; there could be no other South until the North created one.[16] The image of the South which Phillips labored to evoke in the Northern mind embodied deformities that were designed to call up repugnance, anger, and fear. It violated the cherished ideals of the North. He conjured up a land of whipping posts and auction blocks, a feudal society in which newspapermen, politicians, and clergymen were vassals. The nobility controlled family, church, and government. The slave power he described as a cable of three strands: the prejudice of race, the omnipotence of money, and the almost irresistible power of aristocracy. Nobility and aristocracy were evocative terms in the New England of his day. And the most summary abstraction of them all was Phillips' epithet, "The South is the thirteenth and fourteenth centuries."

The three-strand cable would not be easily broken, and could not without involving bloodshed. Phillips, who did not share Garrison's philosophy of nonresistance, often spoke of the possibility of armed rebellion in the South. "I can imagine the scenes of blood through which a rebellious slave-population must march to their rights." But his thoughts of the battlefield, he assured his audience, were no more dreadful than his thoughts of slavery. The most ghastly battlefield, he asserted, would seem "white as an angel's wing" in comparison with "the blackness of that darkness which has brooded over the Carolinas for two hundred years." Actually Phillips was weighing not two realities but two imagined entities; for in his comparison Waterloo and Thermopylae, with their heroic connotations, stood for the one,

[16] References in this and the following paragraph are to Phillips, *Speeches, Lectures, and Letters* (J. Redpath, Boston, 1863), pp. 85, 86, 152, 278, 362–63, 534, 538. See also *The War for the Union: A Lecture Delivered by Wendell Phillips in New York and Boston, December, 1861* (E. D. Barker, New York, 1862), p. 16.

Wingate College Library

while nothing less than hell itself stood for the other. Phillips' method was that of induction from isolated fact, for which he developed a style of presentation well suited in its cumulative movement. In a characteristic sequence, for example, he began by picturing a specific wrong, "some young, trembling girl sent to the auction block." He then asked his hearers to "multiply this individual agony into three millions; multiply that into centuries." Next he led them through a catalogue of general evils, selected to suggest a threat to the sanctity of family life. In this way he prepared his listeners for a summarizing charge: the South was "a daily system of hell." Phillips became adept at establishing an abusive epithet as a kind of algebraic sign standing for the South itself, a scarlet letter separating the South from the North and justifying its banishment from the community of respectable citizens.

The agitator must continually intensify his attack if he is to maintain the appearance of vitality. With the years, Phillips grew more vitriolic. The growing hostility between the regions seemed to add justification to his mounting virulence. In 1853, surveying the achievements of the abolition movement, he said: "To startle the South to madness, so that every step she takes in her blindness, is one step more toward ruin, is much. This we have done." Nothing shows more clearly that Phillips had become a victim of his own program. By this time he could summarize his view of the South in one image: the South was "one great brothel where half a million women are flogged to prostitution, or, worse still, are degraded to believe it honorable." By the time of the Harper's Ferry incident, Phillips was able to say that Brown had more right to hang Governor Wise than the Governor had to hang Brown. "I mean exactly what I say. I am weighing my words now," he said as he called Virginia a pirate ship and Brown the Lord High Admiral commissioned to sink it by the Almighty.[17]

As Phillips grew more outspoken, some of his listeners became indignant, and the abolitionists were forced to form bodyguards. Young Thomas Wentworth Higginson, who often served as captain of the guards for Phillips, showed initiative and talent in this phase of the activity. Looking back over the ante bellum period, Higginson noted that in Wendell Phillips the reformer had become the gladiator. "The

[17] For references in this paragraph, see *ibid.*, pp. 108, 153, 272.

better his fencing, the more he [became] the slave of his own talent.
. . . The position once taken must be maintained,—the opponent
must be overwhelmed by almost any means."[18] After 1856, when he
traveled to Kansas in behalf of the Emigrant Society, Higginson never
questioned that "the absolute and increasing difference between the
two sections" would bring about a "farther conflict of some sort." He
took fencing lessons, read books on military tactics, and approached
the conflict with clenched fists and flexed muscles. On a river boat
he had seen the swagger of Southern youths, "drunken, gambling,
quarrelsome boys, but otherwise affable enough, with the pleasant
manners and soft accent of the South." He was struck by their braggadocio and scandalous talk of drunkenness, and especially by their
casual manner of speaking of Negroes as property. Higginson recalled
a scriptural passage which he had seen in Mrs. Stowe's *Dred:* "Woe
unto them, for they have cast lots for my people, . . . and sold a girl
for wine, that they may drink."

Higginson knew more about the South than did Phillips. He had
visited a Virginia plantation where the Negroes and whites lived together in comfortable domesticity. "The slaves seemed merely to
share in the kindly and rather slip-shod methods of a Southern establishment." His parents knew the South, too, from personal visits they
had made to the homes of Southerners whose sons had been under
the direction of Higginson's father at Harvard. It is interesting to
note that Higginson traced his conversion to abolitionism, despite his
personal contact with certain aspects of the South, to his reading of
Harriet Martineau's *The Martyr Age in America* and Lydia Maria
Child's *An Appeal in Favor of That Class of Americans Called Africans.* He also accredited Whittier with strong influence in leading
him to become a reformer. Higginson was a vigorous convert. In the
skirmish to free a fugitive slave from a Boston jail, Higginson was
wounded and even jailed for a few hours. To watch the ante bellum
career of Higginson is to understand better the extent of the excitement that was called up by the antislavery agitation. To read his

---

[18] For references in this and the following paragraph, see Higginson, *Wendell
Phillips,* p. xvii; *Cheerful Yesterdays* (Houghton Mifflin Co., Boston, 1901),
pp. 123–26, 212–13, 235–36; *John Greenleaf Whittier,* "English Men of Letters"
Series (The Macmillan Company, New York, 1902), p. 94–95.

rather oddly named *Cheerful Yesterdays* is to realize, too, that the reformers were not without their bravado and self-conscious dramatics.

There was an ambiguity inherent in the program of Garrison and Phillips in respect to its primary aim: Was it to free the slaves or to free the North from a slaveholding society? By 1843 Garrison trumpeted the idea that there must be no union with slaveholders.[19] His contempt for the Constitution is well known, as is the sensational ceremony in which he publicly burned a copy of it. Both he and Phillips assumed, of course, that disunion would be effected without war. Upon the news of actual secession, Phillips delivered his "Disunion" speech in which he uttered triumphantly, "The Lord reigneth; let the earth rejoice! 'The covenant with death' is annulled; 'the agreement with hell' is broken to pieces."[20] What Southern independence would mean for the slave was a problem which he solved facilely by a contention, never logically defended, that secession would bring the end of slavery. "Disunion is abolition! . . . The music of disunion to me is, that at its touch the slave breaks into voice, shouting his jubilee." This hypothesis depended on two assumptions: a South that was weak and a Negro that was hostile to it. And without this hypothesis, of course, he could well have been accused of abandoning the Negro. But over the years Phillips had repeatedly emphasized the great power of the South in its competition with the North. The gloss of his eloquence could not conceal the essential incompatibility between this and another favorite contention of his that without Northern power the South would be unable to hold her slaves in subjection. In the "Disunion" address Phillips revived this latter claim to support his prognosis of Southern disaster: "What supports slavery? Northern bayonets, calming the master's fears. . . . Disunion leaves God's natural laws to work their good results. God gives every animal means of self-protection. Under God's laws, insurrection is the tyrant's check. Let

[19] Austin, *The Life and Times of Wendell Phillips,* p. 144. See also Lindsay Swift, who traces the disunion speech to 1841 in *William Lloyd Garrison* (G. W. Jacobs, Philadelphia, 1911), pp. 300–301.

[20] Phillips, "Disunion" (speech delivered Jan. 20, 1861), *Speeches, Lectures, and Letters* (J. Redpath, 1863). See especially pp. 343–44, 359–62, 364, 369–70. See also his speech delivered at the grave of John Brown (Dec. 8, 1859), *ibid.,* p. 292.

us stand out of the path, and allow the Divine law to have free course."

Phillips had never been in the South, and, except for his Harvard days, he had no Southern friends. In 1830, Garrison went to Baltimore to help edit the *Genius of Universal Emancipation*. Convicted of libel, he saw the inside of a Baltimore jail. That was his only trip South until after the Civil War, when, ironically, this former advocate of disunion joined in the ceremony of raising the American flag over Fort Sumter. Late in life, when Phillips was addressing an audience at Harvard, he stated that "one half of history is loose conjecture, and much of the rest is the writer's opinion. . . . Most men see facts, not with their eyes, but with their prejudices."[21] The pertinence of this observation to much abolitionist writing is obvious. Phillips had helped establish loose conjecture and prejudice as fact. He and Garrison had striven to create a public opinion in the North that was hostile not only to slavery but to the South itself. Their desire to stamp out slavery in America was commendable, but in devoting themselves to this ideal they added the fuel of their eloquence to the fires of sectionalism, stirring up the emotionalism and misjudgments of their age. In the name of benevolence, they helped to build up an atmosphere of hate. Their work had been not so much "a searching into abuses," to use Mrs. Stowe's expression, as it had been a conjuring up of a monstrous image of evil which they named "the South."

[21] Phillips, "The Scholar in a Republic" (Phi Beta Kappa address delivered at Harvard, June 30, 1881), *Speeches, Lectures, and Letters* (Lee and Shepard, 1892), pp. 334–35.

· 2 ·

Whittier

IN 1826, while editing the *Newburyport Free Press,* Garrison published a poem by an unknown farm boy named John Greenleaf Whittier. It was Garrison's first paper and Whittier's first published poem. The Whittier family, subscribers to the *Free Press,* had been drawn by "the humanitarian tone" of the paper.[1] Garrison, on the other hand, had perceived the true though uncultivated genius of young Whittier. This recognition was a timely and much needed encouragement to the nineteen-year-old Quaker who saw sixteen more of his poems printed in Garrison's paper before a year had passed. Although Whittier later found himself among those of the abolition movement who could not support Garrison in the resolve to remain aloof from political action and to associate feminism, temperance, and other reforms with abolitionism, he nevertheless retained a personal loyalty to Garrison, late in life speaking of him as one of his "earliest and most intimate friends."[2] When he himself became an editor, Whittier gave whatever support he could to Gar-

---

[1] Oliver Johnson, *William Lloyd Garrison and His Times,* with introduction by John Greenleaf Whittier (Houghton Mifflin Co., Boston, 1880), p. ix.

[2] *Pennsylvania Freeman,* IV, No. 21 (Aug. 2, 1838). Hereafter cited as the *Freeman.* Some eleven years later, however, in speaking of Garrison to Higginson, Whittier confided: "I know him thoroughly, and know that he is a despot. . . . Garrison identifies the movement absolutely with himself. He is a *Robespierre* with the same perfect self-consecration and the same absolute incapacity of tolerating those who differ from himself." *Letters and Journals of*

rison—frequently reporting his activity, often quoting his speeches, and, in 1838, defending him against charges of self-seeking.[3] The schism in the ranks of abolitionists had related only to methods of advancing the cause of antislavery, for there seemed to be no disagreement among them about the nature of life in the South.

Whittier never traveled south of Washington. But he responded as a youth to what he called "the high and manly truth" of Garrison, and his conscience focused on the evil of slavery and shaped his entire image of the South. The subjectivity of the Quaker doctrine of soul no doubt disposed him to rely on his intuition of evil. Since the Inner Light took precedence over tradition and formal learning, it would not have seemed necessary to him to corroborate by study and observation of life in the South the idea of the hatefulness of slavery. "My heart echoes thy words," he said in the poem "To Garrison," which he wrote when the *Liberator* was nearly one year old.[4] He described Garrison's spirit as soaring above the cloud of human ills and assured his readers that God was on Garrison's side. A year later, in 1833, Whittier published at his own expense an antislavery tract, *Justice and Expediency*. The thoroughness of his preparation has been acknowledged, but what has been overlooked is that his research dealt with such documents as the Constitution and the writings of Jefferson and Milton, where he of course found adequate support for his philosophy of freedom. In so far as his preparation touched on the problem of slavery in its particular relation to the South, his reading consisted of "a fresh examination of anti-slavery writings."[5] Whittier's generation of abolitionists did not follow the example of Benjamin Lundy, an early Quaker antislavery reformer, who traveled in the South and addressed himself directly to Southerners. In 1833, accompanying Garrison to the Philadelphia Anti-Slavery Convention, Whittier helped launch a movement which called for immediate, mass

---

Thomas Wentworth Higginson 1846–1906, ed. Mary Thacher Higginson (Houghton Mifflin Co., Boston, 1921), pp. 8–11.

[3] *Freeman*, IV, No. 21 (Aug. 2, 1838).

[4] *The Complete Works of John Greenleaf Whittier* (Fireside Edition), (Houghton Mifflin Co., Boston, 1910), III, 9–10. All quotations from Whittier's published works are taken from this edition. Hereafter cited as *Works*.

[5] John A. Pollard, *John Greenleaf Whittier, Friend of Man* (Houghton Mifflin Co., Boston, 1949), p. 117.

reform. In such an atmosphere, there could be little chance of systematic and direct observation of slavery as a way of life.

Whittier journeyed to Philadelphia in 1838 to become editor of the *Pennsylvania Freeman,* which was a front-line post in the ideological battle over American slavery. His office was located in the newly constructed Pennsylvania Hall, where the Anti-Slavery Society held its meetings. Seeing this building burned by an angry mob gave Whittier a vivid lesson in the destructiveness inherent in the struggle, and it probably shook his faith in the usefulness of reasoned arguments. Nevertheless, he tried dealing with slavery in terms of principle. In "The True Character of Slavery," one of his earliest editorials in the *Freeman,* he sought to identify the essence of slavery and to explore some of the fundamentals of human relationships.[6] His mind lacked sustaining power on the conceptual level, however, for he slipped, as he invariably did, from the intellectual to the imaginative. He theorized that "the seizure of the entire man" was the essential evil of slavery, to which the particular abuses, for all their wickedness, were incidental; nevertheless, his mind was more at home with the particular abuses, and his emotionalized presentation of them characterized his writing on the subject.

It is substantially true to say that in Whittier's writings there is no Southland; there is only an evil specter of slavery which, to him, was the South. Regarding slavery as intrinsically evil, Whittier reasoned as did Garrison that any slaveholder was responsible for all abominations. By holding slaves the Southerner marshaled himself in the rebellion against God. "The law never made any man a slaveholder. The serpent held forth enticingly the forbidden fruit of Eden: The criminality of our first parent consisted in this, that *she put forth her hand* and received it." Those who distinguished between the benevolent slaveholder and the insensible exploiter of the slave were charged by Whittier with "ecclesiastical hair-splitting." He maintained that "the praying slaveholder does far more to uphold the system than the swearing one. He gives it a credit and a countenance by his direct participation in it, without which it could not stand at all." Whittier's attitude, of course, condemned the Valentine St. Clares equally with the Simon Legrees. His refusal to acknowledge the worth of kind

[6] *Freeman,* IV, No. 5 (Apr. 12, 1838).

slaveholders got him into difficulties with readers who recalled that some of the greatest American patriots had been holders of slaves. Charged with maligning George Washington by implication, Whittier defended himself in the *Freeman* by saying that because Washington had wished to free his slaves, he died "a practical abolitionist." After all, Whittier added, one does not revile Paul for having been Saul. And Washington, like Paul, had repented.[7]

With the assumption that the slaveholder was Satan's agent in the eternal warfare between good and evil, Whittier quite instinctively pictured him in terms of opposition to those values which he held dearest. An example of his vivid conjectures about the Satanism of the slaveholder can be found in a *Freeman* article which told of a sick Negro in Tennessee who was to be sold by a sheriff in order to pay the jail fees and doctor bills involved in his keeping.

The poor wretch will probably be bought by some hardened monster as a matter of speculation. If he recovers, it will be a good bargain; but if the doctor pronounces him incurable, he will be compelled to exhaust his remaining strength in toil, and the torture of the whip will be added to the agony of disease. And who shall estimate the horrors of the dying hour of that miserable being. . . . Who will lift the cordial to his lips.

Whittier then embellished his sentiment with a Gothic tale of a dying Negro who narrowly escaped premature burial—a story told to him by one who lived in South Carolina. The particular way in which Whittier shuffled from fact to conjecture can be seen in his description of the system devised by these agents of Satan. In a passage typical of his antislavery writings he spoke of Southern slavery which

holds two millions of God's creatures in bondage, which leaves one million females without any protection save their own feeble strength, and which makes even the exercise of that strength in resistance to outrage punishable with death! which considers rational, immortal beings as articles of traffic, vendible commodities, merchantable property,—which recognizes no social obligations, no natural relations,—which tears without scruple the infant from the mother, the wife from the husband, the parent from the child.

[7] *Ibid.*, IV, No. 20 (July 26, 1838); V, No. 33 (Apr. 25, 1839); *The National Era,* I, No. 27 (July 8, 1847).

Thus his chain of associations carried him swiftly and without need of investigation to the firm conviction that the Southern system was unmixed wickedness without rival anywhere. This passage from *Justice and Expediency* antedated by four years the beginning of the public career of Wendell Phillips, who built this type of sequence into a finished art. And as Higginson remarked of Phillips' work, "It was not heroic, but it was war."[8]

Whittier's concept of Southern law, which he discussed in the Preface to *The Narrative of James Williams,* was subject to the characteristic vagaries of his mind. The circuit of his associations went like this: Southern statute books made property of men; they therefore substituted the will of the master for the moral government of God, annihilated the rights of conscience, enjoined disobedience to the Divine Lawgiver, discouraged purity and chastity, legalized concubinage, encouraged crime, and in other ways proved that the code was unrivaled in its abhorrence. By way of citing authority, he quoted John Wesley: "American slavery is the *vilest* beneath the sun!" Whittier supported this charge with the theory that "the antagonistic laws of liberty and tyranny," an "unnatural combination" which made the American system unique, forced the American slaveholder to "exceed every other in severity and cool atrocity."

The Preface also expressed the conviction that the practice as well as the theory of the Southern system was without peer in vileness. Whittier did not test this conclusion by investigating actual conditions in the South; he considered it confirmed by Priestley's principle: "No people ever were found to be better than their laws, though many have been found to be worse." He did read the Southern papers, however. From advertisements and printed speeches of the slaveholders, he gleaned supporting evidence for the following summary of the Southern code in respect to the treatment of the Negro: perfect obedience is required of the slave who is made to feel that there is no appeal from his master; authority is maintained only by fear, by "a reign of terror"; the lash is the main support of authority with stocks an auxiliary; the economy of slavery is to get from the slave as much as possible while giving in return as little as possible; slaves are

[8] *Freeman*, IV, No. 8 (May 3, 1838); Whittier, *Works,* VII, 13; Higginson, *Wendell Phillips* (Lee and Shepard, 1884), p. xvii.

branded and scarred; iron collars are fastened on the necks of women; runaway slaves are chased by dogs trained to hunt them as beasts of prey; runaway slaves may be shot with impunity by any white; masters offer rewards for killing their runaway slaves.[9]

In *The Narrative of James Williams,* Whittier fictionalized, though unintentionally, an account of slave life in the South. An escaped Negro recounted to him a narrative which he called his true, personal experiences in the South and his final escape to freedom. Whittier wrote the story and prepared it for publication. The *Narrative* suggested Mrs. Stowe's later story of Uncle Tom in several ways. Williams was the favorite slave of a generous, kindly, aristocratic family in Virginia. Through the caprice of fortune, however, he met the ever dreaded fate of being sent away from his wife and children into the deep South, being promised, of course, that the family would be reunited. The new plantation was comparable to Simon Legree's as a place of cruelty, though it lacked the Gothic elements of the latter. Williams was ordered to be a slave-driver on this plantation. Unlike Tom, he did not refuse; but, like Tom, he did refuse to whip a woman and consequently sustained a brutal, nearly mortal, whipping himself. Like Legree, the overseer kept a Negro mistress and often drank excessively. In his drunkenness his cruelty knew no bounds. Fiendishly he devised ways of increasing the sufferings of his slaves. Pregnant women were whipped until they miscarried; Negroes who tried to escape were mercilessly left to the dogs; a proud Negro was ruthlessly shot. James Williams finally escaped, making a long, pathetic trek in pursuit of the North Star.

For verification of the story the reader was referred to John Greenleaf Whittier, of Amesbury, Massachusetts, and to about six named persons, all of whom had heard the story from the Negro's lips and attested to its truth. No doubt Whittier was sincere in writing and sponsoring the story, but he failed to establish its veracity. Janet Wilson, in her article "Early Anti-Slavery Propaganda," called the

[9] *The Narrative of James Williams, an American Slave, who was for several years a driver on a cotton plantation in Alabama* . . . (published by the American Anti-Slavery Society), (Isaac Knapp, Boston, 1838), pp. iii, iv, vi–vii. Near the end of the Preface, Whittier quotes several pages of admissions and testimonies of slaveholders to establish the validity of the nine-point indictment which has been summarized in this paragraph.

book a fiasco because Southern editors had triumphantly proved it spurious.[10] The Negro had fabricated, and the Executive Committee of the Anti-Slavery Society ordered the book withdrawn. However, it had gone through six editions in eight months, and its appeal was enormous. There can be no question about Whittier's writing the story, for it was a matter of common knowledge at the time, and, in 1886, Whittier wrote a letter to a friend in which he spoke of his having written the story of James Williams.[11] Many abolitionists believed that, in spite of the charge of falseness, the book described the sort of thing that went on in the South. The *Freeman* quoted a statement that anyone acquainted with the slave system would recognize that "there is not an item in [the book] that does not find its counterpart in Southern Slavery."[12] In considering the reception of *The Narrative of James Williams,* it is not hard to understand how, after twelve years of conditioning, the American mind was well prepared for *Uncle Tom's Cabin,* which, in addition to antislavery sensationalism, presented the attractions of Gothic romance, more intellectualized debates of social and moral problems, and a style of remarkable sustaining power.

Whittier's verse dealing with slavery suffered because of his remoteness from the life that he was supposedly portraying. It was weakened, first, by the falseness of his image of the South, and, second, by his attempt to substitute sentiment for truth. For in his antislavery poetry Whittier enlisted the services of such sentiments as mother love, family solidarity, piety, and other values dear to the American heart. And the Southerners in his poetry were cut to the abolitionist pattern. Whittier's Southern gentleman usually carried a driver's whip or a tyrant's rod. He mocked all God-fearing Northerners. He was haughty and rich (though, as will be seen, his plantations were in a state of

[10] Janet Wilson, "Early Anti-Slavery Propaganda," *More Books* (bulletin of Boston Public Library), XIX (1944), 393–405. Miss Wilson cites executive committee minutes for the history of this episode.

[11] Thomas F. Currier, *A Bibliography of John Greenleaf Whittier* (Harvard University Press, Cambridge, Mass., 1937), pp. 32–39; see also Whitman Bennett, *Whittier, Bard of Freedom* (University of North Carolina Press, Chapel Hill, N.C., 1941), p. 149; Vernon Loggins, *The Negro Author; His Development in America* (Columbia University Press, New York, 1931), pp. 100–102.

[12] *Freeman,* IV, No. 26 (Sept. 6, 1838).

decay). He was a lank-haired hunter of men who trampled down images of God. The overseer or auctioneer was a bully, a fighter, a gambler, and a crooked politician. He was garrulous. His speech was filled with pious phrases, his mind with filthy jests. His social and economic system was a foul temple of Moloch where Nature was outraged. It was doomed ultimately to the wrath of God and financial failure. The Southern village showed both vulgar newness and premature decay. The centers of interest were its tavern with mad whisky brawls and its slave auction.

The Negro pictured in Whittier's poetry groaned in chains. Though he was low, despised, and miserable, he still retained nobleness. In fact, he usually uttered prayers. He loved freedom. He was physically superior to the Southern white, who had become flaccid through sloth. (Whittier, however, also claimed that two-thirds of the Negroes were incapable of productive labor.) The Negro had a broken heart and a clouded mind. With fetters clanking he crouched on the plains where "freedom" had been won from the British. The Negro woman had shrinking flesh upon which the lash of the slave whip fell. She was riven from her children and separated from her husband. She was marked and branded, tasked and plundered. She shrank beneath the tyrant's rod. She toiled by day in the fields and by night submitted to dark ignominies of lust. She, too, was often in an agony of prayer. The image of the runaway slave woman staggering down the center aisle during a Sunday morning church service so gripped Whittier's imagination that he composed a poem on the subject which he printed in *The National Era* the year of the compromise.[13] This poem, like so much of his antislavery writing, showed a characteristic juxtaposition of sentiments carrying special power for his generation: reverence for God, for woman, and for freedom. In "The Panorama," Whittier described the entire South as a once-noble woman who had fallen— a metaphor excelled only by Phillips' "brothel" in bad taste and misrepresentation. Nevertheless, it reflected Whittier's idea of a degenerate South, and he expressed the hope that one day she would resume her old attire and seek "to smooth/Her unkempt tresses at the glass of truth."[14]

[13] Whittier, "The Sabbath Scene," *Works*, III, 160.
[14] Whittier, "The Panorama," *Works*, III, 201–202. The comments in these

The nonslaveholding white was not pictured in Whittier's polemical verse. In his editorials, however, the nonslaveholding white was usually identified with the poor white and regarded, like the Negro, as noblehearted and wretchedly oppressed. Assuming that these "disfranchised free laborers" shared his own views on slavery, Whittier asserted confidently that they were one with the Negro in wanting to break "the chain and dungeon bar." They were somehow spiritually allied with the North, remaining silent through fear alone, and therefore were not included in Whittier's abstraction, "Southern character." Rather, they were its victims. The poorer classes of Southern whites who were obliged to work for a living were pariahs of a society in which manual labor was regarded as disgraceful for white men.

In his newspaper prose Whittier frequently departed from the picture of the noblehearted slave whose manacled hands were raised to Heaven. Such an image was not supported by his theory that enslavement had inevitably demoralized Negro and white alike. To support this theory he reported that two-thirds of the Negro slaves were too young or too old, too sick and decrepit or too slothful and vicious for work and that those available for labor were about one-third as efficient as free workers. He sometimes spoke of a middle class in the South, but in his characteristic oversimplification of Southern society there were in effect only the aristocratic slaveholder, the poor white, and the slave. Since the plantation demanded a large investment of capital, he reasoned that agriculture in a slaveholding community would eventually come exclusively under the control of the wealthy. He recognized in this a fateful parallel to the plight of the Roman Republic, which, he said, had been robust only in its early days, when warriors and statesmen themselves cultivated the fields. He saw the fate of Rome "written legibly upon the soil of Virginia."[15]

two paragraphs on the Southerner and the Negro have been assembled from all of Whittier's antislavery verse. See, especially, such poems as "To Garrison," "Toussaint L'Ouverture," "Expostulation," "Hymn," "The Yankee Girl," "Stanzas for the Times," "The Hunters of the Men," "Clerical Oppressors," "The Crisis," "Official Piety," "The Haschish," "The Kansas Emigrants," "For Righteousness' Sake," "Arisen at Last," "A Song for the Time," "A Word for the Hour."

[15] For references in this paragraph, see *The National Era*, II, No. 49 (Mar. 30, 1848); II, No. 61 (Apr. 20, 1848); IV, No. 51 (Mar. 28, 1850); *Freeman*, V, No. 13 (Dec. 6, 1838); Whittier, *Works*, VII, 45, 68–70.

Persistently Whittier advanced the idea of a decaying South.[16] His image of the plantation was not the sumptuous mansion of broad, white-pillared porches, and well-trimmed, rolling lawns of greenness and vista which marked the romanticized retrospection of post–Civil War days. In 1833 he expressed the opinion that Virginia, although originally one of the most beautiful and fertile regions on earth, had become sterile through waste, neglect, and improvidence. He imagined "the half-finished mansion already falling into decay, the broken-down enclosures, the seed-grown garden, the slave hut open to the elements, the hillsides galled and naked, the fields below them run over with brier and fern." He spoke again of "the abandoned plantation where the profitless fern and thistle have sprung up under the heel of slavery." The notion of physical and economic as well as moral decay of the South remained firmly fixed in Whittier's mind throughout the entire period of his agitation. In 1847 he quoted in *The National Era* the reports of a traveler to demonstrate that although soil and climate were the same in Ohio and Kentucky, the former was prosperous, the latter impoverished. Like every other state suffering the sickness of slavery, Kentucky was marked by unweeded fields, dilapidated enclosures, squalid children, languid slaves. In "The Panorama," published in 1856, Whittier spoke of

> A slave plantation's slovenly repose
> Where, in rude cabins rotting midst their weeds,
> The human chattel eats, and sleeps, and breeds;
>
> .   .   .   .
>
> Of ampler size the master's dwelling stands,
> In shabby keeping with his half-tilled lands;
> The gates unhinged, the yard with weeds unclean,
> The cracked veranda with a tipsy lean.
> Without, loose-scattered like a wreck adrift,
> Signs of misrule and tokens of unthrift.

[16] For references in this and the following paragraph, see Whittier, *Works,* III, 199; VII, 32–33, 64, 81, 83, 84; *Freeman,* V, No. 2 (Sept. 20, 1838); V, No. 13 (Dec. 6, 1838); *The National Era,* I, No. 9 (Mar. 4, 1847). One exception to this portrayal of a decayed plantation can be found in Whittier's poem "The Yankee Girl" in which the "haughty Southron" is rich and his plantation is beautiful.

Whittier found some support for his theme of ruin in a speech delivered before Congress in 1838 by the Honorable Mr. Clowney, of South Carolina. Complaining about legislation that favored other parts of the country, the Congressman said that other states surpassed what South Carolina had been in the "happiest and proudest days of her prosperity." He complained, too, that the sparse population in the interior of the state prevented the development of good elementary schools. Whittier quoted this speech in the *Freeman,* labeling it "The Confessions of Chivalry." He believed that the difficulty of maintaining schools was detrimental chiefly to middle-class society because the Negro was intentionally kept illiterate, whereas the children of the wealthy planter, independent of community schools, were left wholly to their parents and private tutors to be instructed in prejudice, sloth, and despotism. Characteristically, Whittier assigned the backwardness of the South not to the frontier but to "chivalry." In Jefferson's *Notes on Virginia* he had read that the Negro child soon learned "degraded submission," while the planter's son got a firm grounding in the theory and practice of tyranny. The bad effects of slavery upon children impressed Whittier keenly. As time went by, it mingled in his mind with his Puritan fear of carnality and other dark sins that beset the sons of men. In 1856 he wrote a description of life on a Southern plantation, pointing out how contagion passed from parent to child.

> There, all the vices, which, like birds obscene,
> Batten on slavery loathsome and unclean,
> From the foul kitchen to the parlor rise,
> Pollute the nursery where the child-heir lies,
> Taint infant lips beyond all after cure,
> With the fell poison of a breast impure;
> Touch boyhood's passions with the breath of flame,
> From girlhood's instincts steal the blush of shame.

Whittier held no hope for organized religion in the South because the Southern clergy did not take up his hue and cry for abolition.[17] He called Southern ministers paid hypocrites who sold truth, bartered for wrong, and fed fat on the fettered and plundered slave. Western

[17] Whittier, *Works,* III, 39, 170, 174, 181; *The National Era,* I, No. 40 (Oct. 7, 1847); VII, No. 21 (Feb. 10, 1853).

cotton was their "hempen Haschish of the East" which induced their exotic dreams of heaven as a plantation and angels as Negro overseers. The church in a slaveholding community was a slaveholding church. In an abusive poem called "Official Piety" he pictured the Southern clergy locking the door of hope against three million souls and, with uprolled eyeballs, whining a prayer for help to hide the key. Despite these claims of religious neglect, he usually spoke of the Negro as pious. There was, of course, the great example of Uncle Tom—Mrs. Stowe's book had appeared serially in the *Era* in 1851. And in the year "Official Piety" was published, 1853, he reviewed for the *Era* a book entitled *Cousin Frank's Household; or Scenes in the Old Dominion*. Whittier devoted nearly an entire column to a quotation comparing the intensity, sincerity, and simplicity of Negro worship to the fashionable detachment of the whites in their tastefully decorated church. Like Uncle Tom, one of the Negroes had just been sold to a Texas planter and was facing separation from his wife and baby. The Negroes knew the "Man of Sorrows," and they kept repeating the Biblical phrase, "How long, O Lord!" During the Kansas-Nebraska struggle Whittier painted a scurrilous portrait of a Methodist missionary in Kansas who sanctioned the use of the bowie knife in carrying the Southern gospel into the West. Manifest Destiny was Providence to this minister, who led the laity in cruelty to the Negro, treachery to the Yankee, and prayer to God. Whittier never acknowledged intentionally the dilemma which faced the clergy in the South. Nor did he seem to recognize that its members could have been concerned with problems of charity and humanity in a slave society. That the Southern clergy were hypocrites remained his firm and settled conviction.

From the age of twenty-one, when he first became an editor, Whittier was well trained in the ways of American politics and had learned to follow the newspaper exchanges regularly. His antislavery writings brought him into close association with the political arena, in which he became a hard-hitting editor. When the abolitionists founded *The National Era* in Washington, January, 1847, Whittier was invited to serve as corresponding editor. He was a good choice for a paper which declared in its first issue that its aim was to cover current events, congressional proceedings, general politics, and literature. From Amesbury he submitted antislavery poems, book notices, and controversial articles, frequently political in nature. His respect for political dexterity reflected itself in his comments on Clay, Calhoun, and Benton, who formed what he called the triumvirate of Southern leaders. There were times when Whittier was hopeful for both Benton and Clay, since one wanted slavery excluded from the territories and the other advocated emancipation in Kentucky. But, to him, Calhoun had a prototype in Milton's Satan. "Scarcely since the fall of the Bad Angel has so noble an intellect been devoted to a cause so unholy and abhorrent."[18]

One wonders how consistent with his theme of a decaying South was Whittier's repeatedly expressed fear of Southern political power. He was apprehensive lest the North never match the South in producing resolute, incisive leaders. He feared "the union, persistent energy, and audacity of the South." In his journalism he strove to create in the North a sectional identification which might give it a sense of solidarity for protection against the Southern union. To him, one of the compensations which rose from the Nebraska trouble was that it revealed a "North." He exhorted this "North," which he had helped to create, to oppose the South and strive to "denationalize" it. He denounced as weak and opportunistic those Northern politicians whose voting record did not show complete and uncompromising opposition to the South. Those congressmen who failed to vote for the Wilmot Proviso were labeled by *The National Era* as modern Judases who, having cursed the world by their treachery, lacked the conscience to hang themselves. These abusive words came from a paper which was only six issues old, but the tone of the paper was already established. It marked the intensity and pugnacity that persisted in most antislavery journalism until, with the horrors of a fratricidal war, its work was finished.

The book notices which Whittier sent to the *Era* show how com-

[18] For references in this and the following paragraph, see *The National Era*, I, No. 6 (Feb. 11, 1847); I, No. 31 (Aug. 5, 1847); VIII, No. 54 (Apr. 6, 1854). Whittier's view of the American cultural struggle had the Manichaean flavor of eternal opposition between good and evil. His slaveholder, "leagued with the Power of Darkness," participated in the "struggle with the Almighty for dominion over His rational creatures." See *Freeman*, IV, No. 5 (Apr. 12, 1838); IV, No. 6 (Apr. 19, 1838).

pletely this literary man was absorbed in the grimly practical business of agitation. On June 5, 1851, the editors of the *Era* devoted three and two-thirds columns of the front page to the first installment of *Uncle Tom's Cabin; or Life among the Lowly*. When the story was brought to a close the following April, the editors observed: "We do not recollect any production of an American writer that has excited more profound and general interest. Since the commencement of the publication in our columns, we have received literally thousands of testimonials from our renewing subscribers, to its unsurpassed ability." Whittier praised the book, calling it "the Iliad of the Blacks," but he never spoke of it in any detailed way. He accepted the book as a truthful picture of Southern scenes and customs. "Uncle Tom, as well as its subject, is entirely American; it has the 'odor of nationality' about it." Whittier's quip was true, but not in the sense he intended. His angle of vision was too nearly identical with Mrs. Stowe's for him to see its unintended area of meaning. The book was New England much more deeply than he realized. Its sentiment, moral fervor, and predilections were as Yankee as its protagonist. But Whittier did not discuss the book as literature; his mind was on its polemic value. Therefore, he wished to proclaim its fidelity to Southern life. Mrs. Stowe, he said, had "daguerreotype[d] some of the striking features of our 'peculiar institution.' "[19]

Two years later he reviewed William Goodell's *American Slave Code in Theory and Practice,* using it to support Mrs. Stowe's picture of the South.[20] Goodell's book was no romance, he said, it contained the hard facts of slavery, unquestionably true. It would serve as an emphatic refutation to those "pro-slavery divines and politicians" who had answered "the world-wide murmurs of sorrow and indignation awakened by the revelations of Uncle Tom's Cabin" by claiming that Mrs. Stowe exaggerated and libeled. *The American Slave Code,* Whittier affirmed, would end such idle contentions.

Let this book follow in the wake of Uncle Tom's Cabin, and it will be

[19] *The National Era,* V, No. 89 (June 5, 1851); VI, No. 54 (Apr. 1, 1852); VII, No. 21 (Feb. 10, 1853); VII, No. 55 (Apr. 7, 1853). In August, 1850, the *Era* published Mrs. Stowe's "The Freeman's Dream—A Parable," a story dealing with a toilworn, escaping slave.

[20] *The National Era,* VII, No. 55 (Apr. 7, 1853).

seen that there is not an atrocity or an agony described in that marvelous fiction, which has not been authorized and defended by positive law; recognized as a necessary part of the slave system, without which that system would lack completeness and vitality.

Whittier's interest in *The American Slave Code* exceeded his interest in *Uncle Tom,* and his comments on the former were more specific and direct. Comparing these remarks with those on the slave code which he had made fifteen years earlier, in 1838, one sees that during the intervening years Whittier's notion of Southern law remained substantially unchanged.

During the early months of 1853, *The New York Times* published a series of letters from Frederick Law Olmsted, who was then traveling through the South. At Amesbury, Whittier probably had no opportunity to read these letters, but three years later he reviewed them for *The National Era* when they were published in book form under the title *A Journey in the Seaboard Slave States.*[21] Whittier and his Anti-Slavery Society colleagues found it difficult to understand Olmsted's position. For, although Olmsted hated slavery, he objected to the abolitionists. His *Journey* was an important book, and Whittier could have learned much from it: first, the salutary example of reporting from direct observation, and, second, a picture of the South presented in its social and geographical variety. Moreover, in Olmsted's book there was the recognition of the continuity of slavery —not as an abstract evil but as a way of life—for the author saw that no one generation or group was alone responsible for slavery. But, above all, Whittier, with his hatred of the evil of slavery, was presented with a South which had been so thoroughly interpenetrated, body and soul, by slavery, that she was more a patient than a criminal.[22] Whittier called the book "a daguerreotype" and accredited

[21] *Ibid.,* X, No. 71 (May 1, 1856); Frederick Law Olmsted, *A Journey in the Seaboard Slave States in the Years 1853–1854. With Remarks on Their Economy* (originally issued 1856), with biographical sketch by Frederick Law Olmsted, Jr., and Introduction by W. P. Trent (G. P. Putnam's Sons, New York, 1904).

[22] I am indebted for the idea of this distinction to Broadus Mitchell, *Frederick Law Olmsted; a Critic of the Old South* (The Johns Hopkins Press, Baltimore, 1924), p. 68.

Olmsted with "the rare faculty of seeing things as they are, undistorted and uncolored."

In the review, Whittier did not turn his attention primarily to the aspect of the South's retarded development, which was an important part of the book—Olmsted's subtitle was *With Remarks on Their Economy*. This omission seems strange, inasmuch as Whittier had so frequently used the theme of ruin in writing of the South. But Olmsted saw that much of the South was still a frontier, which was something quite different from Whittier's notion of decline. Of all the Northern writers on slavery, only Bryant came close to understanding the importance of the frontier in the Southern way of life. Nevertheless, the closest Whittier ever came to freeing himself from his oversimplifications was in this review of the *Journey*. Olmsted's picture was complete, Whittier said, "so far as we can judge." Moreover, Whittier seemed to be approaching a perception of the tragic complexity of the social and economic problem of the South. Its system of slavery "curses not only master and slave, but the very soil on which they tread." But this was 1856. And under the intensified intersectional struggle of the mid-fifties one would hardly expect an agitator with twenty-five years of experience to soften his blows by paying deference to the varied complexion of the system he was fighting to destroy.

Whittier's antislavery writing fell off in bulk after the mid-fifties. The force of events by this time, moreover, made antislavery impetuousness seem like a water sprinkler in a rainstorm. Tempers were high because of the Kansas-Nebraska dispute and the Dred Scott decision. Whittier's production was always subject to the frequent periods of illness that he experienced all his life. He had been writing for twenty-five years, and it took more than Goodell and Olmsted to replenish his armory. Although he continued to hold his position on the *Era* until 1860, by 1856 he had had his say about the South. There is nothing to show, however, that his personal zeal had abated or that he had in any way changed his opinion about the South.

There has always been a tradition that Whittier hated slavery but loved the individual slaveholder, that he fought for principles, not against people. This idea was proclaimed, of course, by Whittier himself and has been carried on by Pickard, Pollard, Bennett, and others. In an unpublished dissertation, Max Griffin quoted the following statement of Whittier's: "I was never an enemy to the South or the holders of slaves. I inherited from my Quaker ancestry hatred of slavery, but not of slaveholders."[23] Griffin accepted this statement, as did Pickard, from whom the quotation was taken. And Vernon Louis Parrington said, "As a Friend, a man of peace, he would not deal harshly with the supporters of slavery; he would not counsel violence."[24] But Parrington also observed that Whittier "was conscience rather than intellect. He felt rather than thought." One cannot deny that Whittier, with his Quaker conscience, considered himself charitable toward all individuals. He stated his willingness to regard the majority of Southerners as kind, and at times he acknowledged some good in them.[25] But the tradition that he loved the individual Southerner is idle because the picture of the individual Southerner, drawn by Whittier in his writings, could only have aroused hatred for him. In spite of his declaration that he felt no animus toward the Southerner, he fell into the tyranny of types, caricatures, and too-easy generalizations. At times he even wiped out the geographic definition of the South: it began where freedom ended. During Frémont's campaign, when war clouds were unmistakably gathering, Whittier thanked God that he could witness the lining up of Good and Evil for a final battle, and he was reminded of Michael and his angels driving back the Spirits of the Night.[26] The unwary reader must have unconsciously passed with Whittier from hatred of slavery to hatred of the Southerner.

[23] Max Liles Griffin, "The Relations with the South of Six Major Northern Writers, 1830–1861" (unpublished dissertation, University of North Carolina, Chapel Hill, N.C., 1944). In his chapter on Whittier, Griffin tells of his contacts with Southerners, mostly those who had moved North and become abolitionists. Griffin's dissertation deals primarily with the friendships between Southerners and Northern writers.

[24] Samuel T. Pickard, *Life and Letters of John Greenleaf Whittier* (Houghton Mifflin Co., Boston, 1899), II, 501–502; Vernon Louis Parrington, *Main Currents in American Thought* (Harcourt, Brace and Co., Inc., New York, 1930), II, 364.

[25] Whittier, *Works*, VII, 64, 80, 81, 85, 91–92, 112 ff. See also *The National Era*, "The Mission of Democracy," II, No. 56 (Apr. 13, 1848); II, No. 61 (Apr. 20, 1848).

[26] Whittier, *Works*, III, 191–92.

By the time that secession sentiment had become alarmingly strong in the South, Whittier was able to say with composure that since freedom was higher than union and secession preferable to war the North should allow the Southern states to withdraw. In January of 1861, on the eve of the Civil War Whittier could say:[27]

> Draw we not even now a freer breath,
> As from our shoulders falls a load of death
>
> .   .   .   .
>
> Why take we up the accursed thing again?
> Pity, forgive, but urge them back no more
> Who, drunk with passion, flaunt disunion's rag
> With its vile reptile-blazon. Let us press
> The golden cluster on our brave old flag
> In closer union, and, if numbering less,
> Brighter shall shine the stars which still remain.

It seemed not to occur to him that secession meant defeat for his abolition campaign or that emancipation would not solve the enormous problem of racial relations. No reader of Whittier would deny his moral fervor, but his inability to consider the necessary ordering of means to the proper end of his idealism and his constant misjudgment of the world in which he lived made of him a nineteenth-century Don Quixote.

[27] *Ibid.,* III, 218–19.

· *3* ·

Lowell

J AMES RUSSELL LOWELL'S writings about the South were so implicitly bound up with his opposition to slavery that the two can in no way be separated. In 1848, he accredited Whittier with having "made (directly) more public opinion on the right side than any poet we can think of."[1] In this judgment Lowell was too generous to Whittier and too modest about the influence of his own work. It is true, of course, that Whittier was considered first voice in the abolitionist choir. Despite the fact that Lowell was much more of a part-time reformer than was Whittier, he probably contributed more tellingly to the Northern ante bellum hostility toward the South than did Whittier. Lowell had the advantages of formal training and taste which usually saved him from the cant notions and trite phraseology characterizing much abolition literature. The ever widening range of his reading in literary and cultural history counted effectively in the varied allusions and figures employed in his antislavery writing. His wit, irony, and sarcasm helped to catch the attention of America and to focus it on the abolitionist picture of the South.

With characteristic responsiveness to ideological trends, Lowell reflected in his earliest poetry the devotion to freedom that was to dominate his mind throughout what Harry Hayden Clark has called the humanitarian period of his life.[2] His native idealism found sym-

[1] *The National Anti-Slavery Standard,* IX (Dec. 21, 1848), 119.
[2] Harry Hayden Clark and Norman Foerster, *James Russell Lowell, Repre-*

pathy and encouragement in the abolitionist Maria White, whom he met in 1839 and married in 1844. Writing for the first time as an editor, in 1843, young Lowell praised the older abolitionists, calling them martyrs to the gospel of freedom. If they were at times "unguarded in their expressions," it must be remembered that "a great idea has seldom time to waste in selecting what Hotspur would have called 'parmaceti phrases.' "[3] He predicted that although Garrison was "too remarkable to be appreciated in his generation" later ages would recognize him as "a great and wonderful spirit." In a widely circulated poem, "To W. L. Garrison," Lowell trumpeted the message that freedom and truth were born in Garrison's small, friendless chamber.[4] When, in 1849, Horace Greeley attacked Garrison for fanaticism, Lowell maintained that Garrison was gloriously fulfilling a divine mission and thanked God for such fanatics.[5] Wendell Phillips also received support from the young Lowell, who wrote a sonnet in 1843 applauding Phillips for having the courage to join hands with the godly before it was expedient and fashionable to do so. And three years later, Phillips was again praised by Lowell in his "Letter from Boston" for the depth, clarity, and power of his eloquence.[6] Lowell was too close to his age not to be influenced in his own verse by the vogue of oratory. "The Present Crisis," which he wrote in 1844, was a favorite platform piece. George William Curtis testified to its power over New England audiences, particularly when Wendell Phillips read the lines.[7] "For twenty years the solemn monitory music of this poem never ceased to re-echo in public halls."

In December, 1844, Lowell moved to Philadelphia, where he served the Friends of the Anti-Slavery Society as an editorial writer

---

sentative Selections, with Introduction, Bibliography, and Notes (American Book Company, New York, 1947), p. xv.

[3] The Pioneer, A Literary Magazine, ed. James Russell Lowell. Introduction by Sculley Bradley (Scholars' Facsimiles and Reprints, New York, 1947), I, 93. Hereafter cited as The Pioneer.

[4] The Complete Poetical Works of James Russell Lowell (Houghton Mifflin Co., Boston, 1896), p. 103. Hereafter cited as Poetical Works.

[5] The Anti-Slavery Papers of James Russell Lowell (Houghton Mifflin Co., Boston, 1902), II, 83. Hereafter cited as Anti-Slavery Papers.

[6] Lowell, Poetical Works, pp. 23, 112.

[7] Ferris Greenslet, James Russell Lowell (Houghton Mifflin Co., Boston, 1909), pp. 78–80.

for their paper, the *Pennsylvania Freeman,* of which Whittier had been editor about seven years earlier. Lowell's opposition to slavery and Southern aggressiveness mounted rapidly, growing particularly ardent and articulate with the annexation of Texas and the War with Mexico, which he regarded as products of Southern greed. In 1846 he began to contribute steadily as a corresponding editor to *The National Anti-Slavery Standard.*[8] Yet he was never completely at home in the partisan environment. His letters to Sidney Howard Gay, the editor of the *Standard,* indicate that he realized the essential conflict between the journalistic demands of antislavery writing and his steadily growing desire to devote himself to poetry and the life of letters.

The uncertainty arising from this sense of antagonism can best be seen in Lowell's comments on the antislavery poetry of Whittier. Writing for his short-lived *Pioneer* in 1843, Lowell had maintained that in Whittier the poet was martyred in the service of mankind.[9] By means of a conveniently ambiguous metaphor, he thus had been able to support the reformer while at the same time exempting the poet from critical examination. In his *Fable for Critics,* however, written about five years later, Lowell was unwilling to disregard the literary measure of Whittier. That he had come to doubt the suitability of agitation for the full development of literary powers is clear from his lines on Whittier in the *Fable.* Perceiving that Whittier sometimes mistook excitement for inspiration, he observed that torrents of denunciation in verse had flooded over much of the truly poetic in Whittier. But remembering his own antislavery allegiance, Lowell excused the

---

[8] Lowell began contributing occasionally to the *Standard* at least five years before this and continued to do so for some time after 1848. All but a few of these items have been reprinted, either in various editions of his poetry, or in *Anti-Slavery Papers,* which reprints five editorials from the *Pennsylvania Freeman* and fifty from *The National Anti-Slavery Standard.* See George Willis Cooke, *A Bibliography of James Russell Lowell* (Houghton Mifflin Co., Boston, 1906). Cooke's *Bibliography,* however, has many errors and should be used with caution. See F. DeWolfe Miller, "Twenty-eight Additions to the Canon of Lowell's Criticism," *Studies in Bibliography* (University of Virginia, Charlottesville, Va., 1951), IV, 205–10. Miller has checked with the file of the *North American Review,* 1878 index, prepared by William Cushing and has revealed important omissions in Cooke's *Bibliography.*

[9] *The Pioneer,* I, 93.

weaknesses of his colleague's poetry by relating them to the source of his strength, which he found to be the Quaker's "fervor of mind." Reviewing Whittier's poetry for *The National Anti-Slavery Standard* a few months after completing the *Fable,* he avoided the fundamental question of the extraliterary uses of poetry and tried unconvincingly to reconcile poetry and action by praising Whittier as a voice crying in the wilderness.[10] The unresolved conflict in Lowell's mind destroyed the value of the review as criticism. It remains buried, as perhaps it should, in the pages of *The National Anti-Slavery Standard.*

Lowell was in complete accord with Whittier's view of the South, though his manner of attack was less visual and more conceptual than was Whittier's. Understanding that oppression was part of the universal problem of evil and that American slavery was one phase of oppression, Lowell frequently assaulted in general terms hypocrisy, oppression, or discrimination, leaving the reader to make his own application to the Southern system of slavery. His formal education made him aware of the moral and ethical wrong of slavery, but his limited knowledge of current events prevented him from making specific indictments or recommendations. He did not watch the contemporary political and social scene, North or South, as closely as did Whittier. Even while he was contributing regularly to *The National Anti-Slavery Standard,* Lowell confessed to its editor that he saw so few papers other than those on his side that he could not write a controversial article. Lowell recognized that he was in danger of "dealing too much in generalities," for he understood that the most effective way to argue against slavery was not by making generalized analyses based upon ethical principles but by plucking specimens from the tree to hold before the eyes of the masses.[11] Unlike Whittier, he did not paint particularized pictures of the South; but the ideas behind Whittier's pictures of decayed mansions, slave-whipping overseers, and runaway Negro women were all contained explicitly in Lowell. They formed a conceptual core or nucleus around which his attacks

[10] *The National Anti-Slavery Standard,* IX (Dec. 21, 1848), 119. It is erroneously listed in the *Bibliography* as appearing on Dec. 14, 1848. The review has not been reprinted.

[11] Horace E. Scudder, *James Russell Lowell, A Biography* (Houghton Mifflin Co., Boston, 1901), I, 212; Lowell, *Anti-Slavery Papers,* I, 163.

revolved. To identify this core is to realize that, in respect to the South, Whittier and Lowell were in essential agreement.

Lowell considered the South a cultural backwater and foresaw inevitable stagnation. He frequently asserted that the great struggle of the day was not primarily between North and South but between the progressive, enlightened spirit of the nineteenth century and the retrospective, static South. He often charged Southern leaders either with ignorance of history or with stubborn disregard for its meaning. His own view of history in the ante bellum days was that the past taught one to look forward. But in resisting the philosophy of natural rights, the South was closing its mind to the lessons of nature as well. In "King Retro," he ridiculed the South for its opposition to progress. King Retro's peculiar whim—and all monarchs, he said, have their irrational whims—was his determined attempt to keep last year's leaves from falling. The King and his ministers, clinging stubbornly to their "Ruin," legislated against freedom of speech and thought and banished the Bible and Light from their kingdom. The one wise counselor in the King's ministry, protesting in vain, pointed out that, even without the Bible, beaten and mistreated slaves would inevitably turn to God. He warned that the King could not shut out aspiration and love or interfere with nature's benign teaching, for the saneness and health of nature, he said, would always be an eloquent criticism of King Retro's government.[12] Many random comments can be found throughout Lowell's writing to show the persistence of this idea that the South was doomed as long as it resisted the popular New England ideologies of the day. Parson Wilbur's caricature of Calhoun as the mad knight tilting with an entire age is his most famous expression of this idea.

A concomitant of this prediction of doom was Lowell's contention that the Southern mind had steadily declined since the heroic period of American history. Once, steeped in the tradition of freedom and truth, he said, Southern leaders had been willing to discuss openly the question of Negro emancipation. After the Virginia Convention of 1831, they had suffered through self-interest a distortion of intellect

[12] Lowell, *Anti-Slavery Papers*, I, 143–46; II, 189; Thelma M. Smith (ed.), *Uncollected Poems of James Russell Lowell* (The University of Pennsylvania Press, Philadelphia, 1950), pp. 65–72. Hereafter cited as *Uncollected Poems*.

and a deadening of conscience. Southern leadership, which Lowell termed the "Southern oligarchy," received the brunt of his attack. He described it as a disgruntled, imperious, grasping group, which not only enslaved the Negro but also intimidated most whites, both Northern and Southern. Lowell declared openly that he would welcome any event which might exhibit this group in its true light.[13]

South Carolinians were singled out for particular abuse. In 1848, in *The National Anti-Slavery Standard,* he spoke of their "fatal facility for rendering themselves ridiculous." Political meetings in Charleston he stigmatized by "fustian," a favorite word of glib abolitionists. He scoffed at the "great Power" which defied world opinion and at the same time was terrified by the escape of twenty unarmed Negroes. Later, as editor of the *Atlantic Monthly,* he continued his ridicule of the state, again paying particular attention to what he considered was her naïve boasting. By dint of endless repetition alone, the South had convinced itself of the truth of its "sonorous nonsense." The "orgies of loquacity" coming from the South, particularly from South Carolina, reminded him of the proverbial woman who talked of her virtue. Southerners knew their figures of speech but were inept with statistics and deficient in practical wisdom and common sense. The South's dependence upon a single agricultural product brought from Lowell the statement that the whole South Carolina Convention knew less of political economy and laws of trade than any single average Northern merchant. The state's leading political figure, Calhoun, was ridiculed unrelentingly by Lowell. At one time he pictured him trying to put out the sun with a four-ounce squirt. Calhoun's reputation he accounted for by asserting that men admire boldness, even when it is on the wrong side. He presented Calhoun as a ruthless, cunning opportunist.[14]

Lowell's most characteristic attitude toward the South was one of scorn. This scorn he effectively communicated through his own par-

[13] Lowell, *Anti-Slavery Papers,* II, 148; *The Complete Writings of James Russell Lowell* (Houghton Mifflin Co., Boston, 1871–90), V, 4, 60–61. Hereafter cited as *Complete Writings.*

[14] Lowell, *Anti-Slavery Papers,* I, 143 ff; II, 113–18; Lowell, *Complete Writings,* V, 48–50, 58; for Lowell's treatment of Calhoun, see "Debate in the Sennit" and "An Imaginary Conversation." See also Lowell, *Anti-Slavery Papers,* I, 64, 136, 148, 50; II, 128, 152.

ticular kind of satire, as in the popular *Biglow Papers*. Series One of the *Papers* was designed to attack the Mexican War, which Lowell regarded as a sinister scheme of the South to extend the area for abusing Negroes. Birdofredum Sawin, Hosea Biglow, and Parson Wilbur were the spokesmen through whom he conjured up a Southland that violated all the hallowed values of the North. Hosea heaped abuses upon the South. A lover of liberty and peace, he charged the "grasping, over-reaching, nigger-drivin' States" with breaking down the virtue of the North and trying to enslave it. Parson Wilbur ridiculed Southern politicians. In B.O.F. Sawin, a character drawn with deadly irony, Lowell attacked both the South and those in the North who did not oppose the South. Sawin was an opportunistic, slovenly minded Northerner, who allowed himself to be duped by Southern buncombe and continued to be taken in even after sacrificing to Southern greed a leg, an arm, some fingers, and other parts of his anatomy. "The Debate in the Sennit," which Hosea "sot to a nusry rhyme," was his "Kind ov Poetikul lie" designed to establish in the minds of his readers an association between Southern politics and humbug. The ignorant, selfish cant of Calhoun, Foote, Cass, and others who supposedly engaged in this debate suggested as characteristics of the Southern mind such qualities as arrogance, smugness, mock piety, sloth, and defiance.[15]

The dramatic form was an effective vehicle for Lowell's irony. His puppets revealed themselves devastatingly. A longer, more detailed prose version of the "Debate in the Sennit" was published as "An Imaginary Conversation" in the May, 1848, issue of *The National Anti-Slavery Standard*.[16] It enabled Lowell to develop more fully several themes which were popular in abolitionist literature. His Machiavellian politicians of the South were contemptuous of the common man and cynical about the role of the public servant. Bragging of the advantage which Southern representatives enjoyed in Washington, one speaker wondered whether Northern noses were not "beginning to redden at the vicarious tweekings they [had] so long received through their waxen representatives." The "Conversation" supported the common abolitionist position that Southerners despised

---

[15] Lowell, *Poetical Works*, pp. 181 ff, 197 ff.
[16] Lowell, *Anti-Slavery Papers*, I, 68–84.

the American patriots of the Revolution. One of the imagined speakers reviled Jefferson for making concessions to the vague instincts of the people; another suggested that Jefferson knew well the difference between words and action and that, after all, it had been his words that had elevated him to the Presidency; a third added ironically that America owed a debt of gratitude to Jefferson because his words had enabled the South to purchase the votes of Northern democracy without spending any of the real specie of government. The Calhoun of the "Imaginary Conversations" was the most outspoken of the group. He professed his willingness to exploit the North whenever the opportunity presented itself and averred that cotton thread alone held the nation together. At the same time, he confessed to his circle of friends that the South was essentially weak and could not maintain itself without the support of the North. For this reason he acknowledged that disunion talk, although sometimes useful, was very dangerous and could not be pushed too far.

In a fearfully short time from the period of rupture, the South would be a Black Republic. We should be obliged to strain the cord so tightly that it would snap. At present, the piety and respectability of the North is the wet blanket which keeps our roof from taking fire. Remove that, and how long should we be safe under the shower of sparks from all parts of the civilized world?

Lowell's Calhoun valued piety. He realized that it was "as cheap as irreligion and vastly more profitable."

Lowell developed the knack of suggesting in a single passage various facets of Southern depravity and ignorance. In "An Imaginary Conversation," one of his Southerners reacted with a mixture of self-indulgent wistfulness and resentment to a news report that a beautiful slave girl had been kidnaped from a poor, pious widow. This Southerner knew of the Bible's admonition against stealing from widows and poor people, because, as he himself said, his spiritual adviser had told him so.[17]

The wench was nearly white, and of a figure approaching in beauty to Power's Greek Captive, though more voluptuous in proportions. Her mistress had lately refused fifteen hundred dollars for her. I assure you

[17] *Ibid.*, I, 75.

she was well worth that and more, but this noble woman refused it. She denied herself the many luxuries which the money might have procured, in the hope of bequeathing her as a widow's mite to the Methodist Episcopal Church South. What punishment is severe enough for monsters who would cross the path of piety such as this?

Through spokesmen such as these, Lowell called up a South that was offensive to his credulous readers: a South that trampled on Northern loyalty to the patriots who fought for American independence, that profaned their sacred sentiments of family solidarity, sexual purity, piety, thrift, and industry.

Blending themes of Southern sensuality with those of Southern misuse of organized religion was particularly popular with the abolitionists. In the "American Tract Society," Lowell charged Southern religion with being "blandly silent about the separation of families, the putting asunder whom God had joined, the selling of Christian girls for Christian harems." Then he asked: "Was there ever a Simony like this,—that does not sell, but withholds the gift of God for a price?"[18] Lowell felt with Whittier that true religion was basically humanitarian and therefore closed to slaveholders. He scoffed at an invitation extended by Dr. Bullard, a St. Louis clergyman, to an ecclesiastical committee of Northerners to make a firsthand study of conditions in the South. Lowell could imagine the representatives being dined by genial Southern hosts who cleverly restricted them to Southern parlors. He feared that the committeemen would be molested if they tried to see the plantation from the back, because he recalled that "it [was] only ten years since two persons had their ears cropped for entering into private conversation with 'servants' in Dr. Bullard's own city of St. Louis."[19] Admitting that even Dr. Bullard acknowledged slavery in the abstract to be morally evil, he concluded that slavery in practice must be "we know not what" in its wickedness; for Lowell ascribed to the principle popular among abolitionists that no institution was so perfect in practice as it was in theory. Dr. Bullard had wanted the committee to determine this "know-not-what" for themselves, but Lowell had not considered such a direct study necessary. "The horns of a dilemma, we fear, are not so com-

[18] Lowell, *Complete Writings,* V, 11.
[19] Lowell, *Anti-Slavery Papers,* I, 159–63.

fortable a refuge as those of the altar, to which theologians commonly fly when pursued by the justice of anti-slavery."

The Southern slave was regarded by Lowell as an essentially noble and capable person who was as yet unchallenged and therefore undeveloped. His usual reference to the Negro was to the man in bondage, the man doomed to despair under the system of slavery. His legacy from the white man, he said, was Pandora's box containing all evils and lacking the one important item, hope. The lot of the slave, as slave, could not be improved. Yet Lowell's Yankee distrust of leisure led him to affirm that the drudge was Nature's nobleman as surely as the idle man was selfish and decadent.[20] In the *Biglow Papers* Lowell drew a picture of the runaway slave. He created a dramatic incident in which the Negro, Pomp, turned the tables on B.O.F. Sawin, the prejudice-packed, obtuse, renegade Northerner. Since Sawin loved his "gunnin'," he went in search of a runaway slave whom he captured, taking the Negro's whole family. Pomp managed to get Sawin's gun, however, and, in making a slave of his captor, proved himself both more resourceful and more merciful than Sawin. Pomp was clearly the master of Sawin. He was firm, coolheaded, resourceful, genuinely religious, intellectually curious, industrious in raising corn and "taters" and in other ways caring for his family, and, above all, merciful toward those who would exploit his race. Pomp's great desire was to follow the North Star to the land of freedom and opportunity.[21] Unlike his fellow-reformers, Lowell usually avoided the repetitive use of emotion-stirring clichés about the Southern Negro. But his picture of the noble Pomp trying desperately to care for his "woolly-headed cubs" undoubtedly appealed effectively to the domestic sympathies of the Northern reader. The episode was a well-chosen "specimen" of bad fruit for the Northern masses to use in judging their Southern neighbors.

Lowell was more outspoken in his references to the slaveholder. His ideal of treating slavery on a theoretical level did not prevent him from falling into the abusive epithets that were characteristic of much abolition writing. Lowell considered idle any talk about kind and generous planters because he held that a slaveholder, as slaveholder,

---

[20] *Ibid.,* I, 195, 205; II, 12.
[21] Lowell, *Poetical Works,* pp. 212–17.

could not be kind or generous.[22] The terms were mutually repugnant. When his widely scattered comments are assembled, Lowell's notions of slaveholders become visible: they were ruffians who knew the craft of tyranny; they had sleek, catlike predatory instincts of selfishness; they were hypocrites professing piety but engaging in impious traffic in human flesh; they were ignorant of history; they were idle and soft handed; they were thieves holding their brethren in bondage; they were haughty and sneering; they loved fustian and hated truth; they demanded every form of sacrifice from the North without giving anything in return except scorn and rebuke; they were the cursed race of Amalek; they were tyrants and devils who offered the vilest arguments in defense of their vilest of tyrannies; they were pimps of slavery; they perpetrated daily enormities worse than those of the Inquisition. Their land was sin's stronghold.

Thus did Lowell continue piling his literary stones on the barrier separating North and South. Running throughout all his works on the South was the implication that the Southern cousins were the black sheep of the family who gave it a bad name abroad. Lowell insisted that the manifold evils of the South could not be localized and that the entire family of states, North and South, would inevitably be infected. His Siamese twins carried this idea effectively. Actually, the careful reader could see that by the one sick twin Lowell meant not the South but slavery itself. But imperceptibly this twin became associated in the mind of the reader—and doubtless in Lowell's mind too—with the South in general, so that the impression derived from the reading was that of a well-meaning, innocent North that was being dreadfully abused and victimized by a diseased, dissolute South. Lowell also referred to the North as a Sancho Panza who was unwilling to accept self-inflicted punishment in order to be rid of the wicked enchantment and whose ideal was enslaved by a self-indulgent, unscrupulous neighbor. Yet the North, Lowell charged, would only beat trees in a vain effort to be rid of the curse. One of his methods of attack, when he became editor of the *Atlantic Monthly*, was to talk of the North as a province of the slaveholding states. Pointing out that

[22] References in this paragraph are as follows: Lowell, *Anti-Slavery Papers*, I, 62, 96, 143–46, 207; II, 12, 15, 55–56, 113, 120; Lowell, *Poetical Works*, 82–83, 197 ff; Smith (ed.), *Uncollected Poems*, 42, 43.

the free states were without their fair share of influence in the federal government, he predicted that things could only get worse unless the North asserted itself resolutely. The slave power, he said, had forced upon the entire country a falseness which clashed with its sense of right. Therefore a "moral disintegration" had set in; "beginning with our public men, it [has] gradually spread to the Press, the Pulpit, nay worse than all, the Home, till it is hard to find a private conscience that is not tainted with the contagious mange." Repeating a figure of speech which he had used earlier, he compared the slave power to a Swiss glacier which slowly surged forth, covering everything in its path.[23]

In the schism of abolitionists, Lowell's attachments were stronger to the Garrisonians than to the "new organization," to which Whittier had allied himself, for, unlike Whittier, Lowell believed the abolitionists should remain free of political commitments.[24] He was disappointed in the uncompromising harshness of Garrison, however, and tried hard to understand Garrison's faults, calling them faults of his position. In 1848 he observed: "There never has been a leader of Reform who was not also a blackguard. Remember that Garrison was so long in a position where he alone was right and all the world wrong, that such a position has created in him a habit of mind which may remain, though circumstances have wholly changed."[25] About this time Lowell's zeal for agitation began to wane, and his antislavery writing diminished both in bulk and in ferocity. He had never shared the shallow optimism that characterized so much of the movement, and his wit and imagination made him chafe at its restrictions. More-

[23] Lowell, *Anti-Slavery Papers,* I, 156–57; II, 6; Smith (ed.), *Uncollected Poems,* pp. 74–75; Lowell, *Complete Writings,* V, 21, 43; *Atlantic Monthly,* I, 758–59.

[24] Leon Howard said that Lowell was not always so sure of himself on this point. When he went to Philadelphia he was ready to have his mind made up for him. And Lowell also found himself on the fence at times between free-soil and disunion. See Leon Howard, *Victorian Knight-Errant: a Study of the Early Literary Career of James Russell Lowell* (University of California Press, Berkeley, 1952), pp. 192, 280. But in a *National Anti-Slavery Standard* editorial dated February 22, 1849, "The Moral Movement against Slavery," Lowell expressed emphatically his belief that since political action was subject to temporary set backs, it was more expedient for the reformer to avoid any political commitment.

[25] Scudder, *James Russell Lowell,* I, 189.

over, the breadth of his personal studies helped him to develop toler-
ance and restraint.[26] The steady emergence of conservatism which
marked his intellectual development had set in. Profoundly discouraged by the Compromise of 1850, he expressed a wish to leave his
special vineyard and to get as far away from American slavery as
possible.[27]

There were other causes, too, for the waning of Lowell's spirit of
agitation. Between 1847 and 1853 death struck his family relentlessly,
taking from him three of his four children, his mother, and his wife.
The tragedy in his private life deepened the meditative and reflective
side of his temperament. Two trips to Europe and a professor's chair
at Harvard broadened his perspectives and turned his mind and pen
to other subjects. When he became editor of the *Atlantic Monthly* in
1857, his attention was focused once again on the American scene.
His re-enlistment in the ideological war was dictated by the intensified hostility between the North and the South in the final years before
the Civil War.

Nevertheless, Lowell's own writing in the *Atlantic Monthly* during
the years immediately preceding the war revealed a marked change
from his earlier attitude. He had grown dissatisfied with abolitionist
agitation, even satirizing Wendell Phillips under the name Philip
Vandal and deriding those who claimed to love their fellow-men but
had nothing but brickbats for them.[28] This was in December, 1860.
In the previous issue he had reviewed Olmsted's *Back Country,* expressing great admiration for Olmsted and saying that "no more important contributions to contemporary American history" could be
found than in his work. "To discuss the question of Slavery without

---

[26] In one of his letters to Sidney Gay, the editor of *The National Anti-Slavery
Standard,* Lowell observed that nature everywhere, even in the South, must
have its healing powers which work slowly but inevitably upon social ills. Never
able to understand a religion that sanctioned human slavery, he nevertheless
observed philosophically that each person revolves about God in his own orbit
and that after all Christ walked with sinners. Charles Eliot Norton (ed.),
Letters of James Russell Lowell (Harper & Brothers, New York, 1894), I, 158.

[27] *Ibid.,* I, 48.

[28] Reprinted in James Russell Lowell, *The Function of the Poet and Other
Essays,* coll. and ed. Albert Mordell (Houghton Mifflin Co., Boston, 1920).
Ferris Greenslet identified "Philip Vandal" as Wendell Phillips. (Greenslet,
James Russell Lowell, p. 151; Mordell's Preface, p. ix.)

passion or even sentiment seemed an impossibility; yet Mr. Olmsted has shown that it can be done, and, having no theory to bolster, has contrived to tell us what he saw, and not what he went to see." In acknowledging that Olmsted was a good observer, Lowell attested to the value of the fact. In the "really new fact," he said, lay "the germinal principle of knowledge." He was praising a method quite alien to that of the abolitionists. One sees also that Lowell's concern for slavery as a moral issue had yielded a good deal to slavery as a political force. The political "lead" article (April, 1858), of which Lowell wrote the last six of fourteen pages, contained a fervent attack upon the Buchanan administration for its support of Southern policies, and it scoffed at secession threats. Other articles, such as "The Election in November" (October, 1860) and "The Question of the Hour" (January, 1861), demonstrate the predominantly political nature of Lowell's hostility toward the South. In November, 1860, Lowell reviewed Whittier's *Home Ballads and Poems*. This time Lowell found the essential character of Whittier's poetry to be lyrical, and not, as in 1848, oratorical. The poet had changed, but so had the reviewer. Whittier, he said, was exhibiting "a softer and more meditative mood." Now, a backward glance at Whittier's antislavery verse could bring a slight arch to Lowell's eyebrow. "The years deal kindly with good men, and we find a richer and clearer quality in these verses where the ferment is over and the *rile* has quietly settled."[29]

Lowell's world had broader horizons and more varied associations than Whittier's, but, when it came to the South, his attitudes were substantially the same as Whittier's. Although his opinion of abolitionism had altered with his emerging conservatism, there is no indication of any change either in his image of the South or in the conceptual core around which his attacks had always revolved: under the plantation system the rich become richer, the poor poorer. The system inevitably impoverishes the soil. It weakens the moral and spiritual life of society. Politicians, newspapermen, and clergymen must go to unnatural extremes in protecting the fraudulent system. As natural forces join in opposition, the slaveholder necessarily becomes more repressive and cruel, the politician more militant and aggressive, and

[29] *Atlantic Monthly,* I, 759; VI, 635–39; VII, 120; Lowell, *Complete Writings,* V, 20 ff.

the minister more contradictory to the spirit of true Christianity. Lowell saw the South as a society marked by those characteristics which had produced revolt in Europe, only the small landowner and the free worker—the keel of society—were lacking. With these factors of revolt present, it appeared certain that the irrepressible conflict would be surely developing within the South itself.[30]

The full ironic force of this notion can be appreciated only when one looks back over the battlefields of the Civil War to the controversies which brought them about. One must admire the underlying cause for Whittier's and Lowell's agitation—the love of liberty and the undaunted recognition of the right of every individual to guide his own life. Understandably, Lowell and Whittier were alienated by the Southern theory of slavery; but they were shocked by its practice, not as it was in its day-to-day reality, about which they knew little, but as they viewed it in their suppositions. The important question here is not what resemblance these suppositions had to actual conditions in the South, for no doubt there were many instances of cruelty and wickedness among slaveholders. Moreover, the failure of slavery in respect to certain social and moral consequences is simply a matter of record—though when judged economically it was certainly not a failure, as recent studies have convincingly demonstrated.[31] The point here is the willingness of these men to impute the limitations of a system to what they regarded as the wickedness of the men who were part of it, to trust the validity of their blackest assumptions about these men, and to apply one indictment to all Southerners. Theirs was a propaganda of hatred and fear. The conflict which they were helping to make irrepressible cannot be separated from the distrust and resentment generated by a growing body of extremists, North and South. In their failure to perceive the complexity and depth of the evil they opposed, Whittier and Lowell committed themselves, in the final analysis, to the ugly business of creating for the popular imagination a villain whom the people of the North would soon be quite willing to meet in battle.

[30] Lowell, *Complete Writings,* V, 32, 60–61; Lowell, *Anti-Slavery Papers,* I, 171, 195, 200, 212; II, 55, 56, 78, 138, 163.
[31] See, for example, Kenneth M. Stampp, *The Peculiar Institution: Slavery in the Ante-Bellum South* (Alfred A. Knopf, Inc., New York, 1956).

· 4 ·

Emerson and Thoreau

R|ALPH WALDO EMERSON'S interest in the South, unlike that of Whittier and Lowell, antedated the abolitionist movement in New England. At Harvard, 1817–21, Emerson knew some Southern students, and although his opinion of them was not complimentary—he thought them spoiled children who were good for nothing but further spoiling[1]—this acquaintance aroused in him an interest in Southern character. After graduation he invited a correspondence with one of his Southern classmates, stating that he wished to inquire deeply into "the peculiar and striking distinctions which we see at Cambridge separating our Northern and Southern countrymen."[2] Nothing came of the invitation, however, and Emerson was obliged to wait for an opportunity to learn more about Southern character until 1826, when he traveled South for his health. Nevertheless, his observations of Southern character at Harvard no doubt accounted in part for his treatment of the Southern slaveholder in the "Vision of Slavery," which he wrote a year after graduation. He argued against slavery, but his objections were based on principle and not on alleged cruelty or mistreatment of the slave by the master. "For it is true that many a slave under the

---

[1] *The Journals of Ralph Waldo Emerson* (Houghton Mifflin Co., Boston, 1909–13), IV, 312–13. Hereafter cited as *Journals*.

[2] Ralph Leslie Rusk (ed.), *The Letters of Ralph Waldo Emerson* (Columbia University Press, New York, 1939), I, 108. Hereafter cited as *Letters*.

warm roof of a humane master, with easy labours and regular subsist-
ence enjoys more happiness than his naked brethren" in Africa.[3]

Emerson traveled in the South during 1826 and 1827, long before
antislavery agitation had made Northern travelers self-conscious and
tutored in their responses to life in the South. Emerson's concern was
for his health, and the intellectual and spiritual adjustments which he
found necessary to make because of his illness meant that he was not
circumspective as a traveler. Nevertheless, he was pleased by the cordiality and gracefulness of Southern manners, noting that as one
traveled South one could not miss "the amelioration of manners." He
noticed, too, the relaxed, leisurely pace of the Southerners. He remarked in his journal that he had "never seen an awkward Carolinian." And later, in a letter to Lidian, he wrote that "the bland
speech and courtly manners" of Baltimoreans were "a kindly contrast" to the "more selfish manners" of the Northerners. "If I may
ask my way in the street, there is sure to be some gracefulness in con-
veying the information, and service of the negroes in the hotels is
always courteous."[4]

The Southern personality always held a fascination for Emerson.
During his lecture tour of the British Isles, in 1847 and 1848, he told
his audiences that the "Southern people are almost all speakers, and
have every advantage over the New England people, whose climate is
so cold that 'tis said we do not like to open our mouths very wide."[5]
In his extensive lecture tours in America, Emerson again had the opportunity to observe Southern manners. From St. Louis he wrote a
droll description to Lidian of the men he saw on the river boats, of the
planters who carried pistols in their breast pockets, of the "amiable
gentlemen" who gambled ostentatiously with large sums of money
and, Emerson fancied, hoped to lure the reticent Yankees into the
game. They "professed to be entire strangers to each other, and, if
asked any question respecting the river, 'Had never been on these
waters before.' "[6]

The quiet-mannered, thoughtful Emerson was sometimes awed

<hr>

[3] Emerson, *Journals*, I, 184.   [4] *Ibid.*, II, 141–42; III, 129.
[5] *The Complete Works of Ralph Waldo Emerson* (Houghton Mifflin Co.,
Boston, 1883–93), VII, 68–70.
[6] Emerson, *Letters*, IV, 210–11.

by the swagger, the lustiness, and the self-confident assertion of the Southerner. He spoke of "tall, restless, Kentucky strength" and the willingness of the Kentuckian to drink and fight.[7] He always considered the Southerner a better fighting man than the Northerner and thought it proof enough that "a Southern minority prevails, and gives the law." The secret of Southern power he placed in "the private heats and courages" of Southern individuals. He was of the opinion that the Southern way of life, with its "slavery and hunting, sportsmanship and the climate and politics," gave the men self-reliance.

The Southerner always beats us in politics. And for this reason, that it comes at Washington to a game of personalities. The Southerner has personality, has temperament, has manners, persuasion, address, and terror. The cold Yankee . . . has not fire or firmness, and is coaxed and talked and bantered and shamed and scared till he votes away the dominion of his millions at home! He never comes back quite the same man he went; but has been handled, tampered with.

Emerson feared the Yankee was outclassed both in the salon and on the field. "The South is well officered, and, with some right, they despise the peaceful North people, leaning on the law and on each other." Yet despite the Southerner's strength and energy, which he freely acknowledged, he considered Southern culture too raw and hurried to be well developed and finished. Nature had hastened there, he thought. When the war broke out, Emerson assumed that the Southerner welcomed it as "a chivalrous sport to him, like hunting, [which] suit[ed] his semi-civilized condition." Emerson's attitude toward Southern personality and manners can best be summarized by quoting from his letter to James E. Cabot, written in August, 1861:

At first sight, it looked only as a war of manners, showing that the Southerner who owes to climate and slavery his suave, cool, and picturesque manners, is so impatient of ours, that he must fight us off. And we all admired them until a long experience only varying from bad to worse has shown us, I think finally, what a noxious reptile the green and gold thing was . . . these spit such unmistakable venom, that I think we are *desillusionnés* once for all.

[7] References in this paragraph are to Emerson, *Journals,* VII, 257, 294; VIII, 100, 101; IX, 85, 297, 308; Emerson, *Works,* XI, 213, 284; Emerson, *Letters,* V, 253.

To follow Emerson through this "long experience" is to realize that, despite his critical independence, many fixed notions of the South drifted beyond his critical fences and gathered in the corners of his mind. The promise that the young college graduate showed of studying Southern character perceptively in its ideological environment was never realized.

After 1844 Emerson no longer looked upon the Southerner as affable and courteous. In this year he delivered an address honoring the tenth anniversary of West Indian emancipation.[8] The evils of the plantation system, as Emerson found them in his preparatory reading, impressed his mind vividly and formed the basis for his judgments of all slaveholding communities. In his address he described a society which despised the familiar signs of a thriving middle-class community. The whistle of the railroad, the newspaper, the mailbag were not loved, Emerson said, by slavery. Nor did it love the scholar or the preacher who had "the absurd whim of saying what he thinks." Under conditions of slavery, Emerson affirmed, "everything goes to decay." A creation of man's greed, the system was nevertheless unsound economically. As the British tradesmen had recognized, the slave laborer, unlike the wage-earner, could never be a customer. Ugly questions of ethics and rumors of homicide and adultery were simply drowned out by the tolling bells and pious organ tones of the white man. In this system every house had its dungeon and "every planter was the spoiled child of his unnatural habits." The Negro was a victim of a tragic racial myth which taught him that the Great God was punishing him for the greed of his ancestor. Although relating specifically to the West Indies, Emerson's view applied to slave plantations everywhere, the "peculiar institution" of the South not excepted.[9] Moreover, his concept of life under the system of slavery remained fixed in its fundamental features: The Negro was docile, simple, easily exploited; the planter was indolent, licentious, material-

---

[8] Emerson, *Works,* XI, 103, 118–19, 123–26.

[9] Emerson spoke of the painful comparisons: "Whilst I have read of England, I have thought of New England." Paragraph 2 of this address contains the implication that Emerson regarded the plantation system in the United States as essentially the same as that in the British West Indies. Elsewhere Emerson says that slavery is slavery wherever it is found. Emerson, *Works,* XI, 101, 129–30, 228.

istic, and cruel; religion in the slave area was only a comforting cover for the ugliness and vice of the system; the economics of the system was unsound, and it was shortsighted as an agricultural program. Emerson approved of the British method of emancipating the slaves by purchasing them from the planters and tried unsuccessfully to interest his fellow-Americans in the plan.[10]

It was about four months after the West Indies speech that Emerson's friend Samuel Hoar, who had gone South to investigate the seizing of Negro citizens of Massachusetts from Northern ships in Southern harbors, was expelled from South Carolina. This cavalier treatment of Hoar, which seemed to Emerson an unmistakable indication of the barbarity of the South, created in him an enduring antipathy. In its retarded culture the South revealed only animal nature, brute strength, and therefore it was inferior to Massachusetts, which had achieved a moral nature.[11] Emerson compared South Carolina to the troublesome, crime-infested areas of the world and stated that it was to America what Algiers was to Turkey, Calabria to Naples, Alsatia to London. "We must go there in disguise and with pistols in our pockets, leaving our pocketbooks at home, making our wills before we go." Every man of honor, humanity, and freedom had been excluded from the state, he said. Emerson charged further that its people were degraded, that their lips were padlocked, and that they were a people of but one opinion—Calhoun's. From this time on, Emerson regarded the South as the stronghold of immorality, of force, of thought control.

Subsequent events during the late forties and the fifties merely intensified Emerson's hostility toward the South, and his attitude became virtually indistinguishable from that of the abolitionists. He shared their apprehension over expansion in the Southwest. The annexation of Texas was to Emerson "one of those events which retard or retrograde the civilization of ages." When American troops invaded Mexico he prophesied both victory and disaster, proclaiming that Mexico would poison the United States. Noting the commercial ties between North and South, he charged that Massachusetts and New York co-operated with the South only because of their mortgages

---

[10] Emerson, *Works,* XI, 208; Emerson, *Letters,* IV, 484 and note.
[11] Emerson, *Journals,* VII, 14–15, 21, 191–92; Emerson, *Works,* XI, 260.

on Southern property. "Cotton thread holds the Union together; unites John Calhoun and Abbot Lawrence." The Fugitive Slave Law he denounced as immoral, for it enacted the crime of kidnaping, and he resolved to do all in his power to oppose its execution. Four years later, during the agitation over the Kansas-Nebraska territories, Emerson's anger mounted even higher. "What effrontery it required to fly in the face of what was supposed settled law, and how it shows that we have no guards whatever, that there is no proposition whatever, that is too audacious to be offered us by the Southerner." By this time, Emerson believed that the country was divided irremediably between right and might. On the fourth anniversary of Webster's "Seventh of March" speech, Emerson declared in an address given in New York that it was too late for the position of compromise, too late to find good and plausible things to say for the South. Webster had treacherously bowed before might, he said. "This is not a question of ingenuity, not a question of syllogisms, but of sides. How came he there?"[12]

Emerson's anger reached its peak two years later, in 1856, when his friend Charles Sumner was assaulted in the Senate by Brooks, of South Carolina.

I do not see how a barbarous community and a civilized community can constitute one state. . . . The whole state of South Carolina does not now offer one or any number of persons who are to be weighed for a moment in the scale with such a person as the meanest of them all has now struck down. . . . It is the best whom they desire to kill. It is only when they cannot answer your reasons, that they wish to knock you down. If, therefore, Massachusetts could send to the Senate a better man than Mr. Sumner, his death would be only so much the more quick and certain.

In February of the following year Emerson heard John Brown speak in the Town Hall and announced that Brown gave a good account of himself. Emerson considered the Harper's Ferry raid a "fatal blunder," but one which made Brown's virtues clear to all. "The man is so transparent that all can see through him, that he has no second thought, but was the rarest of heroes, a pure idealist, with no by-ends

[12] Emerson, *Journals*, VII, 26, 201, 206; VIII, 179, 442–43; Emerson, *Works*, XI, 187, 225–26.

of his own." Although he acknowledged that the Governor, of Virginia, had praised Brown for his courage and idealism, Emerson's antipathy toward the South was by this time so complete that he could only accuse the United States Court in Virginia, "in its present reign of terror," of requesting Northern witnesses, not for legitimate legal purposes, but for party purposes. "It wants [them] for meat to slaughter and eat."[13]

The events of the fifties confirmed Emerson's fears of Southern political power. It was "the ascendency of Southern manners" that drew the public men into the support of the South. As his alarm increased, distorted antislavery imagery began to color more vividly his picture of the South. At the same time, his attitude toward the North grew more sentimental and less critical. He drew more sharply the line between the slave states and the free states. Expressions such as "party of darkness" versus "party of light," "aristocracy" versus "plebeian strength" began to appear in his journals and addresses. Like his fellow-abolitionists, he assumed that the goodness of the individual was simply lost in the badness of the slavery system. "No excess of good nature or of tenderness in individuals has been able to give a new character to the system, to tear down the whipping-house." With the facility of an experienced pamphleteer, he passed from the general concept, "system," to the particularized image, "whipping-house," an image which had become in his mind synonymous with the Southern system. Emerson maintained that no slaveholder could be free. "Is a man free whose conscience accuses him of thefts and lies and indulgences without number? No." He fell into the abolitionist assumption that nobility and sincerity were inevitable concomitants to the Negro's ignorance and simplicity. Those who ran away were fleeing from plantation whips and hiding from hounds. "The poor black boy, whom the fame of Boston had reached in the recesses of a vile swamp, or in the alleys of Savannah . . . had taken the risk of being shot, or burned alive, or cast into the sea, or starved to death, or suffocated in a wooden box, to get away from his driver."[14]

[13] Emerson, *Works*, XI, 247–48, 272; Emerson, *Letters*, V, 179–80; Emerson, *Journals*, IX, 248.

[14] Emerson, *Journals*, VIII, 186–87, 242, 301–302, 382–83; Emerson, *Works*, XI, 185, 187–88, 193, 238.

Those who co-operated with the South were stigmatized. Any judge who obeyed the Fugitive Slave Law by returning a runaway slave to the South made of his bench an extension of the planter's whipping post. Emerson sarcastically remarked that although Everett spoke eloquently and ornamentally of liberty, he acted "with the planter's whip in his buttonhole." Emerson's disappointment in Webster overpowered his judgment. He saw Webster as a spineless, opportunistic sycophant to Southern power, one who had "deliberately taken out his name from all the files of honour . . . from all association with liberal, virtuous, and philanthropic men, and read his recantation on his knees at Richmond and Charleston." The following quotation demonstrates that Emerson not only misjudged the personal power of Webster in national politics but also permitted his anger to blur his picture of America.[15]

It will be Webster's distinction to have changed in one day, by the most detestable law that was ever enacted by a civilized state, the fairest and most triumphant national escutcheon the sun ever shone upon, the free, the expanding, the hospitable, the irresistible America, home of the homeless, and pregnant with the blessing of the world, into a jail or barracoon for the slaves of a few thousand Southern planters, and all the citizens of this hemisphere into kidnappers and drivers for the same.

Emerson's anger over Brooks's assault on Sumner led him to exaggerate uncritically his account of both Northern and Southern values.

Life has not parity of value in the free state and in the slave state. In one, it is adorned with education, with skilful labor, with arts, with long prospective interests, with sacred family ties, with honour and justice. In the other, life is a fever; man is an animal, given to pleasure, frivolous, irritable, spending his days in hunting and practising with deadly weapons to defend himself against his slaves and against his companions brought up in the same idle and dangerous way. Such people live for the moment, they have properly no future, and readily risk on every passion a life which is of small value to themselves or to others.

Emerson's letter to his brother William in June of 1856 revealed the extent of his pessimism. He stated that he was looking at the map to

---

[15] Emerson, *Works*, XI, 198; Emerson, *Journals*, VIII, 184, 190, 213.

find a place to go with his children when Boston and Massachusetts should surrender to the slave trade. "If the Free States do not obtain the government next fall, which our experience does not entitle us to hope, nothing seems left, but to form at once a Northern Union, & break the old."[16]

The events of the next few years did not restore his hope, and by 1858 he was calling for a *"cordon sanitaire"* to isolate the pestilence of the South. In 1859, he affirmed that the slaveholder who "chains and chops" such men as Brown fails to realize that many other opponents will emerge. These opponents will be men who breathe the air of liberty and who regard slaveholders as "felons who have disentitled themselves to the protection of law, as the burglar has . . . and therefore no matter how many Browns he can catch and kill, he does not make the number less, for the air breeds them, every school, every church . . . every home of courtesy, genius and conscience is educating haters of him and his misdeeds." Emerson's myopia was at its worst when he declared of Brown: "There is a Unionist,—there is the strict constructionist for you. He believes in the Union of the States, and he conceives that the only obstruction to the Union is slavery, and for that reason, as a patriot, he works for its abolition." In June, 1861, Emerson wrote to his Aunt Mary Moody: "It does not now look probable that the foot of any slave-owner or slave-catcher will pollute that ground [Sleepy-Hollow Cemetery]. Let us hope that the very South wind will come to us cleaner & purer of that taint, until it is sweet as the air of Maine Mountains." Two months later Emerson wrote a letter to James E. Cabot which contained an excellent summary of his position:[17]

And yet, gulf as it is, the war with its defeats and uncertainties is immensely better than what we lately called the integrity of the Republic, as amputation is better than cancer. I think we are all agreed in this, and find it out by wondering why we are so pleased, though so beaten and so poor. . . . If the abundance of heaven only sends us a fair share of light

[16] Emerson, *Works,* XI, 247; Emerson, *Letters,* V, 23.
[17] Emerson, *Journals,* IX, 146–47, 241–42; Emerson, *Works,* XI, 268–69; Emerson, *Letters,* V, 249, 253.

and conscience, we shall redeem America for all its sinful years since the century began.

One cannot miss the depth of Emerson's dismay as he viewed the tragic course of events during these years. As this man of thought considered the mountains of cotton and sugar and the obedience of the American people, both Northern and Southern, to the dictates of trade, he felt like Prince Hamlet. There was an irresolvable conflict in his mind regarding the abolitionist societies. His hatred of slavery made him fundamentally sympathetic toward them, but his distrust of reform disposed him to doubt their value. He recognized that most reform was negative. He was clear-sighted enough to see that the reformer must indemnify his victim or turn out to be merely a thief. A fundamental tenet of Emersonianism, after all, was that each man and woman, black or white, must save himself.

Nature will only save what is worth saving, and it saves, not by compassion, but by power. It saves men through themselves. . . . If the black man carries in his bosom an indispensable element of a new and coming civilization, for the sake of that element no wrong nor strength nor circumstance can hurt, he will survive and play his part.

Emerson's hope, therefore, was for the emergence of strong individuals among the Negroes, men who were capable of contending with the whites. A Toussaint or a Douglass, "if he is of pure blood," would outweigh all the antislavery societies of the world. "If you have man, black or white is an insignificance." With this perspective, Emerson was able to caution wisely those who assumed "the dangerous pretension of being abolitionists."[18]

Another facet of Emerson's attitude toward the South was reflected in his personal response to the abolitionists. In 1835, he perceived what Higginson later expressed in his backward glance over the ante bellum era, that the agitators, in their vanity and "thirst for notice," were groping for "what is called a cause." It was also in 1835 that he cautioned the abolitionists Samuel J. May and George Thompson against polluting their cause with personal feelings, warning them "to adhere religiously to the fact and the principle." In 1844, however,

---

[18] Emerson, *Letters,* IV, 484; Emerson, *Journals,* VI, 532, 533, 535.

the year of his "Address on the West Indian Emancipation" and of Hoar's expulsion from South Carolina, Emerson praised Wendell Phillips highly, saying that Webster, Everett, and all political aspirants should learn their eloquence from him. The following year he recommended Phillips to the curators of the Lyceum because, he said, "slavery had a commanding right to be heard in all places in New England." And in this same year, 1845, he praised Garrison, calling him "a virile speaker." Garrison, he said, "brings his whole history with him, wherever he goes, and there is no falsehood or patchwork, but sincerity and unity."[19] In a speech given at Dedham on July 16, 1846, and printed in *The National Anti-Slavery Standard,* Emerson expressed his gratitude to the abolitionists. Theirs was the school of love and action, he said, already consecrated by the blood of martyrs.[20]

At the same time, Emerson had always feared the exaggeration of the abolitionists. Stated mathematically, without the colorings of imagination and emotion, the position of the abolitionists, he thought, was right. But he feared "the personal feelings" and the "adverbs that went to colour their mathematical statement." He understood the dangers to fact and principle that lay in the current craze for oratory. He realized that abolition meetings easily became sheer recreation for the audience and intoxication for the speakers. One New England meeting suggested to his mind a medical experiment. At another he wished for the Locrian halters of old which had enabled audiences to choke off the flow of words. Emerson followed the careers of Garrison and Phillips with mixed response, sympathizing with their hatred of slavery, admiring their oratory, but disapproving their methods and fearing their exaggerations. In 1853, he confessed that although Garrison and Phillips were "inestimable for workers on audiences" he had no desire to associate with them personally. He sensed the element of self-deception in both men. Indeed, he feared that Phillips had no personality, that he had only a "*platform*-existence." Three years earlier he expressed disappointment in Garrison's lack of receptivity to new ideas. "He cannot understand anything you say, and

---

[19] Emerson, *Journals,* III, 546, 548; VI, 542–43; VII, 5–6, 97.
[20] *The National Anti-Slavery Standard,* VII (July 16, 1846), 319–20. This speech is not reprinted in his *Works.*

neighs like a horse when you suggest a new consideration, as when I told him that the *fate*-element in the negro question he had never considered."[21]

Nevertheless, Emerson understood the greatest of all the difficulties besetting the reformers' attempts to arouse the North against the evils of slavery. "In this mercantile country, there is a thrift which lays its grasp on almost all the forcible and well-organized individuals. It makes the law of its actions." It accounted for the tameness of the North in the face of Southern threats. "The Southerner said frankly, if not very civilly, through the mouth of John Randolph, 'Gentlemen of the free States, we shall drive you to the wall: We have done it, and we shall keep you there.' " But "old traders," Emerson said, "make it a rule rarely to shoot their customers, and never until the bill is paid."[22] Emerson knew that the bonds and securities for many plantations were held in State Street and Wall Street and that the Northern tradesmen were joined with the financiers in their willingness to humor the "bad temper and vicious politics" of the slaveholder. It was against this background of commercialism that Emerson regarded the antislavery society as a wholesome symptom. It was the "Cassandra that has foretold all that has befallen."[23]

Thoreau was also a critic of America's acquisitive culture, and he was more militant about it than was Emerson. The true enemy of individual freedom in America was to Thoreau the tyranny of getting and spending. Against this insensitive materialism he fought with vigor and conviction. Its embodiment in Southern slavery was a particularized evil about which he knew little. He therefore never intentionally joined his neighbors in their literary jousts with the South. But he inevitably became entangled in the ideological struggle over the question of slavery, and his attitude toward the South can be determined only by viewing his part in this struggle. His involvement,

[21] Emerson, *Journals*, III, 504, 546; VII, 96, 178; VIII, 99–100, 433–34; IX, 116–17.
[22] *The National Anti-Slavery Standard*, VII (July 16, 1846), 319–20.
[23] Emerson, *Works*, XI, 244.

however, was ineffectual, for he failed to help his countrymen toward a peaceful solution of the most urgent problem of their day. His failure was largely the result of two causes: His information about the actual nature of Southern slavery was both limited and distorted, and his philosophy of extreme individualism was inadequate for a problem which called for co-operative group action.[24]

Thoreau's individualism demanded a relatively simple and completely free society. He instinctively withdrew from the reports of a world to the south which was neither simple nor free. It had always been more congenial to his temperament to hunt for turtle eggs than to hunt for news items. What little he learned of a more complex world, of gold-diggers in the West, "Filibustiers" in Washington, and slave economy in the South strengthened his desire to ignore the times for the eternities.[25] But his privacy was interrupted by issues he could not ignore—tax demands of a government which was, he thought, unjustly at war with Mexico, runaway slaves who needed his help, and, finally, the capture and execution of John Brown, whom Thoreau had met personally. These issues disturbed him with insistent questions which embarrassed his philosophy of individualism and aroused him, if not to vote, at least to go on record openly and resolutely.

Throughout most of this period, Thoreau maintained the attitude that Northerners should occupy themselves in opposition to private forms of servitude instead of being concerned about "the gross but somewhat foreign form of servitude called Negro slavery." Nevertheless, two abolitionists received Thoreau's approval. He wrote an essay in praise of N. P. Roger's antislavery sheet, the *Herald of Freedom,* quoting from it extensively. He praised Wendell Phillips for his eloquence and integrity, speaking of him as a Redcross Knight

[24] I am indebted in part to Joseph Wood Krutch for the idea that Thoreau's philosophy of individualism was hardly capable of meeting the problem of America's cultural difference. See, for example, Professor Krutch's discussion of "Slavery in Massachusetts" in *Henry David Thoreau* (William Sloane, New York, 1948), p. 235.

[25] *The Writings of Henry David Thoreau* (Houghton Mifflin Co., Boston, 1906), VI, 250, 378–79. All references to Thoreau's work are to this edition. Hereafter cited as *Writings.* Volumes VII–XX contain the journals of Thoreau.

fighting the paynims of error. But he disapproved of the American Anti-Slavery Society and was one of the few men of his generation who felt that Phillips "[did] himself an injustice when he remind[ed] us of the American Society, which he represent[ed]."[26] In this judgment, Thoreau anticipated the recent findings of scholars concerning the final importance of Garrison in the antislavery movement.[27]

The abolitionists dropped further in Thoreau's estimation when they rejected Bronson Alcott's offer of help. "This is very much to their discredit; they should have been forward to secure him. Such a connection with him would confer unexpected dignity on their enterprise."[28] Alcott had traveled through Virginia and the Carolinas early in the eighteen twenties. Even before the founding of the *Liberator*, Alcott had been aware of Garrison, and in October, 1830, he heard him speak on two successive nights.[29] Of the first speech he said: "His lecture was full of truth and power." Of the second: "This lecture consisted chiefly in a statement of facts concerning the cruelty with which many slave-holders had treated their slaves at the South." It is significant in view of his firsthand knowledge of the South that Alcott's only criticism of these lectures was Garrison's occasional failure to discriminate between the "slaveholder who keeps his slaves from motives of expediency and the one whose principles are in favor of slavery." Alcott attended many of the early antislavery meetings in Boston, and upon one occasion exchanged words with some fiery Southerners—travelers who had been attracted to the meeting—who were attempting to intimidate George Thompson.

Before they left the door . . . one of them said . . . "We will give five hundred dollars for him in any one of the slave-holding States." I said, "And what would you do with him?" "Do with him!" said he, with a

[26] Thoreau, *Writings,* II, 14; IV, 306–10, 311–15; see also Thoreau, *Writings,* XX, 292–93.

[27] See Gilbert Hobbes Barnes, *The Antislavery Impulse, 1830–1844* (D. Appleton-Century Co., Inc., New York, 1933). See also Richard Hofstadter, *The American Political Tradition: And the Men Who Made It* (Alfred A. Knopf, Inc., New York, 1948), p. 144.

[28] Thoreau, *Writings,* XI, 365.

[29] The Alcott references in this and the two following paragraphs are to *The Journals of Bronson Alcott,* selected and edited by Odell Shepard (Little, Brown & Co., Boston, 1938), pp. 25, 60, 188, 230, 272.

look of mingled malignity and scorn, uttering at the same time an oath, "we would hang him!" "Sir," said another, "if we had him at Vicksburg we would bring Lynch's Law to bear upon him at once." With that they departed.

In 1847, Alcott harbored a fugitive slave for one week. The comment in his journal enables one to see something of the emotional effect of the experience upon the mind of a liberal New Englander:

He is scarce thirty years of age, athletic, dextrous, sagacious, and self-relying. He has many of the elements of the hero. His stay with us has given image and a name to the dire entity of slavery, and was an impressive lesson to my children, bringing before them the wrongs of the black man and his tale of woes.

As Boston faced the crisis of the Fugitive Slave Law, Alcott joined the Vigilance Committee. It was he who drove his friend Higginson from Worcester to Boston at the time they agitated daringly in behalf of Anthony Burns, the fugitive slave.

Nevertheless, Alcott's perception of the complexity of the slavery problem in the South enabled him to utter words of caution when he heard Parker, Phillips, and Garrison at Faneuil Hall denouncing Webster for his "Seventh of March" address.

The speeches were eloquent for freedom and humanity . . . but a little more time must pass to enable the nation to discern the scope and tendency of affairs and Webster's true place, his merits and demerits as a statesman. I am incapable of becoming a partisan; and while I accept and am proud of the declarations of my friend who pleads the cause of civility and justice with an eloquence so fervent and convincing, I yet must cry for the awards of justice and civility to Webster, Clay, Calhoun, and the conservatives of slavery even.

There was little room for this sort of balance and perspective among the abolitionists. Alcott could have helped them heed Emerson's advice to adhere to fact and principle.

Unlike his friend Alcott, Thoreau had never traveled in the South, and he lacked Alcott's awareness of the cultural trap into which America had fallen. In his isolation, he developed certain attitudes that were much closer to Garrisonianism than he realized. In "Civil Disobedience" (1849), Thoreau asserted that the Mexican War was the work of a few individuals who made a personal tool of the American government. His attack was not directed at these few, however, whom he called "far-off foes," but at those in the North who were so enslaved by commerce that they were not capable of helping the Negro or the Mexican. His diagnosis of America's fundamental illness was valid, but he was unwilling to prescribe any medicine to check its immediate manifestations in slavery and imperialism. He stated unequivocally that holding slaves and making war on Mexico were disgraces to the American government. But his doctrine of passivity was hardly adequate to curb the alleged evil policies of those who were in control of the government. Thoreau was actually describing himself when he spoke of those who "hesitat[ed] ... for others to remedy the evil, that they may no longer have it to regret."[30] His assertion that "voting *for the right* is *doing* nothing for it" expressed an attitude toward legitimate political processes which was Garrisonian in itself; and it led logically to the support, ten years later, of John Brown's flagrant kind of individual "doing."

Thoreau had wisely distinguished between America's ubiquitous foe, materialism, and one of its aspects, the exploitation of Negro labor in the South. But this secondary evil was certainly not faraway and foreign, as a consideration of the complicated interrelationship of commercial interests, North and South, would have revealed, or as the growing number of fugitive slaves indicated. But the community concept was always foreign to Thoreau. He distrusted government, or organized group action of any kind, especially when reform was its aim. The functions of the body politic were what he called *"infra-human,"*[31] and one should ideally be unaware of them. This notion of government precluded any concern on Thoreau's part for preventive medicine. Indeed, his public outbursts in 1849 and again in 1853 were late, coming in each case long after the crucial decisions of government had been made. Four years after the Fugitive Slave Law was passed, Thoreau, angered by the return of Anthony Burns into slavery, lashed out against the offensive practice.[32] In the case of Sims and other runaway slaves, he had seen the individual compromised by group action. It was the servility of his own Massachusetts which

[30] Thoreau, *Writings,* IV, 360–63.
[31] *Ibid.,* IX, 103.   [32] *Ibid.,* IV, 400.

angered him most. But it was the sores of Southern slavery which were infecting the entire body politic. In reviling his fellow-Northerners for not being sound enough morally to throw off the poison, he aroused in them not detestation of their own frailty but fear and resentment of the disease in the South to which they were so dangerously exposed.

Thoreau's sense of the fundamental antagonism between the North and the South revealed itself in an incidental though significant remark in *A Week on the Concord and Merrimack Rivers.* Comparing the Indian and the gardener in their relationship to nature, Thoreau commented:[33]

The Indian's intercourse with Nature is at least such as admits of the greatest independence of each. If he is somewhat of a stranger in her midst, the gardener is too much of a familiar. There is something vulgar and foul in the latter's closeness to his mistress, something noble and cleanly in the former's distance. In civilization, as in a southern latitude, man degenerates at length, and yields to the incursion of more northern tribes,—

> "Some nation yet shut in
> With hills of ice."

The value of the passage lies, of course, in its alignment of associations. The Indian lived independently, a natural agent belonging freely to nature, whereas the gardener exploited nature, making a mistress of her. The one suggested the "noble and cleanly," the other, the "vulgar and foul"; with the former was associated "northern," with the latter, "southern." The passage implied, moreover, a prognosis of eventual triumph, through hitherto unrealized power, of the one over the other. Immediately following the quotation above was an observation of indefinite portent: "There are other, savager and more primeval aspects of nature than our poets have sung. It is only white man's poetry."

When John Brown was captured, in 1859, Thoreau did not hurl invectives at the South. His scorn was directed at the American people's woodenness of heart and head. He charged the inhabitants of Massachusetts with the sins of insensibility and self-interest. He pictured the government of the United States as a giant sitting on four

[33] *Ibid.,* I, 56.

million gasping people. He accused it of pretending to be a Christian government while it crucified a million Christs daily.[34] But he applauded the courage and conviction of Brown and denounced those who considered him insane or foolishly rash. He was firing at his own neighbors, but it was the Southerner in the background who sustained the damage. For, in defending Brown, Thoreau claimed the right of the individual to interfere forcibly with the slaveholder. And he backed up his words with personal action in aiding one of Brown's raiders, a man with a price on his head, to escape to Canada. He no longer advocated noninterference with "foreign servitude." He reviled all nonslaveholders for their complicity in America's infamous sin. To convey his view of America he drew upon the time-honored image of the ship of state, which he represented as a slave ship crowded with dying victims.[35] The slaveholders were the crew, the nonslaveholders the passengers. Under the hatches were four million innocent and helpless creatures. Countenanced by a large body of passengers, the crew was gradually smothering the human cargo below. Thoreau could hear the sound as bodies of the dead were cast overboard; they, at least, found deliverance. This passage was perhaps the most eloquent metaphor penned by a Northern opponent of slavery. By implication it contained many of the frightening charges found in current antislavery writing. After all, passangers were no safer than crew, and they had little to say about the destination of the ship. No American could comfortably ignore conditions aboard Thoreau's ship. The metaphor suggested a complicity more ominous and much closer to the truth of the American plight than was implied in Thoreau's flat statement that the state ought to dissolve her union with slaveholders or else the individual ought to break his union with the state.[36] But the metaphor, consistent with the entire "Plea for Captain John Brown" in which it was used, added to the urgency of the North's alarm and indignation.

Thoreau shared the single-mindedness of many New England reformers. This quality of mind at times led him to oversimplifications,

---

[34] *Ibid.,* XVIII, 404, 409.

[35] *Ibid.,* XVIII, 411–12. See also Thoreau's "Plea for Captain John Brown," *ibid.,* XVIII, 424, for the expanded image.

[36] *Ibid.,* XII, 370.

sweeping denunciations, and conclusions based upon insufficient information. He regarded the Unitarian minister as much a slave as the hapless Negro. The editor, the judge, the clergyman were all shallow spokesmen of an acquisitive culture. They were slaves who deemed themselves freemen. An episode in which a Missouri slave killed his would-be kidnaper and fled to Canada drew from Thoreau this comment: "The bloodhounds have tracked him to Toronto and now demand him of her judges. From all that I can learn, they are playing their parts like judges. They are servile, while the poor fugitive in their jail is free in spirit at least . . . . Better that the British Empire be destroyed than that it should help to reinslave this man!" Thoreau thus idealized the fugitive, regarding what was probably a terrified, desperate, defeated man as "free in spirit" while, equally arbitrarily, he assumed the Canadian judge to be a spineless slave of a legal system. At another time, Thoreau's righteous soul lost all patience with Maryland when she added the vice of lottery to her sin of slavery. In both, he maintained, she was utterly lacking in principle. "Maryland, and every fool who buys a ticket of her, is bound straight to the bottomless pit. The State of Maryland is a moral fungus. Her offense is rank; it smells to heaven."[37] He charged Maryland with knowingly working for the Devil and with adding hypocrisy to that sin by her suggestion that she would gladly keep the identity of ticket-buyers a secret. "Consolidated Deviltry!" he concluded.

Thus, despite his reluctance to enter into the political and social strife of his day, Thoreau was carried along on the current of anti-slavery sentiment, and his voice joined the hue and cry that deafened people to the voices of peaceful arbitration. Thoreau never observed social phenomena—even in the North—with the same attention to detail which he devoted to those in nature. He regarded slavery as a moral question, one that could be evaluated without a close and accurate knowledge of social and economic conditions. It was a question to be judged on principle—his principle of uncompromising individualism. His two main sources of information about the South were runaway slaves and the antislavery utterances, both oral and written, of his abolitionist acquaintances. His personal conception of the South was determined largely by the nature of these two sources.

[37] *Ibid.,* XIII, 150–51; XV, 284; XVIII, 429; XX, 292–93.

The few references to the South which can be found in his writings reflect current Northern antislavery opinion. He suspected that Virginia, like Concord, was afraid of its shadow. He referred in one place to the terrors of a Southern mob, in another to the meanness of the slaveholder, to the gasping, fettered slave, to men hunted by hounds and whipped to death. He considered the slave to be intelligent and well-behaved, though superstitious.[38] In these references one can find an implied alignment of three ideas which were to him ugly: slaveholder, government, and authority. With these were associated the emotional terms "tyranny and injustice," "hound and whip." The bulwarks of these evil forces were pulpit, bench, and copy desk. This chain of association was instinctive for Thoreau. It was implicit throughout his utterances on man and society.

But Thoreau never forgot that exploitation and inhumanity among men are not restricted to regions. He deviated from the usual pattern of the abolitionists in not adding North and South to his alignment of freedom and slavery, good and evil, God and Devil. Neither did he fall into the propagandist's vicious habit of allowing emotional epithets to stand algebraically for an entire class of people. Nor did he paint sentiment-inducing pictures of cowering slaves and sneering overseers. He was saved from these errors by his natural dislike of reformers and by his perception of the utilitarianism of the American commercial culture. Over the years, the wisdom of *Walden* has helped this nation immeasurably in its constant need to acknowledge and control this utilitarianism. Furthermore, Thoreau's emphasis upon the spiritual worth of the individual has contributed significantly to America's awareness of the personal meaning of freedom. Nevertheless, in respect to the specific problem of understanding the South, Thoreau failed to help his own generation extricate itself peacefully from the trap in which it was caught.

[38] *Ibid.,* IV, 37, 400, 429, 446; XI, 472; XII, 315; XVIII, 409, 458.

· 5 ·

Longfellow, Holmes, and Hawthorne

LONGFELLOW did not participate in organized antislavery agitation. In answer to Whittier, who suggested that he run for office on the Liberty party ticket, Longfellow said: "Partisan warfare becomes too violent, too vindictive, for my taste; and I should be found but a weak and unworthy champion in public debate."[1] The social atmosphere of New England was alive with controversy, however, and Longfellow was not indifferent to the slavery issue. He attended many abolitionist meetings; he applauded Richard Henry Dana, Jr., the legal champion of fugitive slaves; he gave personal encouragement and approval to his friend Charles Sumner, who was probably the most militant opponent of the South in Congress; and, in 1842, before it had become fashionable to espouse the abolitionist cause, Longfellow wrote the *Poems on Slavery*. It is not surprising, therefore, that Whittier had hoped for a political ally in Longfellow. He congratulated him on the slavery poems; they contained a picture of the South which agreed, so far as it went, with his own.

Reviewing Longfellow's *Poems on Slavery* in *The Pioneer*, Lowell observed that "Longfellow rarely or never touches the deepest in-

[1] Letter to Whittier dated September, 1844. Reprinted in Samuel Longfellow (ed.), *The Life of Henry Wadsworth Longfellow with Extracts from his Journals and Correspondence* (Ticknor & Co., Boston, 1886). Hereafter cited as *Life*.

stincts of our nature, but he runs over the wide scale of natural *sentiment* with the hand of a master."[2] His strength lay in "the spiritual
picturesque," said Lowell. Certainly, these eight short lyrics had the
power to evoke a picture. They expressed not so much "natural *sentiment*" as an artificial sentiment which became more and more familiar to readers of abolition literature.[3]

One of the poems pictured a slave lying in the rice fields, physically
exhausted from overwork and ill-treatment. His hand still gripped the
sickle. His breast was bare, his hair matted. He dreamed of the days
when he had been a king with a "dark-eyed queen" and children who
"clasped his neck and kissed his cheeks and held him by the hand."
This king had been a romantic figure. He had ridden a stallion at
furious speed along the Niger's banks. He had known the lion's roar
and the hyena's scream, but he had been sensitive as well to the bright
flamingoes and the fields of tamarind. This nobleman no longer felt
the driver's whip or the burning heat of day, for death came at the
end of his dream. Another of the poems described a runaway slave
who was crouching in the "dismal swamp" and listening to the
"bloodhounds distant bay." His face was deformed by great scars and
his frame was mangled. The emotional content of the poem is con-
fusing, however, for the fugitive was compared to a "wild beast in his
lair" and then in the next line was called "a poor old slave, infirm and
lame." *Poems on Slavery* expressed also the traditional notion of the
religious zeal of the slave and, in contrast, the lust and greed of the
slaveholder. In one poem the enslaved Negro sang of Zion and chant-
ed at midnight the Song of David. In another the quadroon girl was
sold by her planter-father because he could not resist the slaver's gold.
The last of the *Poems* expressed a not very convincing fear that the
Negro, who was "poor, blind Samson," "shorn of his strength and
bound in bonds of steel," might "shake the pillars of this Common-
weal/Till the vast Temple of our liberties" were destroyed.

This sort of writing, in its striving "to make the beauty of the right

[2] *The Pioneer, A Literary Magazine,* ed. by James Russell Lowell, intro. by
Sculley Bradley (Scholars' Facsimiles and Reprints, New York, 1947), I (No.
2), 93.

[3] *The Poetical Works of Henry Wadsworth Longfellow* (Riverside Press,
Boston, 1887). References here and in the next paragraph are to pp. 41–44.

more apparent," did more good, Lowell said, than that which "inveigh[s] against the loathsomeness of the wrong."[4] As Lowell observed, there was no spirit of controversy in these lines. But there was the bland assumption of the poet and his critic alike that the Northern a priori notion of life in the South was true. This assumption combined with the vogue of sentiment in literature made writing such as this more effective than an energetic, avowedly controversial writing in the ideological battle.

During the late forties and throughout the fifties, Longfellow watched with mounting apprehension the aggressiveness of the slave states and the continued apathy of a large body of Northerners. He believed that Southern aggression began with the purchase of Louisiana and continued with the purchase of Florida and the annexation of Texas. "These three great violations of the compact between the States, and consequent increase of the Slavery power, the North has submitted to, fascinated by increase of territory." He called the Mexican War shabby and disgraceful. In 1850, he traveled to Washington, reporting in his journal that he and Clay talked politics and smoked cigars together "with gusto" and that he also saw Benton, Webster, and Mrs. Frémont. But his journal tells us nothing about these conversations. He heard rumors that the South Carolinians were serious about dissolution. "They think it would be for their advantage; and mean to preach this doctrine. So say all the travelers returning from Charleston."[5] But one is impressed by the lack of personal comment in Longfellow's reporting of these experiences in Washington.

Longfellow's indignation was aroused by the Fugitive Slave Law. That Eliot of Boston voted for it was "a dark disgrace to the city."[6] When a fugitive slave escaped from court, Longfellow expressed pleasure: "Very glad of it. This government must not pass laws that outrage the sense of right in the community." But despite his strong feelings, he held to his resolutions never to express himself publicly on controversial issues. His response to Emerson's address in May, 1851, on the Fugitive Slave Law was complicated by his notion that the

[4] *The Pioneer,* I (No. 2), 93.
[5] Longfellow (ed.), *Life,* II, 168, 183.
[6] References in this paragraph are to *ibid.,* II, 177, 180, 190, 192–93, 194–95.

man of letters ought to remain the genteel observer. It was painful for him to see Emerson "in the arena of politics, hissed and hooted at by young law-students." The New England air was filled with vigorous antislavery oratory. Horace Mann, Theodore Parker, the Negroes Remond and Douglass, and Wendell Phillips all won Longfellow's approval as orators. When Boston complied with the new Fugitive Slave Law, Longfellow's outrage reached its peak. Upon the capture and return of Sims to slavery, Longfellow wrote in his journal: "O city without soul!—When and where will this end? Shame, that the great Republic, the 'refuge of the oppressed,' should stoop so low as to become the Hunter of Slaves." The rendition of Anthony Burns evoked in his journal the comment "I am sick and sorrowful of this infamous business. Ah, Webster, Webster, you have much to answer for!"[7]

While many New Englanders were expressing their disillusionment in Webster, Longfellow simply asked: "What has there been in Webster's life to lead us to think that he would take any high moral ground on this Slavery question?"[8]

In his disdain for Webster, Longfellow was at variance with his friend Oliver Wendell Holmes, who welcomed the Compromise of 1850 and signed a letter of congratulation to Webster on his "Seventh of March" speech.[9] Holmes's attitude toward the South during the ante bellum period was in pronounced contrast to Longfellow's and Lowell's. The difference in attitude was due in large part to family influence. Abiel Holmes had served for seven years as pastor of a congregation in Midway, Georgia. Holmes recalled that his father had been[10]

in contact with slavery in its best and mildest form; and, living among

---

[7] Longfellow (ed.), *Life*, II, 222–23.

[8] *Ibid.*, 162.

[9] Eleanor Marguerite Tilton, *Amiable Autocrat: A Biography of Dr. Oliver Wendell Holmes* (H. Schuman, New York, 1947), pp. 224, 227. Hereafter cited as *Amiable Autocrat. The Poetical Works of Oliver Wendell Holmes* (Houghton Mifflin Co., Boston, 1872), p. 139.

[10] John T. Morse, Jr., *Life and Letters of Oliver Wendell Holmes* (Houghton Mifflin Co., Boston, 1896), I, 300–301, 303. Hereafter cited as *Holmes*.

the best people, learned to look upon it with less abhorrence than if he had studied it from a distance. Though he rarely referred to it, I did not receive from him the strong feeling of hatred and opposition to the institution which many Northern children inherited from their parents.

Holmes recalled, too, that his maternal grandfather had been a slaveholder by inheritance. He also claimed to have acquired a prejudice against the Negro from a book called *Negro Plots,* which he read in his youth. Eleanor Tilton, in her biography of Holmes, has accepted this claim and has added that the impressions which fixed themselves firmly in his mind from this book were strengthened by the influence of his father.[11]

Oliver Wendell Holmes accepted the Southerner's belief in the superiority of the whites over the Negroes, and its corollary that the whites must always have the upper hand in the South. His view, however, was not irreconcilable with the belief in natural aristocracy held by Longfellow and Lowell, and the Brahminism of Holmes was less provincial, if more racial, than theirs. The important difference, after all, was not in respect to racial theories or to slavery as an institution— Holmes thought slavery "a dreadful business" and told Charles Sumner that he would have fought for the freedom of the Negro in Kansas—but rather in their respective opinions of slavery as it was practiced in the South. Holmes's early experiences enabled him to view the abolitionist picture of the South more critically than was possible for many of his New England contemporaries. He was scornful of the vituperative force of abolition eloquence, and he thought that there was "nothing so flat and unprofitable as weakly flavored verses relating to [slavery]." In his respect for the Union, Holmes was grateful to Webster and others who struggled to preserve it. Holmes shrank from the thought of disunion, for he realized that it would mean war. He therefore resented the "ultra-abolitionists" because, failing to temper the "law of conscience" with the "law of love," they fed the fires of sectional hostility. In 1856, four years after the death of Webster, Holmes honored his memory in a poem of praise. He assured his readers that despite "the envious tongue[s]" which upbraided Webster, his name would remain in the nation's heart.

[11] Tilton, *Amiable Autocrat,* pp. 7–8.

Longfellow's friend and next-door neighbor, Richard Henry Dana, Jr., was equally concerned about the problem of returning men into slavery. Dana had no objections to the aristocracy of the South. He accepted social stratification, North and South, and regarded the ruling classes of both as a caste of gentlemen. His opposition was directed at the attempts of the Southern aristocracy to extend slavery into the territories. He was a free-soiler and a constitutionalist, not an abolitionist. He admitted to a friend that he became a free-soiler because he was "of the stock of the old northern gentry."[12] Dana looked upon the slaveholding oligarchy as a competitor, and he resented any suggestion that the New England aristocracy was subservient to Southern aristocracy.

In deference to the Constitution, Dana was willing to accept a compromise law, even a fugitive slave law, if it was fair and just. But he despised "the iniquitous form" of the particular law passed in 1850.[13] Some of its provisions, he said, were outrageous. He donated his legal services generously, first, in the defense of those who had helped in the escape of Shadrach, a Boston Negro who was being held for rendition into slavery, then in the defense of Burns and Sims, two fugitive slaves. But he retained his respect for the Southern gentleman. "You are not assembled in any hostility to the South," he told his audience in a speech before the Free-Soil meeting in Boston, July, 1848. "There is much to admire in the Southern character; there are some points in which it is superior to our own, as some in which we think it otherwise." Even during the greater excitement of the fifties he was careful to say that slave-catchers, after all, were not of the Southern aristocracy. He asserted that Southern gentlemen shared the Northern feelings of repugnance for slave-dealers and those who tracked down fugitives. "They use them as we use spies, informers, and deserters in war." The operators of slave markets were social outcasts in the South, he said. "They look upon this occupation with as

[12] Charles Francis Adams, *Richard Henry Dana, a Biography* (Houghton Mifflin Co., Boston, 1891), I, 126. Hereafter cited as *Dana*.

[13] *Speeches and Letters of Richard H. Dana, Jr.,* ed. with intro. by his son, Richard H. Dana, III (Houghton Mifflin Co., Boston, 1910). The quotations in this and the following paragraph are from pp. 146, 164, 200, 214–215. See also Adams, *Dana*, I, 183, 211.

much contempt, aye with more contempt than we seem to, now; for there is a higher spirit in their aristocracy than in the ruling classes of our own Northern cities at this moment."

Nevertheless, Dana understood the intersectional competition and the danger of indifference in the North. He parodied the Fugitive Slave Law in a satire called "Great Gravitation Meeting at Faneuil Hall," in which he portrayed Webster as the Great Expounder and attacked the property-hungry, pompous men who had been responsible for the unjust law. He rarely resorted to the type of pleading that marked the antislavery eloquence. In defending the fugitive Burns, however, he strove to convince his audience that this was a test case in the eyes of the nation, that, "with all the pride of the Old Dominion aroused in him," the Virginian was watching for the results of the trial. Then he indulged in conjecture that was very much in the abolitionist manner.

The man you send away would be sold. He would never see the light of a Virginia sun. He would be sold at the first block, to perish after his few years of unwonted service, on the cotton-fields or sugar-fields of Louisiana and Arkansas. Let us have, then, no chance for a mistake, no doubt, no misgiving.

Though the enforcement of the Fugitive Slave Law had won many supporters for the antislavery forces, defending Burns still meant social stigma in many Boston circles. But there was a rapid change in Northern opinion after the Kansas-Nebraska Bill. In 1854, Dana observed: "I do not know how many who hardly spoke to me from 1850 to 1853, and whom I heard of in all quarters as speaking against me bitterly, come up to me with the freedom and warmth of old friends, and talk as though there had never been any differences between us." Longfellow wrote to their mutual friend, Charles Sumner, that in trying to prevent the rendition of Burns, Dana "had done nobly, acting throughout with the greatest nerve and intrepidity." Longfellow kept in close touch with Sumner, who often shared his Sundays with Longfellow and Dana, having dinner with one and tea with the other. Of those who had entree to the drawing rooms of Park and Beacon streets, Dana and Sumner were among the few who represented, in the words of Charles Francis Adams, "the unfashionable side."[14]

Much can be learned of Longfellow's attitude toward the South by considering the support and approval which he constantly gave to Sumner.[15] The two men often discussed the political scene. They were both opposed to the annexation of territory, particularly if it was slave territory, and they agreed that the Mexican War was caused by the lust of the slave states for power. When Sumner formulated these notions as "Resolutions" which he introduced, unsuccessfully, to the Boston Whigs, Longfellow observed in his journal: "I don't see why they should have been rejected; they are very good." When Sumner became active in the newly organized Free-Soil party, Longfellow urged him "to take ground against any coalitions, by which the anti-slavery principles of the Free-soil party may be suppressed, as in New York."[16] This advice was hardly necessary, however, for Sumner was vehement in opposing slavery.

When Sumner went to Washington as senator in 1851, Longfellow sent him many letters of encouragement, complimenting him on his firmness in the face of threats of violence to his person. Longfellow liked Sumner's Nebraska speech, in which the Senator looked forward to the time when "there will really be a North, and the Slave Power will be broken,—when this wretched Despotism will cease to dominate over our Government." Longfellow judged it one of Sumner's best speeches, "with a pulsation of freedom in every line of it; a noble rebuke to the foul iniquity about you."[17] Needless to say, Longfellow was outraged on behalf of his friend when the news reached him that Sumner had been assaulted by Brooks, of South Carolina. "I have no words to write you about this savage atrocity . . . this great feat of arms of the Southern 'chivalry.' A brave and noble

[14] Adams, *Dana*, I, 128, 214, 285; Longfellow (ed.), *Life*, II, 272.

[15] In addition to Charles Francis Adams and Samuel Longfellow, see Thomas Wentworth Higginson, *Henry Wadsworth Longfellow* (Houghton Mifflin Co., Boston, 1902), p. 289. "[Longfellow] took an unfeigned interest in public matters, always faithful to the traditions of his friend Sumner."

[16] Longfellow (ed.), *Life*, II, 93, 150; for Sumner's "Resolutions," see *The Works of Charles Sumner* (Lee and Shepard, Boston, 1871), II, 55. Hereafter cited as *Works*.

[17] Longfellow (ed.), *Life*, II, 247; Sumner, *Works*, III, 343–44.

speech you made; never to die out of the memories of men!"[18] This
was probably Sumner's "Crime against Kansas," a speech designed
to expose the "Power Behind, which succors and sustains the Crime"
and which required two days (May 19–20, 1856) to deliver in the
Senate. It called for the redemption of the Republic from "the thraldom of that Oligarchy which prompts, directs, and concentrates the
distant wrong." It charged the South with "a vaulting ambition
which would hesitate at nothing . . . a control of public opinion
through venal pens and prostituted press." Sumner accused the South
of subsidizing crowds and making tools of politicians, lawyers, and
judges. Pointing to the slave power, he said: "There, Sir, stands the
criminal, all unmasked before you, heartless, grasping, and tyrannical."[19] The Senator received praise from Whittier also, who regarded
this speech as his best. It is worthy of immortality, he wrote Sumner,
"a grand and terrible Philippic."[20]

In 1860, when Sumner had delivered "The Barbarism of Slavery,"
a speech on the bill to admit Kansas as a state, Longfellow wrote him:
"You have done your work fearlessly, faithfully, fully! It was disagree-
able, but necessary, and must remain as the great protest of Civilization against Barbarism in this age." This speech was Sumner's most
systematic denunciation of the slave system, which he called the greatest organized barbarism on earth. He outlined the five "essential elements" of slavery's law: It claimed property in man, abrogated marriage, abrogated parental relation, closed the gates of knowledge, and
appropriated all the toil of its victims. These, he said, were sometimes
called "abuses," but if they were taken away, slavery would cease to
exist. He then outlined the practical results of slavery. In spite of
natural climatic and geographic advantages, the South had failed to
keep pace with the North in development. In agriculture, manufacture, mining, mechanical arts, commerce, railroads, canals, postal
service, voluntary charity, educational establishments, public libraries,
the press, number and value of patents—in all these areas the South
was inferior to the North. The Southern system had caused the degradation of free labor and had prevented the growth of the white

[18] *Ibid.*, II, 280.   [19] Sumner, *Works*, IV, 141–42, 143.
[20] Samuel T. Pickard, *Life and Letters of John Greenleaf Whittier* (Houghton Mifflin Co., Boston, 1899), I, 381.

population. It inevitably demoralized the slave master. "Unconscious of their true condition, they [the slave masters] made boasts which reveal still further the unhappy influence. Barbarous standards of conduct are unblushingly avowed. The swagger of a bully is called chivalry; a swiftness to quarrel is called courage; the bludgeon is adopted as substitute for argument; and assassination is lifted to be one of the Fine Arts." Longfellow observed of the speech: "Its great simplicity gives it awful effect. In rhetoric you have surpassed it before; in forcible array and arrangement of arguments, never!"[21]

Longfellow's uncritical acceptance of abolition literature may be seen in his attitude toward Harriet Beecher Stowe and Hinton R. Helper. *Uncle Tom's Cabin* was "pathetic and droll . . . a book of power." Longfellow knew Mr. and Mrs. Stowe socially and entertained them in his home. He was awed by the sales of *Uncle Tom.* "She is shaking the world with her Uncle Tom's Cabin! At one step she has reached the top of the stair-case up which the rest of us climb on our knees year after year. Never was there such a literary *coup-de-main* as this." His emotional involvement in antislavery was deepened by reading *Uncle Tom.* "Every evening we read ourselves into despair in that tragic book. . . . It is too melancholy, and makes one's blood boil too hotly."

In the summer of 1857, Longfellow wrote Sumner: "I say nothing of politics. There is nothing very cheering except the anti-slavery movement in Missouri, and Mr. Helper's book, from Carolina."[22] To appreciate fully the state of mind revealed in this comment, one must know something of the book which Longfellow found "cheering." It was *The Impending Crisis of the South: How to Meet It.* According to the title page, Helper was a native of North Carolina, and the book was dedicated to the nonslaveholding whites of the South. Helper declared that his intention was primarily to discuss the economic plight of the South. He proposed to use statistics to prove that the South was inferior to the North because of slavery.[23] Although stating that it was not his purpose "to cast unmerited opprobrium upon

[21] Sumner, *Works,* V, 50–51; Longfellow (ed.), *Life,* II, 354.

[22] Longfellow (ed.), *Life,* II, 222, 223, 233, 303.

[23] Hinton R. Helper, *The Impending Crisis of the South: How to Meet It* (A. B. Burdick, New York, 1860). References are to pp. v, 28, 33, 42–45.

slaveholders," Helper's hatred of the slaveholder stamped itself on every page. His abusiveness was unmatched by any of the Northern abolitionists.

Nothing short of complete abolition of slavery can save the South from falling into the vortex of utter ruin. Too long have we yielded a submissive obedience to the tyrannical domination of an inflated oligarchy; too long have we submitted to their unjust and savage exactions. Let us now wrest from them the sceptre of power, establish liberty and equal rights throughout the land, and henceforth and forever guard our legislative halls from the pollutions and usurpations of pro-slavery demagogues.

Helper played cleverly upon the sense of intersectional rivalry, stressing the condescension the Southern slaveholder showed toward the Northerner, despite the fact that economically the North had outstripped the South.

Agriculture, it is well known, is the sole boast of the South; and strange to say, many pro-slavery Southerners, who, in our latitude, pass for intelligent men, are so puffed up with the idea of our importance in this respect, that they speak of the North as a sterile region, unfit for cultivation, and quite dependent on the South for the necessaries of life!

Helper also managed to reveal the planter's scorn of such Northern ideals as sexual purity, democratic fellowship, and patriotism. His planter was all the abolitionist had dreamed of: He was boastful, arrogant, cruel, boisterous, belligerent, dishonest.

On the other hand, the nonslaveholding white in Helper's picture must have been equally displeasing to the Northern reader, and it no doubt stimulated more contempt than sympathy for the Southern underlings. Certainly the Yankee could find no more flagrant violation of his ideals of independence, self-reliance, and respect for knowledge than in the following statement:

The lords of the lash are not only absolute masters of the blacks, who are bought and sold, and driven about like so many cattle, but they are also the oracles and arbiters of all non-slaveholding whites, whose freedom is merely nominal, and whose unparalleled illiteracy and degradation is purposely and fiendishly perpetuated. How little the "poor white trash," the great majority of the Southern people, know of the real condition of the country is, indeed, sadly astonishing. The truth is, they know nothing of public measures, and little of private affairs, except what their imperious masters, the slave-drivers, condescend to tell. . . .

Helper's picture of an unscrupulous oligarchy holding in subjection an uninformed, inert mass of Americans was calculated to flatter Northern superiority while it outraged its republican sentiments. "Never were the poorer classes of a people, and those classes so largely in the majority, so basely duped, so adroitly swindled, or so damnably outraged." Helper pictured a South which "weltered in the cesspool of ignorance and degradation."

A journal entry of 1857 indicates how derisive Longfellow's attitude became toward Southern statesmen and their policies. He intentionally stayed away from a celebration at Bunker Hill, for he did not like "this everlasting talk, talk. I see by the papers that Senator Mason of Virginia was there, powwowing about the Union and carrying on the government 'acording to the Constitution,' by which he meant catching runaway slaves." The day of John Brown's execution in Virginia, Longfellow wrote in his journal: "This will be a great day in our history; the date of a new Revolution,—quite as much needed as the old one. Even now as I write, they are leading old John Brown to execution in Virginia for attempting to rescue slaves! This is sowing the wind to reap the whirlwind, which will come soon."[24]

During the fall of 1860 and the spring of 1861, Longfellow anxiously watched the troubled skies for signs of the breaking storm. "I hope the North will stand firm, and not bate one jot of its manhood," he wrote in his journal. "Secession of the North from freedom would be tenfold worse than secession of the South from the Union." He observed that South Carolina talked "nothing but fire and fury," that South Carolina "thinks too much of herself." He grew a little disdainful over Southern claims of aristocracy. " 'Old Huguenot families,' and the rest of it! It sounds very grand, but it is only sound. To be a Huguenot is no title of nobility. The Huguenots were only the Puritans of France. The Puritans of England were quite as grand as they." On January 28, 1861, after six states had left the Union, Longfellow said: "It is now too late to put the fire out. We must let it burn out."

[24] Longfellow (ed.), *Life*, II, 300, 347.

A week later: "The South arrogant; the North like a giant weak in the knees,—at least, a part of it. . . . How a few cowards infect a whole land!" "The dissolution of the Union goes slowly on. Behind it all I hear the low murmur of the slaves, like the chorus in a Greek tragedy, prophesying Woe, woe!" When the news reached him that Fort Sumter had been attacked, he commented: "If South Carolina had not been so self-conceited and precipitate, this war might have been avoided." Later the same month he was indignant over the response of England to the Secession. England "is not behaving well about this Rebellion." England "chooses to put Civilization and Barbarism on an equality."[25]

This balancing of civilization against barbarism was the final over-simplification toward which Longfellow had been moving through the forties and the fifties in his attitude toward the cultural differences between North and South. Longfellow the man viewed the South like an abolitionist. Longfellow the poet, however, succeeded in keeping himself free from involvement, except, of course, for the *Poems on Slavery,* written nearly twenty years before the Civil War.

Hawthorne was out of sympathy with Northern hostility toward the South. He held himself aloof from the antislavery agitation, not because of a theory of the proper relation of the artist to society, but because of his concept of evil. Of the New England writers, perhaps only Hawthorne could have understood the full import of Emerson's statement to Garrison that there was a "fate-element" in the plight of the Negro.[26] To those who were militantly indignant about life in the South, Hawthorne pointed to an alternative view: Slavery may be "one of those evils which Divine Providence does not leave to be remedied by human contrivance." To a people who were turning their reformative impulse from the theological to the moral, however, this view was not popular; and there were times when it required moral courage to express it in Boston. Hawthorne was a student of the human heart, and his wisdom told him that the evil of this agitation

[25] *Ibid.,* 358–67.
[26] *The Journals of Ralph Waldo Emerson* (Houghton Mifflin Co., Boston, 1909–13), VIII, 99–100.

was certain, while its good was only a possible contingent.[27] In his *Life of Pierce,* a campaign biography which he wrote, somewhat reluctantly, for his friend of college days, he made the following observation:[28]

There is no instance, in all history, of the human will and intellect having perfected any great moral reform by methods which it adapted to that end; but the progress of the world, at every step, leaves some evil or wrong on the path behind it, which the wisest of mankind, of their own set purpose, could never have found the way to rectify.

The second determining force in Hawthorne's attitude toward the South was his belief in the value of the Union. Hawthorne spoke of the United States as a "country which Providence brought into one nation, through a continued miracle of almost two hundred years." Julian Hawthorne said that his father had instilled in him such an ardent love of country that when he went abroad he felt almost hostile toward the British. Aware of the cultural differences between North and South and the threat they offered, Hawthorne advocated conservatism as the only intelligent, consistent way. He feared that "merely human wisdom and human efforts [could] not subvert [slavery], except by tearing to pieces the Constitution and destroying the unity of the nation."[29] Hawthorne, who thought Brown justly hanged, was shocked when he learned of Emerson's statement that "the death of this blood-stained fanatic has made the Gallows as venerable as the Cross!"[30]

Because Hawthorne was not involved emotionally in the antislavery movement, his mind was relatively free of the abolitionist's image of the South. Properly speaking, he had no vision of the South. That he was not entirely unaffected by current hostility toward things Southern, however, is suggested by one of his *Twice-Told Tales,* "The Wed-

[27] *The Complete Works of Nathaniel Hawthorne,* intro. and notes by George Parsons Lathrop (Houghton Mifflin Co., Boston, 1903), XVII, 163–64. Hereafter cited as *Works.*

[28] *Ibid.,* p. 166.

[29] *Ibid.,* pp. 163–64. Julian Hawthorne, *Nathaniel Hawthorne and His Wife* (Houghton Mifflin Co., Boston, 1885), II, 270–71.

[30] Ralph Leslie Rusk, *The Life of Ralph Waldo Emerson* (Columbia University Press, New York, 1949), p. 402.

ding Knell." As a curious side light to this story, the reader is told almost parenthetically that Mrs. Dabney, a wealthy New York widow, had married again, this time a Southerner who was many years younger than she. Her life with him in Charleston was described vaguely as "uncomfortable," and it was said that the Southerner's "unkindness" was such that it "had inevitably driven her to connect the idea of his death with that of her comfort." There was nothing in the story itself to demand that the husband be a Southerner, but there were growing numbers of New England readers for whom the South was an appropriate source for fictional villains. Hawthorne's device of understatement must have been particularly effective for them. Moreover, the evils of the South Carolinian, only hinted at, allowed the reader the widest range of speculation according to accepted ideas of Southern depravity.

Aside from the varying shades of implications which Mrs. Dabney's experience in Charleston may have possessed for Northern eyes, Hawthorne did not offer his readers any opinion of Southern character until after the war had begun. Man's willing exploitation of his fellows was to Hawthorne a human mystery which he refused to ascribe to Southerners alone. In his *American Note-Books* (1838), he recorded a casual remark made to him by a young man from Wisconsin as they watched a respectably dressed, self-possessed Negro stop at an inn to get oats for his horse and a brandy-and-water for himself. "I wish I had a thousand such fellows in Alabama," the Westerner said. The remark left "a strange impression" on Hawthorne. "The negro was really so human!" he observed. "—and to talk of owning a thousand like him."[31]

Hawthorne retained his faith in the solidarity of the Union until events preceding and immediately following the early period of the Civil War forced him to reconcile himself to the dissolution of the states. His love of Union had been a concomitant of his respect for the Constitution and for the continuity and oneness of purpose of the United States. He did not know the South itself, either through travel or study. Understandably, his attachments to New England were such

[31] Nathaniel Hawthorne, *Passages from the American Note-Books* (Houghton Mifflin Co., Boston, 1903), pp. 244–45.

that under the stimulus of open hostility he was able to join in the cry that the "country" would be better off without the South.[32] Unlike the abolitionists in the chorus, however, Hawthorne had no optimism about easy solutions to the problem of racial differences and discrimination, nor did he regard a separation of the states as a threat to his life's work.

When South Carolina seceded from the United States, Hawthorne's alarm belied his earlier faith in the solidarity of the Union, and he was forced to acknowledge openly the cultural differences between North and South. In an overstatement that was rather characteristic of the temper of the times, Hawthorne said: "We never were one people, and never really had a country since the Constitution was formed." When the war broke out, Hawthorne was aware, as few of his fellows were, of the cross-purposes and confusion of causes. During the summer of 1861, he wrote to a friend in England:

We also have gone to war, and we seem to have little, or at least a very misty idea of what we are fighting for. It depends upon the speaker; and that, again, depends upon the section of the country in which his sympathies are enlisted. The Southern man will say, "We fight for State rights, liberty and independence." The Middle Western man will avow that he fights for the Union; while our Northern and Eastern man will swear that from the beginning his only idea was liberty to the blacks and the annihilation of slavery. All are thoroughly in earnest, and all pray for the blessing of Heaven to rest upon the enterprise.

Now that the nation was at war, Hawthorne expressed the belief that the only possible way to attain a future union of North and South was through the annihilation of slavery. Therefore, he said, the nation ought to set about preparing Negroes for future citizenship by allowing them to help win their own freedom and by "educating them through heroic influences."

In March, 1862, Hawthorne journeyed to Washington, going on to Harper's Ferry, where he saw a group of rebel prisoners.[33] The experience was illuminating in that it revealed to him an entirely new aspect of American life. In the *Atlantic Monthly* he described these

[32] References in this and the following paragraph are to *Hawthorne and His Wife,* II, 277, 290–91.

[33] *Ibid.,* p. 308.

Southerners as "a breed of men . . . such as [he] did not suppose to exist in this country."[34] They were "simple, bumpkin-like fellows . . . [with] faces vacant of meaning." The signs pointing to frontier life in the South were before him, but he was not able to read them. For the most part, the New England view of the South centered around the plantation, excluding other aspects such as the frontier. It is significant that Hawthorne ascribed the backwardness of these men, not to frontier conditions, but to slavery. He could have seen equally simple, bumpkin-like fellows in the backwood companies of the Union forces. Hawthorne explained to his *Atlantic Monthly* readers that no other consideration so well justified the war as "the probability that it [would] free this class of Southern whites from a thraldom in which they scarcely [began] to be responsive beings." Southerners had been denied the moral and intellectual development that Yankees had received, and therefore such men as these were not capable of "the degree of mercy and benevolence that exist in us." In fact he hazarded what for Hawthorne was a bold generalization: "So far as the education of the heart is concerned, the negroes have apparently the advantage of [this class of whites]; and as to other schooling, it is practically unattainable by black or white."

This was in 1862, however, and the nation was being purged by the bitter medicine of war. The mind of Hawthorne, never responsive to new experience, had by this time lost much of its penetration and imaginative power. It was too late for him to be a Goodman Brown journeying into the dark forest of the war front. By virtue of his spiritual insight into evil, Hawthorne would have been the writer of his generation most capable of re-creating for all time the American tragedy of his time. He did not stay at the center of this tragedy, however, and he produced nothing more than a magazine article on the subject. Perhaps it would have been impossible for any one American of that day to have grasped the totality of American life in the same imaginative way that Hawthorne had grasped the Puritan life. Late in 1862, Walt Whitman, fifteen years younger than Hawthorne and still in the prime of his poetic powers, journeyed to Washington and down to the front in search of his wounded brother. With neither the

[34] Reprinted in Hawthorne, *Works*, XVII. See pp. 398–402 for the quotations in this paragraph.

molding power nor the depth of Hawthorne, Whitman was neverthe-less free of the Hawthorne barriers of solitude and instinctive attach-ment to region. Possessing the most spontaneously sympathetic heart of his literary generation, Whitman remained at the nation's heart during this tragic period, identifying himself with the American experience completely enough to weave its texture into poetry.

· 6 ·

New England Magazines

AFTER assembling every comment on the South which can be found in the writings of the major New England men of letters, one is forced to conclude that apart from the slavery question this group of writers had almost no awareness of the South and apparently no desire to learn more about it in order to understand it better. Occasional signs of interest in such things as Southern personality and manners which can be found in their writings, most notably in Emerson, became virtually indistinguishable, in the atmosphere of intersectional animosity, from the fictionalized South of the abolitionist. In so far as the South was to them a cultural abstraction, it was equated with slavery as an abstraction. These writers came of age at a time when the portion of America which lay below the Mason-Dixon line became the subject of various portraits. In the early eighteen thirties many Southerners—attempting to justify the remunerative blend of cotton and slave labor—began to picture themselves in romanticized tones of a pre-Jeffersonian past, while at the same time the abolitionists in the North began to portray the planters in the much darker but equally unreal tones of villainy. The darker picture grew in popularity, especially in New England, and because most of the major men of letters mistook this portrait for the South itself, one wonders to what extent a more sympathetic and less distorted view was available to the New Englander. Turning to such New England journals as the *North American Re-*

view, the *New England Magazine,* and one of the gilt-edged weeklies, the *Waverly Magazine,* one finds a South sharply contrasted to the South advanced by the writers previously considered. Whereas the major New England writers were for the most part either hostile or silent in respect to the South, there is evidence that these journals were both sympathetic and expressive in their treatment of it.

In April, 1833, the *North American* published a long review of John Pendleton Kennedy's *Swallow Barn, or a Sojourn in the Old Dominion.*[1] The review praised the book highly, observing that its great value lay in the truth and spirit with which it described the manners and customs of Virginia. Quotations from *Swallow Barn* were unusually long, even for the *North American,* which during this time often quoted extensively in reviews. Its interest in the Southern plantation was revealed in both the selection and the length of the passages quoted. They were extensive enough to show that Kennedy's opening simile of "the aristocratical old edifice, which squat[ed] like a brooding hen, on the Southern bank of the James River" caught the tone of his entire picture of life under the beneficence of the plantation system. At Swallow Barn, Negro and white alike lived in security and ease. Moreover, in calling Frank Meriwether "the thorough-bred Virginian," there was a suggestion that he and his ménage were representative. Swallow Barn was the true, the real Virginia. The characteristics of "the very model of the landed gentleman" were all included in the *North American* quotations: Frank Meriwether prided himself on his appearance, both in figure and dress; he opened his home readily to strangers as well as to friends; he had a well-stocked library; Richmond he considered "emphatically" to be the center of civilization, though he disparaged both city life and mercantile pursuits; he made long speeches, was impatient of contradiction and sensitive about his honor; he considered himself High-Church, though he rarely attended services; he loved horses and was amusingly indulgent toward the eccentric and "pragmatical old negro" who ran his stables; his slaves, who held him in "profound reverence," were happy under his dominion. If Kennedy's book was more of an idyl than a report on life in the South, his title promised an idealized Southern farm. And one could suppose, as the reviewer obviously did

[1] *North American Review,* XXXVI (April, 1833), 519–44.

in pronouncing it a truthful picture, that a barn may be as justly celebrated for its swallows as exposed for its dung. It is characteristic of the *North American* that it preferred to keep its eye on the swallow with Kennedy while the abolitionists were pointing more and more insistently to the dung.

The *New England Magazine* also regarded *Swallow Barn* as an essentially faithful presentation of life on a Southern plantation. It praised Kennedy for the accuracy and minuteness of his observations, for his genial humor, and for the beauty of his style. It described the principal characters as "good-natured, worthy persons" and noted that they were kind, hospitable, liberal, and honorable. But it also noted that their lives were trivial, involving nothing more important than the concoction of mint juleps. "They visit each other, eat, drink and are merry, and that is all. They have excellent qualities, but no occasion calls them forth." Kennedy's picture, quipped the *New England,* was a "still life." Because Kennedy had portrayed his characters as "humorously conceited, pompous, ignorant and dogmatic," the *New England,* without denying the truth of the picture, concluded that *Swallow Barn* was "a gentle satire on the pride, aristocratic feeling, and ignorance of a certain class, rather numerous in the south." Three years later, in November, 1835, in reviewing Kennedy's *Horse-Shoe Robinson,* the *New England* paid a tribute once again to *Swallow Barn,* this time saying nothing of satire. It spoke of Kennedy's ladies, the "gay, bold, dashing" Bel Tracy, and the noble Mildred Lindsay. *Horse-Shoe Robinson* was even worthier of a warm reception than was *Swallow Barn,* said the *New England,* and declared that it wished "to add [its] tribute of praise to the universal voice of the reading public. In this case, at least, the *vox populi* has shouted for the right man." Once more the *New England* asserted Kennedy's fidelity to Southern life. "All his descriptive sketches and pictures of character and manners, are life-like and correct."[2]

William Gilmore Simms was also applauded by the *New England Magazine,* which reviewed his *Guy Rivers* in November, 1834, and *The Yemassee* in June, 1835. "We have some doubts whether we ought not to rank Mr. Simms first of American novelists." It adjudged

---

[2] *New England Magazine,* III (July, 1832), 76–80; IX (November, 1835), 390–91.

Guy Rivers to be as good as most of Cooper's novels, and *The Yemassee* superior to *The Last of the Mohicans* in plot, style, and execution. The *New England* objected to the extravagance, verbosity, and occasional incorrect expression which it found in Simms's work. Nevertheless, it commended *Guy Rivers* for having "very respectable powers both in thought and style" and described the central character as "a high-spirited Southron, chivalrous, talented, handsome, and enthusiastic."[3]

Despite its regional title, the *New England Magazine* was remarkably receptive to Southern materials and presented to its readers a rather well-defined and homogeneous picture of the South. In the first two volumes (1831 and 1832) appeared a series of sketches of South Carolina, Virginia, and Kentucky, which paid tribute "to the great number of rich and intelligent cultivators who live on their plantations, after the manner of the old English country gentlemen." Their influence was beneficent, giving "a high tone to public sentiment"; and, the magazine added, "a similar class would be of advantage in New England."[4] As pictured in these sketches, the Virginian was bold and open. He loved horses, bet confidently and hugely on the races, and paid his losses cheerfully. His generosity and profuseness led to frequent borrowing. Although he considered himself a supporter of the church, he evinced little piety and rarely attended services. The plantations were famous for their sumptuous dinners, Virginia ham, good wine, and fellowship.

The *New England* correspondent found this spirit of conviviality prevailing in South Carolina, too.[5] "A common visiting distance for dinner is twenty miles; and, at the races, all Carolina comes up to Charleston." In the city, the Carolinian lived "like a gentleman among his peers" and, in the country, like the "patriarch of old." But

[3] *Ibid.,* VIII (June, 1835), 489–90; VII (November, 1834), 422–26. For an example of the *New England*'s harsh treatment of Cooper, see VII (August, 1834), 154–57. In 1834 and again in 1835 the *New England* reviewed William Alexander Caruthers, both times unfavorably. Of *The Kentuckian in New York,* it said that the characters were feeble, common, and not amusing, the style not remarkable. VII (August, 1834), 157–59. It called *The Cavaliers of Virginia* dull and preposterous. VIII (April, 1835), 324–26.

[4] *Ibid.,* II (January, 1832), 37–45.

[5] "South Carolina," *ibid.,* I (September, 1831), 246–50; I (October, 1831), 337–41.

the *New England* also reflected that the planter is more powerful than it is safe for men to be. "He [was] entrusted with everything relating to the happiness and welfare of hundreds of his fellow men." Generally speaking, however, the planter was equal to the trust placed in him. The Carolinian's virtues were many, said the *New England,* while his faults were those of his institution: he knew little of the New England ideals of industry and thrift. Even a small planter would scatter more money in a year or two than many New England farmers could earn in a lifetime of toil and close economy. Despite the nullification excitement of the time, the *New England* maintained that the Carolinian, for all his ardor, was essentially patriotic and devoted to the common country. And it saw the "true spirit of Carolina" in the patriotism and heroism which she had displayed in the Revolutionary War.

Special emphasis was placed on the mutual affection of master and slave. "[The planter] has grown up among his slaves; many of them have that tenacious hold upon his heart that comes from early companionship as playmates, and some of them are his foster-brothers." It was noted that in Charleston the Negro was better fed, clothed, and conditioned than he was in New York, that he seemed to be "well at ease, and comfortable, if not rising in the world." In respect to the Negro in Virginia, the correspondent expressed the wish that he "could paint the cheerful, undescribed and indescribable negro, whose laugh is so ready, and is such an explosion of joy, that it is a pity, when it is so easy to make him laugh, that he should ever cry."[6] According to the *New England,* the evils of slavery were softened by the humane treatment of the Negro.

The lowest class in Virginia is that of the "poor white man;" or, as the negro calls him, the "poor buckra." He is an object of pity and derision even to the negro himself. These men are gipseys in all but wandering life, having not only no possessions, but no very definite notions of property, scarcely making a distinction between *meum* and *tuum.* Brought up in ignorance, they live in idleness, and their lives are practical homilies of the importance of common schools, and laws to compel attendance thereon.

In presenting Kentucky as the eldest daughter of Virginia, the *New*

6 *Ibid.,* I (January, 1832), 44.

England Magazine recognized the impact of the frontier on Southern character. Kentucky inherited from Virginia its hospitality and courtesy as well as some customs, such as the barbecue and the candy pull, but the new environment had heightened the boldness and self-assurance of its people. The correspondent noted that the dignity of the Kentuckian was "dashed with humor and gaiety."[7] A later sketch told of the "unostentatious cordiality" of Kentucky manners, though it also noted that the Kentuckian was aroused to speedy and resolute action if he suspected an imposition.[8] In describing a portly Negro violinist named "Pompey," the sketch tended to portray him as gifted but eccentric, and it also followed the trend to repeat trite but supposedly colorful names. Paulding, in 1832, had used the names "Pompey the Great" and "Pompey the Little" in his *Westward Ho!*, which the *New England Magazine* had reviewed.[9] Judging from the story, one would assume that the Kentuckians had established a workable and mutually satisfactory relationship between Negro and white. In 1834 there appeared in the *New England Magazine* another representation of society in Kentucky.[10] Emphasizing the loquacity of the Southerner, the sketch maintained that the Kentuckian could talk a Yankee peddler dumb in five minutes—not with blustering or bullying,

but with a stream of words, words, words, uttered in a high key, with a certain dogmatical precision, a drawing down of the brow and sustained monotony of tone, bespeaking unfailing confidence and a solemnity of visage, all which it [was] necessary he should assume to impress his hearers with the required quantum of belief in his infallibility.

[7] "Kentucky," *ibid.,* II (March, 1832), 235–38. "I could parody the phrase of Alexander, and say were I not a Yankee, I would be a Kentuckian. The Kentuckian is worthy of his beautiful country."

[8] *Ibid.,* IV (March, 1833), 202–206.

[9] *Westward Ho! A Tale,* By the Author of "The Dutchman's Fireside" etc. (J. & J. Harper, New York, 1832), I, 28–29. For the review of this book in the *New England,* see III (November, 1832), 424. The review found Paulding deficient in invention and drama, but the story, it said, was well told. "Mr. Paulding's name to an American novel is as good as the impression of the mint upon North Carolina gold: if we are to 'speak or die' which is the American novelist, we should name him in preference to Cooper. He has more wit, humor, and knowledge of character. His actors are not technical, they belong to the great family of man."

[10] *New England Magazine,* VII (July, 1834), 46–50.

As early as 1833 the *New England* perceived the importance to American welfare of mutual respect and understanding between Northerner and Southerner. In an open "Letter on Slavery" to a Southern paper, it asked the South to respect New England principles of freedom. It appealed to Americans, Northern and Southern, to recognize the value of America as a cultural experiment. Furthermore, it foresaw that as the country expanded the question of equality would become increasingly critical. It therefore asked for intelligent and candid discussions of points of difference, and it denounced those who excited harsh feelings.

Most deeply do I lament that there is not more community of feeling, more accurate knowledge of each other's character, between the people of the North and those of the South; I regret that our population do not more fully appreciate the high spirit, the generous and confiding disposition, the frank and open hospitality of the Southerner; and that yours does not more honor the intelligence, the enterprise, the moral worth, and the public spirit, of the Yankee. Did they know each other better, depend upon it, there would be fewer here to raise a hue and cry about the cruelty of slave-masters, and fewer among you to talk of Yankee trick, or Yankee interference in Southern affairs.

In the following year, the editors of the *New England* asked again for more toleration between Northerners and Southerners; for knowledge and understanding, they believed, would check the dangers of prejudice and distrust.[11] But as sectional differences grew so did expressions of disapproval, even in the *New England Magazine*. In a review of the "Letters of John Randolph, to a Young Relative" (July, 1834), the *New England* expressed disdain for "Virginia pride" and complained about the Southern custom of "chewing tobacco, spitting, drinking mint julep in the morning, and toddy at noon, horseracing, fisticuffing, and other like genteel accomplishments."[12] Despite its caustic tone, this complaint of bad manners and unruliness was a far cry from Whittier's picture of the blackhearted villain. But it should be noted, too, that the review reflected the current picture of the South. A year later, though, there appeared an item which was much more ominous in its implication, an account by a Northern traveler

[11] *Ibid.,* V (August, 1833), 122–29; VII (November, 1834), 407–408.
[12] *Ibid.,* VII (July, 1834), 78–79.

in the South who was tarred and feathered by "a posse of Judge Lynch" because the ruffians thought him an abolitionist.[13] Nevertheless, the tone expressed in these two items was in marked contrast to the prevailing mood of the *New England Magazine*.

During the eighteen thirties the *North American Review* expressed an attitude toward the South which was essentially the same as that found in the *New England Magazine,* and one cannot find in its pages even the occasional outbursts of disapproval such as those from the *New England* mentioned above. The *New England* was absorbed by the *American Monthly Magazine* of New York in 1835, but the *North American* continued as an influential New England publication throughout the entire pre–Civil War period. Beginning as early as 1824, when Jared Sparks left his Unitarian congregation in Baltimore to become the editor, the *North American* revealed a continuous interest in things Southern, often numbering Southerners among its contributors.[14] Throughout this long prewar period it consistently adhered to Sparks's policy of leaving slavery to the Southerner and emphasizing the common cultural and economic ties between North and South. In its treatment of the South, the magazine consciously and determinedly held the path of moderation between the extremes of panegyrics and condemnations. To justify its *via media* it drew heavily upon travel literature, especially Sir Charles Lyell's during the forties and Frederick Law Olmsted's during the fifties. The tone of confidence in which the editors received the writings of these men implied that they sought to canonize an authoritative literature which might save their readers from either abolitionist or proslavery heresies.

In October, 1845, the *North American* reviewed Lyell's *Travels in North America in the Years 1841–1842; with Geographical Observations on the United States, Canada, and Nova Scotia.*[15] The book contained many observations on men and manners in the United States, from which the *North American* quoted extensively. "As our

---

[13] "The Inconveniences of Being Lynched," *ibid.,* IX (October, 1835), 270–73. The two items cited in this paragraph were the only hostile ones which came to my attention in examining the issues of the *New England Magazine*.

[14] Frank Luther Mott, *A History of American Magazines, 1741–1850* (D. Appleton-Century Co., Inc., New York, 1930), II, 229, 233.

[15] *North American Review,* LXI (October, 1845), 498–518.

object is to present Mr. Lyell's views, not our own, we give the following series of pretty copious extracts, without comment." The review commented pointedly on Lyell's qualifications, however. It admired his scientific habits of close, accurate observation and his independent thinking; it asserted that his interest in geology took him away from main-traveled routes and therefore brought him into more informative contact with slavery. The *North American* believed that these "copious extracts" presented a corrective for what it regarded as the monstrous misconception in New England of the relationship between master and slave. Pointing to a reciprocity of affection and service between master and slave, Lyell observed that the Negro had a sense of belonging to the family of his master. He told of the paternal care over the slave which the planter and his wife were obliged to exercise, partly out of affection and partly through expedient. This paternalism was particularly important when the slaves were ill. The slaves, he noted, never seemed to be overworked, and he found them "better fed than a large part of the laboring class of Europe."

As reported in the *North American,* Lyell paid tribute to Southern character and described a believable South. Nevertheless, the English scientist noted to what extent slavery hindered the growth and development of the South. He maintained that slave labor was less efficient and therefore more expensive than free labor and that there appeared to be no place in Southern society for the "poor white." Unlike others who pointed to the failure of the South "to keep up" with the North, Lyell never mistook the victim for the disease. It was the system rather than the individual that was bad. Lyell recognized the enormous demands that slavery necessarily placed upon the individual planter. "The prudence, temper, and decision of character required to manage a plantation successfully are very great." He spoke of an almost irresistible temptation which the planters faced: "If they are rich, their slaves multiply, and from motives of kindly feeling toward retainers, and often from false pride, they are very unwilling to sell them. Hence they are constantly tempted to maintain a larger establishment than is warranted by the amount of their capital." There were no whips, chains, or auction blocks in his picture. Many years before Mrs. Stowe's creation of that renegade Northerner, Simon

Legree, the archetype of all cruel slave-beaters, Lyell observed: "It is notorious, that the hardest taskmasters to the slaves are those who come from the northern free States."

Four years later (1849), the *North American* welcomed *A Second Visit to the United States of North America,* by Lyell, now Sir Charles Lyell, F.R.S., president of the Geographical Society of London.[16] The review emphasized Lyell's wide experience with human nature, commenting on his shrewd and thoughtful observations and his "conscientious desire to tell the exact truth and leave the facts to make their own impression." Lyell visited the Southwest on his second trip, seeing Tennessee, Arkansas, and Missouri. As reported in the *North American,* he told of Southern hospitality under the hard conditions of the West. In a little frontier town an elderly bachelor from New Orleans gave up his room in the middle of the night to the Lyells, his sense of courtesy compelling him to do what no sum of money would have bribed him to do. On this second trip, Lyell spent a fortnight on a large rice plantation in Georgia. The *North American* quoted lengthy excerpts from his descriptions of conditions there. As in his earlier book, Lyell criticized the system of slavery, primarily for its inefficiency. The *North American* reminded its readers that Sir Charles Lyell had studied the condition of the slaves carefully, that he attested to "the uniform kindness with which they [were] treated by their masters." The editors regarded Lyell's work as the most "complete and trustworthy" picture of the South to be found in any book of travels in America.

The *North American* was obliged to wait seven years for another picture of the South which it could wholeheartedly recommend to its readers. In July, 1856, it reviewed Frederick Law Olmsted's *Journey through the Seaboard Slave States,* pronouncing the author a "first-class authority" and predicting that his book would prove to be of permanent interest. The editors asserted that Northerners and Southerners alike knew surprisingly little about the system of slavery; that the Southern apologist saw only a part of the system, while the abolitionist, "acting with perfect consistency on the simple principle that it is wrong for man to enslave man, is willing to acknowledge a cer-

[16] *Ibid.,* LXIX (October, 1849), 325–53. Special references to pp. 327–29, 348–49, 353.

tain indifference as to the details of his enslavement." The editors believed that Olmsted's fair and objective report would help to correct
the "false notions of a region and people unjustly handled in the proverbial speech of the North." Olmsted's "practical, deliberate eye"
had seen several "social systems" as he had traveled slowly southward.

These systems, it must be remembered, differ widely from one another.
The tobacco and wheat culture of Virginia, the rosin and turpentine
manufacture of North Carolina, the rice crop of South Carolina and
Georgia, the sugar crop of Louisiana, each presents the system of slavery
in a different light. Each requires hands to be bought and sold, bred,
nurtured, trained, and kept in its own way. The planter in Virginia
knows scarcely more, by his own experience, what slavery is in Louisiana,
than he knows of the working of a steam-engine in the Cornwall mines.

Olmsted, ventured the editors, would lift the discussion of slavery "to
a range decidedly higher than it has ever held before," and they predicted that his views would be gratefully received by those who regarded slavery "as a problem requiring a practical solution." The
following year the *North American* reviewed *A Journey through
Texas; or A Saddle Trip on the Southwestern Frontier* and predicted
that the calm, candid, impartial statements of Olmsted would do
more to hasten emancipation than passionate speeches and works of
fiction however exciting and pathetic. Olmsted's third volume, *A
Journey in the Back County,* which the *North American* reviewed in
the autumn of 1860, was equally well received, and again the editors
emphasized Olmsted's freedom from prejudices and "sectional antipathies."[17]

The existing institutions of the South he regards as not susceptible of
immediate or speedy change,—least of all would he advocate political
interference with them. ... But if they actually prevent the full development of the country's resources, true policy, he maintains, dictates a
course of discussion, and, when opportunity presents, a line of action
which shall look toward the essential modification or the ultimate extinction of slavery.

Although the *North American* drew most heavily upon Lyell and

[17] *Ibid.,* LXXXIII (July, 1856), 278–79; LXXXIV (April, 1857), 565–66;
XCI (October, 1860), 571.

Olmsted to support its middle position, there were other travel books which served to confirm the magazine's point of view. In 1852, the *North American* reviewed a travel book written by the Earl of Carlisle.[18] "He expresses his opinions regarding slavery with a manly and temperate frankness, which would probably not quite please the zealous opponents, or the zealous defenders, of the institution, and which may therefore be supposed to be rational and just." The Earl of Carlisle, said the review, pointed out the bad effects of large-scale plantation agriculture upon the soil and noted the lack of neatness and cleanliness in the South. But the Earl, as quoted in the *North American,* found the Southern planter a pleasant reminder of the English country gentleman. This class of Southerner, he said, was "more easy, companionable, fond of country life, and out-of-door pursuits" than any other class of Americans. In 1858, the *North American* reviewed *Letters from the Slave States,* by "an intelligent and highly educated Scotchman" named James Stirling, who was, it said, "candid, earnest, discriminating and humane."[19] It was the *North American*'s opinion that Stirling had proved, through a series of comparisons between North and South, that the Southern system was economically and socially injurious. But, it added, Mr. Stirling also refuted the charge, so repeatedly leveled at the South, of systematic and habitual cruelty toward the Negro. The editors commented that the book would not be popular in the North because "it entirely lacks that delightful element of recrimination and abuse, without which a work on slavery would fall dead in our market."

Over the years, John P. Kennedy continued to receive the same kindly treatment from the *North American* that he had enjoyed in the review of his *Swallow Barn.* In January, 1850, the *North American* reviewed his *Memoirs of the Life of William Wirt, Attorney General of the United States.* Although the *North American* objected to the length of the book and thought that Kennedy had been perhaps too easy with his praise, it softened both criticisms by conceding that the author had given his readers many pleasant sketches of prominent Virginians.

William Gilmore Simms and Joseph G. Baldwin also received

[18] *Ibid.,* LXXIV (January, 1852), 197–216.
[19] *Ibid.,* LXXXVI (January, 1858), 290–91.

favorable treatment from the *North American Review*. As late as October, 1859, three pages of praise were devoted to Simms, and the reviewer declared that he had read most of the long list of Simms's books, "and though there are very great differences in their merits, we have read none of them without interest, and most of them with great satisfaction." With the authors of *The Scarlet Letter* and *Moby Dick* still actively writing, the *North American* declared: "Indeed, in our own deliberate opinion, since the demise of Cooper there is no one who can be reckoned his superior among American Novelists." On the other hand, thirteen years earlier, 1846, the *North American* had published a flippant, condescending review of Simms, denouncing the Southerner for his "great pretensions," for his deficiency in originality, grace and picturesqueness.[20] This critical tone was decidedly an exception to the usual amicability of the *North American* toward Southern writers. Joseph G. Baldwin was hospitably received by the *North American* with its reviews, in 1855, of *The Flush Times of Alabama and Mississippi* and *Party Leaders*.[21] His series of pictures of the Southwest were "for the most part intensely comic" though not overdrawn. They contained enough "verisimilitude to assure [one] that the outlines were copied from life."

One can learn very little of the antislavery movement in New England from the *North American*. With but few exceptions it ignored the writings, speeches, and activities of the abolitionists. In July, 1835, it expressed regret that Lydia Maria Child had used her pen for *An Appeal in Favor of That Class of Americans Called Africans*. It was a dangerous subject, the *North American* said, and Mrs. Child had been unfair in suggesting that all slaveholders were bad. Eight years later, in July, 1843, it reviewed William Lloyd Garrison's *Sonnets and Other Poems*.[22] The review acknowledged that

[20] *Ibid.*, LXXXIX (October, 1859), 559–61; LXIII (October, 1846), 357–81.

[21] *Ibid.*, LXXX (January, 1855), 266. *Party Leaders,* it adjudged, deserved even greater approbation than did *Flush Times*.

[22] *Ibid.*, XLI (July, 1835), 170–93; LVII (July, 1843), 253–54. The length of the review of *An Appeal* did not reflect an interest in Mrs. Child. It contained a historical sketch of slavery, noting that there has always been slavery, that England, France, and Holland were guilty of the slave trade and thus really forced slavery upon America, and that compromise is the only workable solution to the problem in America.

some of the sonnets possessed clearness, purity, music, and fancy. However, it added, Garrison had "but little of the poetical element" and that had been diminished by his "dwelling perpetually on a single theme." The *North American* was obviously less interested in Garrison's poetry than it was in discussing its own theory that poetry did not belong in the political arena. The magazine held that a poet's powers were inevitably dissipated by quarreling with the world. The article asserted—with specific reference to Garrison—that, in clinging to his single idea, he had sacrificed any claim "to the catholic character of a scholar or a poet."

In 1848, the *North American* maintained that Lowell had been injured and Whittier spoiled by abolitionism. It held that although Lowell had "too much good sense and good taste to go all lengths" with the "insane fanaticism" of the abolitionists, "the tone of his mind . . . [had] been injured by contact with them." The *North American* objected to such a poem as "The Present Crisis" because it supported those who "inculcate toleration with savage intolerance . . . who generously take it for granted that cowardice, selfishness, and meanness are the only reasons why all their fellow-mortals do not shout their war-cry, advocate their measures, and worship them as the only great and good reformers and iconoclasts of modern times." In the following year, however, *The Biglow Papers* was recognized by the *North American* as "successful humor" and praised for its "droll and felicitous portraiture of the Yankee character and dialect," for its successful barbs at our national passion for military glory.[23] But the editors did not absolve Lowell from what they regarded as the sins of the abolitionists, for they felt that the "fierce denunciations and self-glorifying spirit" of the abolitionists were made only less repugnant to reasonable people by the wit and humor of Lowell.

It was in a review of Lowell that the *North American,* borrowing an expression from Sidney Smith, the English critic, described the abolitionists as "moral bullies and virtuous braggadocios."[24] The editors were angered and not a little alarmed by "the amazing increase of the number of small poets, who were emboldened by their multi-

[23] *Ibid.,* LXVI (April, 1848), 476–78; "Humorous and Satirical Poetry"; LXVIII (January, 1849), 186–87.
[24] *Ibid.,* LXVI (April, 1848), 476–78.

tude." In July, 1854, ostensibly reviewing five of Whittier's books, the *North American* took the opportunity to sketch the history of slavery in America and also to recount Whittier's life, with special emphasis upon his abolitionism. Whittier was charged with a harshness and an intensity that conflicted with the mildness of his Quaker doctrines. The juxtaposition of the historical and the biographical sketch carried unmistakably the suggestion that Whittier simply did not see the complexity of the slavery problem. In October, 1843, the *North American* had objected to the "virulent tone" of Whittier.[25] Now, in 1854, it called him the Tyrtaeus of the abolition movement. Whether intentional or not, the appellation had a certain portentous force, since it likened Whittier to the Greek poet who hardened the hearts of the Spartans with his songs of war.

The attitude of the *North American* toward those who advocated immediate abolition reflected its vision of the South as a social organization whose laws, customs, industrial pursuits, and social habits were all controlled and thoroughly interpenetrated by slavery.[26] "The whites need to go through a training for freedom scarcely less than the blacks. The master is as much fettered to one end of the chain, as the slave to the other; and it would be difficult to say which is least prepared for emancipation." The *North American* maintained confidently that in the South one could find "the same moral sensibility" in respect to slavery as could be found in the North. There were a great number of Southerners, it held, who wished to abolish slavery. But there were legal difficulties involved in individual emancipation, and freedom in the South was precarious for the slave.

The only antislavery books which received careful attention from the *North American* were *Uncle Tom's Cabin* and *A Key to Uncle Tom's Cabin,* which were reviewed together in October, 1853.[27] Continuing a tradition that reached back some twenty years to the review of Kennedy's *Swallow Barn,* the *North American* chose to see the Shelbys as a representative planter family.

[25] *Ibid.,* LXXIX (July, 1854), 31–53; LVII (October, 1843), 509; XCII (April, 1861), 505.

[26] "Slavery in the United States," *ibid.,* LXXIII (October, 1851), 347–85. See especially pages 348–49, 353, 355, for references contained in this paragraph.

[27] *Ibid.,* LXXVII (October, 1853), 466–93. Quotations in this and the following paragraphs are from pp. 467, 470, 472, 487–89.

The Shelbys may be regarded as a fair picture of the majority of masters, because they are a fair specimen of the majority of families of respectability and easy fortune everywhere. With such masters and such treatment, the negro is as well placed as he can be. He has kindness and care, government and guidance, and is exempt from the miseries of poverty, idleness and vice. His position is better than that of most of the free negroes in the North, of the peasantry of many parts of Europe, and infinitely better, in all respects, mental, moral, and material, than that of his brethren in Africa.

The *North American* praised *Uncle Tom* highly, calling it a work of genius. "Thought, imagination, feeling, high moral and religious sentiment, and dramatic power shine in every page." It asserted that Mrs. Stowe had drawn her characters with spirit and truth. As for Legree: "We fear he is not exaggerated. There are many such at the North and South: only, in the North, we do not give them so much power." Though admitting that Uncle Tom was a saint, the *North American* pointed out that "many an old family servant in the South is distinguished for probity, fidelity, truthfulness, and religious feeling, and slave though he be, is the object of respect and attachment."

The real source of power in *Uncle Tom's Cabin,* observed the *North American,* derived from the book's foundation in truth. "It is a highly-colored description of a reality." But, it added, "the charge of exaggeration admits the substance, and to acknowledge the exceptions yields nearly the whole case." Conceding that Mrs. Stowe presented the favorable as well as the unfavorable view of the South, the *North American* did not object to such unsavory elements as the trader, the catcher, the whipper, the auction block, the slave pen, the chains and dogs. Mrs. Stowe's picture of slavery, said the *North American,* astonished people everywhere, even Southerners. The reviewer adopted the tone to be repeated in 1856, with the review of Olmsted's *Journey through the Seaboard Slave States,* when he observed:

Very many in the South, too, are almost equally ignorant of such things. . . . These have seen slavery in its mild and beneficent aspect, in the old homesteads of Virginia and Carolina, where hereditary attachment and enlightened humanity have softened and mitigated the system. . . . The good they know and are familiar with, and it is difficult to make them believe that the evil exists.

The review maintained that Mrs. Stowe unconsciously and unintentionally rendered the South a threefold service: She clearly revealed to all that (1) "the general condition of the slaves, notwithstanding many exceptions, is a happy one, well suited to their nature"; (2) "while the benefits of slavery may be increased and extended, its evils are capable of being remedied by wise and just legislation"; (3) "the Southern people alone can deal with this subject." The *North American* therefore looked beyond what it called the hostility and bitterness of the book to what it predicted would be its "happy influence in convincing the liberal and enlightened among the Southern people of the necessity for reform, and of stimulating them to the work."

The *North American* retained this respect for Southern character throughout the entire prewar period. In July, 1860, it reviewed *The History of North Carolina,* by a native of the state, Francis L. Hawks, and praised without qualification both the state and its historian.

The history of a State in which flourished patriots and statesmen like Davie and Caswell, Johnston and Hooper, which can count among her soldiers such leaders as Nash and Davidson, and can point to men so wise and great as Macon and Stanley and Gaston of later times, as the native outgrowth of her institutions and culture, must be a history for strangers to read with pleasure, and of which her own children may well be proud.

As late as April, 1861, the *North American,* while affirming its disapproval of slavery as an institution, defended the individual Southerner: "Cruelty and harshness are, we sincerely believe, the exception, not the rule. . . . Many are the estates and households in which the Christian master and mistress are not tyrants, but the guardians, of those who are called their property."[28]

The *Waverly Magazine* of Boston was a gilt-edged literary weekly whose policy was to encourage new writers. It specialized in the themes of temperance, love, home life, and health; it printed a floral motif in the margins, an original piece of music on the back page; and the masthead was dominated by what Hawthorne vexatiously termed the scribbling females. In such a periodical one would not ex-

[28] *Ibid.,* XCI (July, 1860), 40–71; XCII (April, 1861), 492–515.

pect to find incisive writing upon the crucial questions of the day. Like the *North American Review, Waverly Magazine* was cordial and sympathetic to the South and receptive to Southern writers. It ignored antislavery agitation, except in so far as the issue was expressed in the fictional person of Uncle Tom.[29] In October, 1853, the *Waverly* directed the attention of its readers to a refutation of Mrs. Stowe's charges against slavery. The book it reviewed was *Notes on Uncle Tom's Cabin. Being a Logical Answer to Its Allegations and Influences against Slavery and Its Institutions; with a Supplementary Note on the "Key," and an Appendix of Authorities,* by the Reverend E. J. Stearns, A.M., late professor in St. John's College, Annapolis, Maryland.[30] This book, promised the *Waverly*, would throw water on the raging fire of antislavery. "It clearly disposes of many allegations in Mrs. Stowe's work, and shows that she is not familiar with the habits and customs of the better class of Southern people, and is unqualified to form a correct idea of the general treatment of their slaves." The editors expressed the hope that all who had read *Uncle Tom's Cabin* would read the *Notes.* "We think it will serve to modify their animosities towards our brethren of the South, for an evil which prudence would not require to be removed too hastily." In the same issue of the *Waverly* there was a statement that indicated how universal *Uncle Tom* had become: "That immortal hero has been dramatized, painted, played, sung and danced . . . exhibited on handkerchiefs, and pictured upon porcelain. There have been Uncle Tom pipes and Uncle Tom candies, Uncle Tom coats and Uncle Tom chariots. And the white characters of the book share in the general glorification."[31]

[29] See, for example, its review of "Anti-Fanaticism—A Tale of the South," by Martha Haines Butt, of Norfolk, Virginia. *Waverly Magazine,* VII (July 2, 1853), 9. Miss Butt had contributed a story, "Eva, or the Mountain Gem," to Vol. VI of the *Waverly.* In "A Tale of the South," the *Waverly* found "a good share of that generous sympathy for which the people of the South are noted." In December, 1853, and again in December, 1854, the *Waverly* urged its readers to read the works of Simms and spoke of the popularity of *The Yemassee,* calling it "an old favorite." For other examples of the magazine's congeniality to the South, see VIII (May 20, 1854), 329; IX (July 8, 1854), 24; IX (Aug. 5, 1854), 94; IX (Oct. 21, 1854), 264.

[30] *Waverly Magazine,* VII (Oct. 15, 1853), 252.
[31] *Ibid.,* VII (Oct. 15, 1853), 244.

How well Mrs. Stowe and all those who prepared the way for her had wrought can be clearly seen in a sketch which the *Waverly Magazine* printed in the summer of 1854.[32] Jeannie, the author of "Elsie's Wedding, A Stray Leaf from Negro Life," had gone South to visit a friend who dwelt on a plantation redolent of Swallow Barn. The writer acknowledged that, living in "the rank region of Abolitionism," she had been tinctured by the spirit of hostility toward the South. But this faded fast in the light of her personal observation of life on a Southern plantation.

Instead then, of the picture I had brought with me—of bowed heads, and tear-bedewed cheeks, of ebony lips that never parted in a smile and bleeding backs and clanking chains—to find happy faces, from out whose ample opening the pure white ivory was forever glistening, and musical voices forever pealing forth glad songs, and merry-makings, and sundry visitings, ornamented with all the cast-off finery of "master's" family, called out my interest in this much eulogized and storied race, in entirely a new channel.

Jeannie saw that the South of the abolitionists was as fictitious as the life of Sinbad the Sailor. On the other hand, her version of "the happy faces" attested to a facility for romanticizing which no doubt suited the tastes of *Waverly* readers but surely brought them no closer to actual life in the South than had the abolitionists. In a milieu in which sentiment flourished so luxuriantly there could be little encouragement for an open-eyed, objective view of the South. There is, however, an obvious contrast between the predominantly caustic tone of the major New England writers and the predominantly sympathetic tone of the representative periodicals.

[32] *Ibid.*, IX (July 15, 1854), 43.

Part II

New York

· 7 ·

New York Backgrounds

BECAUSE the New York writers could speak from their own experience, it is not necessary in this chapter to consider Northern portraits of the South which may have been available to them. Nor is it pertinent to examine the abolition element in the New York environment, for these literary men, unlike their New England contemporaries, did not adopt the abolition sentiment. It is pertinent, however, to consider what factors in the New York milieu created a community of apparent good will toward the South, inasmuch as the major New York writers showed an affection for the South and a sympathetic understanding of its cultural problems.

Two of these factors were revealed by Philip S. Foner in his study *Business and Slavery,* which discloses the innumerable economic ties between New York and the South. "The influence of the South upon New York's economic life started at the port, and proceeded uptown, touching every form of business activity on the way."[1] Foner has pointed out that the cotton trade was dominated by New York, that often 30 or 40 per cent of the price of cotton went to New Yorkers. In one year alone, 1849, the South purchased more than seventy-six million dollars worth of merchandise in New York. Such a productive

[1] Philip S. Foner, *Business and Slavery: The New York Merchants and the Irrepressible Conflict* (University of North Carolina Press, Chapel Hill, N.C., 1941). Specific references in this paragraph are to pp. 3, 8, 9.

relationship was of course carefully guarded by merchants. Moreover, these economic ties, according to Foner, inevitably reflected themselves in social ties. New York merchants gave generously to Southern charities. Partnerships, friendships, even marriages joined New York and Southern families.

Against this background we may consider the major pre–Civil War writers. Through travel and social connections, William Cullen Bryant, Herman Melville, and Walt Whitman knew the South in all its variety and particularity. Thus they were free of the New Englander's tendency to abstract an image which could represent the South algebraically.

This attachment and loyalty to the South also extended back to the older generation of New York writers. James Kirke Paulding, James Fenimore Cooper, and Washington Irving knew Southern men and manners directly through personal friendships and through travel. Of the three, Paulding's ties with the South were the strongest. He liked the manners and merriment of the planter aristocracy, maintaining that their pride helped to preserve their virtue.[2] In his *Letters from the South* (1817), Paulding presented the planter aristocracy in an amiable light. One planter whom he visited owned several hundred slaves and ten thousand acres. He was well educated, lively, good-humored, sensible, hospitable, and water was his only drink. Paulding praised the "domestic education" which was given the daughters of the planters. In the "chaste simplicity of their manners . . . the cultivation of their minds . . . the purity of their hearts," he believed them superior to Northern ladies. He was impressed by the spontaneous laughter of the Negroes and by the excellence of their musical talents. "They are by far the most musical of any portion of the inhabitants of the United States, and in the evening I have seen them reclining in their boats on the canal at Richmond, playing on the *banjo,* and singing in a style—I dare say, equal to a Venetian gondolier. They whistle as clear as the notes of a fife."

There was variety and perception in Paulding's picture of the South. He reported the rivalry between the "Tuckahoes" of Old Vir-

[2] James Kirke Paulding, *Letters from the South* (Harper & Brothers, New York, 1835), I, 106. Unless otherwise indicated the quotations are taken from the 1835 edition. For this paragraph, see I, 26–27, 91, 96–97, 156.

ginia and the "Cohees" of the western part of the state, pointing out that the Blue Ridge was both a natural and a political division of Virginia. He also described the country people of the mountain regions, noting their "striking air of conscious independence," and he told of the "laborious Dutchmen" of the Shenandoah who had moved down the valleys from the North to the frontiers of Georgia, a region, he said, where one sees but few slaves.

Paulding's fiction leaned toward caricature of the Southern planter, though he dealt gently with his weaknesses, emphasizing the planter's eccentricities rather than his ineptitudes. Paulding's planter read little, worked less, and mastered the art of killing time. The early chapters of *Westward Ho!* pictured life on the large estate of Colonel Cuthbert Dangerfield, who belonged to the "ancient gentry of Old Virginia"— a high-spirited and hospitable race which was rapidly disappearing. Prodigality had inevitably brought debt, depletion of soil, and, finally, dispossession. The Colonel lost the last of his fortune vainly betting on his favorite horse. His sixteenth cousin, Ulysses Littlejohn, came uninvited to live with the Dangerfields, for he had dissipated his own estate by paying little attention to his affairs and living regularly beyond his income. Despite loss of fortune, however, he remained one of the most jovial men in the country. There was a good deal of mirth among the planters, but Paulding insisted that the Negroes were "a hundred times merrier than their masters." There was contentment for the Negro on the Dangerfield plantation and joyousness for him at the races in Richmond.

Paulding also spoke of the beautiful wives and daughters, "the pride of Virginia," who came to the races in their "gallant equipages." He paid his respect to Southern women in his portrait of Mrs. Dangerfield, who was delicate and beautiful, yet sensible and accomplished. As a mother she was careful and mild; as a wife she desired never to govern but only to curb the imprudence of her husband. Though elegantly at ease with prestige and wealth, Mrs. Dangerfield possessed the nobility of character to renounce them uncomplainingly when the family, dispossessed, migrated to Kentucky.

Paulding spoke discerningly of the impact of the frontier upon Southern character. His imagination was stimulated by the thought of men and women whose manners had been formed in the drawing-room and whose actions had "figured in the great world as warriors, statesmen, and orators," but who were now living in primitive frontier cabins.[3] Kentucky was about fifty years old when the Dangerfields settled there. The perils of pioneering had passed, and the wandering hunters had nearly disappeared, but the spirit of the early settlers was still observable. The first generation had imparted to its posterity "a character of enthusiasm, vivacity, courage, hardihood, frankness, and generosity."

In 1842 Paulding traveled through the deep South with Martin Van Buren, who had been defeated two years earlier by William Henry Harrison and was beginning once more to seek the Democratic nomination for the Presidency. To his surprise, Paulding found New Orleans "one of the most orderly, decorous cities in the world." He liked the opulence of New Orleans and the wealth and independence of Louisiana, and he enjoyed the hospitality of the sugar planters along the Mississippi River. In a short story called "The Creole's Daughter," he tried to re-create the life of the Creoles, whom he praised for their refinement, simplicity, and hospitality.[4]

The shifting emphasis in Paulding's treatment of the Negro and slavery suggests his awareness of the disruptive potential of abolitionism. In the first edition of his *Letters from the South,* he described some abuses of slavery. He told of slave-dealers who separated couples,

[3] *Westward Ho! A Tale,* by the author of "The Dutchman's Fireside," etc. (J. & J. Harper, New York, 1832), I, 9–10, 12–15, 23–30. For his information on the Kentucky frontier, Paulding borrowed from Timothy Flint's *Recollections of the Last Ten Years Passed in the Valley of the Mississippi.* See Amos L. Herold, *James Kirke Paulding, Versatile American* (Columbia University Press, New York, 1926), pp. 103–105.

[4] Paulding published in *Graham's Magazine,* 1843, "The Mississippi," a sketch of the river journey which he and Van Buren took from New Orleans to St. Louis. It has been edited and reprinted by Mentor Lee Williams, *The Journal of Mississippi History,* X (October, 1948), 317–44. "The Creole's Daughter" has been reprinted with an introduction by Floyd C. Watkins in the *Louisiana Historical Quarterly,* XXXIII (October, 1950), 364 ff. Watkins observed that despite many literary flaws the story is interesting historically, for it anticipated the methods of the local colorists and was probably the first fiction in English about the Creoles. The story originally appeared in July, 1846, in *The Columbian Magazine.* Whitman's *Franklin Evans,* which first appeared in 1842, contained an interesting episode about a "Creole" slave girl on a Virginia plantation.

forcing them to mate with others, of Negroes who were forced to walk, half-naked, in the burning sun. Paulding said that, so far as he knew, the Negroes of the deep South were no more mistreated than they were in the Northern slave states.[5] Paulding deleted much of his criticism of slavery in the second edition of his Letters, published in 1835, and added several passages warning his readers of the dangers of ill-feeling between the North and the South.[6] In *Slavery in the United States,* Paulding argued that emancipation would bring greater evils than slavery itself,[7] and he maintained that the Negroes were for the most part happy and well adjusted as slaves.

It had always been Paulding's practice to play down sectional opposition. In the 1817 edition of his Letters he observed that the Northerner, "loaded with a pack of prejudices as large as a pedlar's," realized when he traveled South that he had been misled about Southern manners. While conceding a difference in manners, Paulding stoutly denied any contrast in morals. The difference in manners and customs, he felt, involved advantages and disadvantages to both sides.[8] His fear of the divisive potential in the national situation was revealed in his assertions of Southern loyalty to the Union. To the 1835 edition of his Letters he added this comment:[9]

As to the little sectional differences, which occasionally exhibit themselves, they originate rather in the rivalry of mischievous demagogues, than in any ill-will or opposition of interests in the states. They may scold, and threaten, and bully sometimes, but there towers at all times above these petty local impulses, a deep and noble and universal attachment to the Union.

In 1849 Paulding published *The Puritan and his Daughter,* a story in which are resolved problems arising from cultural differences between a Puritan and a Cavalier family united in marriage.[10] He was

---

[5] *Letters from the South* (J. Eastburn & Co., New York, 1817), 121–31.

[6] For passages that were added in 1835, see I, 167, 172–73, 182.

[7] James Kirke Paulding, *Slavery in the United States* (Harper & Brothers, New York, 1836), pp. 7–9.

[8] *Letters from the South* (1817), I, 33, 36.

[9] Interpolated passage in 1835 ed., *Letters from the South,* I, 181.

[10] In his study "James Kirke Paulding and the South," Floyd C. Watkins has explained Paulding's view of the Negro and the problem of slavery and has traced Paulding's reaction to abolitionism. Watkins has maintained that al-

then over seventy, but his pen was still employed in the service of national unity. Throughout the entire ideological struggle which preceded the Civil War Paulding remained friendly to the South.

Cooper was both a critic of slavery and a defender of the slaveholding South. He strove to account for the existence of slavery in a country which professed the doctrine of equal rights. In 1827, in an anonymous reply to a French critic of America, Cooper maintained that America was slowly extricating itself from the curse of slavery, a curse which had been inflicted upon it by England, France, Spain, and other countries.[11] A year later, in his *Notions of the Americans*, he asserted that the entire nation was involved in the guilt of slavery. "The slaveholders of the present day (viewed as a body) are just as innocent of the creation of slavery, as their fellow citizens of New-York or Connecticut." Cooper saw that the Southerner had been placed in a predicament "that time and society, and all the multiplied interests of life, render so difficult to change." Yet, he said, progress was moving South.[12]

The evils of slavery, Cooper insisted, did not reside in physical suffering; he denied that the slaves were beaten or overworked. In 1827 he told the French that "the American slave is better off, so far as mere animal wants are concerned, than the lower order of the Euro-

though Paulding was a strong nationalist he expressed willingness to sacrifice the Union when it no longer seemed to him consistent with Southern welfare. *American Quarterly*, V (Fall, 1953), 219–30.

[11] Robert Spiller has reprinted the text of Cooper's original English version of his anonymous reply to J. C. L. de Sismondi, who had criticized America in the January, 1827, issue of *Revue Encyclopédique*. Cooper's reply appeared in the same publication, April, 1827, signed "Un Citoyen des Etats-Unis." "Fenimore Cooper's Defense of Slave-Owning America," *American Historical Review*, XXXV (April, 1930), 575–82.

[12] For this and the following references, see *Notions of the Americans: Picked up by a Travelling Bachelor* (Carey, Lea, and Blanchard, Philadelphia, 1838), II, 257, 260, 264, 265, 268, 276. The book was originally published in 1828. See also *American Historical Review*, XXXV (April, 1930), 580; *The American Democrat, or Hints on the Social and Civic Relations of the United States of America* (Cooperstown, 1838), p. 173–76; *Correspondence of James Fenimore Cooper*, ed. by his grandson, James Fenimore Cooper (Yale University Press, New Haven, 1922), II, 697–98.

pean peasants. They are a race proverbial for their light heartedness. The laugh of the negro is merriment itself." Cooper described the climate and topography of the South and stated that the slaves of the upland regions of Virginia, the Carolinas, Georgia, and large parts of Tennessee and Kentucky were employed as they were formerly in New York. "The farmer is the master of three or four labourers, and works in the field at their sides."

There is still a higher, and a very numerous class of American slaves, who are far better instructed, better clothed, and better fed, and who are altogether a superior race to the lowest class of the European peasants. I mean the domestic servants, and those who labour as mechanics and artisans.

Again, as in 1827, Cooper was explaining the existence of slavery in America and predicting its end. "I think that the influence of free opinions, if I may so express it, is steadily on the increase." He then pointed to a characteristic of slavery that lessened his optimism: "It is not the smallest evil of slavery that it begets in the master an indifference to its existence, and that it gives birth and durability to cruel and lasting prejudices." Like Paulding, however, Cooper believed that the North should not interfere in the internal affairs of the slave states. Liberation in the South had to come from the citizens of the Southern states themselves. Ten years later Cooper acknowledged, in *The American Democrat,* that slavery encouraged "those faults of character that depend upon an uncontrolled will, on the one side, and an abject submission, on the other. It usually limits the moral existence of the slave, too, as there is a necessity of keeping him ignorant, in order that he may be held in subjection." These were disquieting reflections, which suggest that Cooper's confidence had not been strengthened in the years since 1827 and 1828.

Despite his criticism of slavery, however, Cooper never charged the Southerner with any wickedness that was not characteristic of human nature everywhere. In *The American Democrat,* he denied the charges of wanton cruelty that had been made against the Southerner.

American slavery is mild, in its general features, and physical suffering cannot properly be enumerated among its evils. . . . It is an evil, certainly, but in a comparative sense, not as great an evil as it is usually imagined.

There is scarcely a nation of Europe that does not possess institutions that inflict as gross personal privations and wrongs, as the slavery of America.

Unlike the abolitionists, he refused to concede slavery in the abstract to be a sin, holding that one could be an excellent Christian and a slaveholder as well. "The relations of master and slave, may be a means of exhibiting some of the mildest graces of the character, as may those of king and subject, or principal and dependent, in any other modifications of human institutions." This defense of Southern character was given added pertinence because of Cooper's personal friendship with such Southerners as William Branford Shubrick, of South Carolina. Throughout his life Cooper retained his personal association with Southerners. In the year of Cooper's death, he received a note from Shubrick expressing an opinion, shared by both, that there would never be a dissolution of the Union in consequence of agitation over slavery. But this was a time of relatively relaxed tensions, for it was only a few months after the Compromise of 1850.

Washington Irving became aware of the South through his commercial associations with his brothers, William and Peter. In 1811 he journeyed to Washington as an agent of the family's hardware business, and again the following year as a member of a committee of New York merchants. Years later, upon his return from Europe in 1832, after seventeen years abroad, Irving visited the West and the South and attended congressional sessions in Washington. In his travels he toured the prairies, sailed down the Mississippi to New Orleans, visited a plantation during its sugar-making period, and then traveled by stage through Alabama, Georgia, the Carolinas, and Virginia, to Washington. There is no doubt that Irving recognized the prominence of the frontier in the South, for he wrote of it not only in *A Tour on the Prairies,* which relates his experiences in the country drained by the Arkansas River but also in "The Early Experiences of Ralph Ringwood," which describes life in the wilderness of Kentucky. And one finds in *Astoria* a description of St. Louis at the turn of the century with its old French buildings, Creole traders, and Kentucky hunters. But there are other aspects of the South, too, in Irving's writing. With his fondness for the picturesque, he was responsive to New Orleans and the Creole culture of Louisiana, and he thought New Orleans "one of the most motley and amazing places in the United States." He described "a serene and dilapidated" Creole village with its ancient houses of French and Spanish design and its *grand seigneur* who carried a gold snuffbox and was attended by a comical French factotum. Irving was impressed by the Creoles' singing and dancing, which he regarded as an expression of their hereditary love of fun.[13]

The sketches reveal Irving's characteristically unreflective and uncritical attitude. But in his letters home, Irving expressed an interest in Southern opinions and Southern manners when they touched on the larger question of national welfare. He resented both Northern and Southern forces which aggravated sectional opposition. Irving dined with Governor Hamilton, of South Carolina, whom he had known earlier in New York. He considered the Governor

a perfect gentleman, though somewhat a Hotspur in politics. It is really lamentable to see so fine a set of gallant fellows, as the leading Nullifiers are, so sadly in the wrong. They have just cause of complaint, and have been hardly dealt with, but they are putting themselves completely in the wrong by the mode they take to redress themselves.

In Washington, Irving expressed disappointment over the "braggadocio speeches and proceedings of South Carolina," which were exciting indignation. "I grieve to see so many elements of national prejudice, hostility and selfishness, stirring and fermenting, with activity and acrimony." He expressed a hope that Congress would devise a bill that would satisfy "the moderate part of the Nullifiers." These sectional differences, however, did not interfere with Irving's cordial relations with Southern friends. He told of spending a day with William C. Preston, of Columbia, South Carolina, talking and laughing over old times.[14]

[13] *The Works of Washington Irving* (G. P. Putnam's Sons, New York, 1881), VIII, 124–30; X, 441–74, 529–37. See also F. A. Sampson, "Washington Irving. Travels in Missouri and the South," *Missouri Historical Review* (October, 1910), privately bound in New York Public Library (AN p.v. 128), p. 31.

[14] William C. Preston was a member of the Legislature and one of the leading

120

There is no evidence that Irving thought deeply about the cultural antagonism that was dividing America or that he involved himself in any way in the heated controversy over the Wilmot Proviso which was filling the air at the time he returned, in 1846, from his second long sojourn in Europe. During the critical years from 1846 until the time of his death, in 1859, Irving retained to the last his characteristic affability in his Southern associations. One must realize, of course, that Irving was sixty-three when he returned to America in 1846 and that he was soon taken up by domestic concerns at Sunnyside and the problems of publishing a revised edition of his works. His mind moved back to the eighteenth century; he revised and extended his work on Goldsmith and undertook once more his biography of Washington.

While doing research for the latter work, Irving renewed his friendship with John P. Kennedy, whom he had first met in 1832, and visited for several weeks at his friend's home in Baltimore. At this time, Kennedy was the secretary of the navy in Fillmore's administration, but his conversation with Irving was of business and finance rather than of the ideological crosscurrents in politics.[15] Irving's letters also reveal a genuine attachment and respect for Mrs. Kennedy and her daughter Mary. His association with the Kennedy family and their close friends in Baltimore and Washington strengthened his ties with the South and was the only attraction, he declared to Kennedy, that was able to draw him repeatedly from home during these latter days of his life. He told Mrs. Kennedy that he was "bewitched with the South," that, for him, Virginia had always been "a poetical region." At another time he spoke of his "veneration for Maryland in general" and his "love for Baltimore in particular." He also enjoyed the natural beauty of the Southern countryside, praising particularly

nullifiers in South Carolina. See Pierre M. Irving, *The Life and Letters of Washington Irving* (G. P. Putnam's Sons, New York, 1863), III, 44, 48. Hereafter cited as *Life and Letters*.

[15] "Their talk was forever of insurance companies, Wall Street, railroads, and the building of houses." Stanley T. Williams, *The Life of Washington Irving* (Oxford University Press, New York, 1935), II, 209–10. See also Killis Campbell, "The Kennedy Papers," *The Sewanee Review*, XXV (January, 1917), 1–19; Stanley T. Williams and Leonard Beach, "Washington Irving's Letters to Mary Kennedy," *American Literature*, VI (March, 1934), 44–65; P. M. Irving, *Life and Letters*, IV, 124, 144–45, 149–50, 164–66.

the beautiful drives along the valley of the Patapsco and the beauty and fertility of the Shenandoah Valley.

Irving had always remained neutral in the slavery issue, disliking both extremes of defiant proslavery and militant antislavery opinion. And he scoffed at Mrs. Stowe.[16] In his sketches of the South his treatment of the master-slave relationship was bland. The slave was an integral part of the Ringwood estate in Virginia, but his presence was not intrusive. Obviously, however, there was consideration for the slave's welfare and even forbearance of his idiosyncracies. The indulgent elder Ringwood gave his son money but denied the boy's request for a personal servant on the grounds that he was not sufficiently responsible to care for him. Their old black groom was permitted absolute authority over the stables. Irving's picture of the Negro in Creole society had no disquieting tones. Among the Creoles, the Negroes were happier than their masters, said Irving, and he noted their politeness as well as their merriment.

No contrast could be greater than that between Irving's blandness in his treatment of the Negro and Melville's searching portrayal of Pip, the black boy aboard the *Pequod,* who prayed, in fear and loneliness, to the great white God. And by way of contrast, one thinks too of the sympathy implied in Whitman's treatment of the "hounded slave that flags in the race." The difference cannot be explained by characteristics of mind and temperament alone. The generation of Melville and Whitman could hardly have written of the Negro without an awareness of controversy. Irving's treatment of the Negro in the South, although incidental and brief, suggested a benignly aristocratic indifference to the demands of equalitarianism which was anachronistic in the America of Melville and Whitman. Though their approach was different because a generation separated them, there was an area of agreement between Paulding, Cooper, and Irving on the one hand and Melville, Bryant, and Whitman on the other in their treatment of the South. The similarity lay in sympathy and knowledge. But there was a large area of difference, too, which indicated a change in American opinion from the earlier to the later

[16] Letter to Mrs. Kennedy dated Nov. 11, 1853. *The Sewanee Review,* XXV, (January, 1917), ii; P. M. Irving, *Life and Letters,* III, 120–21; IV, 297.

generation. This difference was marked by the growing desire for the extension of freedom and equality. It reflected also, the force of events which had brought cultural antagonisms between North and South into sharp focus.

Chronologically, Bryant was a member of the older generation of New York writers. He was five years younger than Cooper, eleven years younger than Irving, and fifteen years younger than Paulding. Paulding retired to his Hyde Park estate in 1849 and ceased writing, Cooper died in 1851, and Irving, though he lived until 1859, did not identify himself with the current scene in any vital way during the eighteen fifties. Bryant continued to be active long after these men ended their literary careers. In his career as journalist and public figure during the turbulent years immediately before the Civil War, Bryant was in a very real sense a contemporary of Melville and Whitman—men twenty-five years his junior.

During the eighteen fifties a favorable view of the South was available to the New Yorker through the daily papers. Howard C. Perkins has demonstrated in his study of the Northern press on the eve of the Civil War that the really formidable proslavery papers in the North were published in New York City.[17] James Gordon Bennett, of the *Herald*, and Dr. J. H. Van Evrie, of the *Day-Book*, were influential proslavery editors. The New York *Journal of Commerce*, the *Daily News*, the *Morning Express*, and the *Brooklyn Daily Eagle* were among the defenders of the Southern system of slave labor.

To find the suitable frame of reference in which to view Bryant, Melville, and Whitman in their attitudes toward the South, one must find in New York a body of opinion which objected to slavery without cursing the slaveholding South. An important avenue of approach to this kind of opinion can be found in *Putnam's Magazine*, a leading New York literary journal of the eighteen fifties. Unlike its chief rival, the eclectric *Harper's Monthly*, *Putnam's* reflected a body of American opinion, and it did so on a consistently high literary and critical

[17] Howard C. Perkins, "The Defense of Slavery in the Northern Press on the Eve of the Civil War," *Journal of Southern History* (November, 1943).

level.[18] Unlike the *Knickerbocker Magazine,* which cautiously walked the fence to avoid offending either North or South, *Putnam's* was remarkably successful in maintaining during a period of pervasive intersectional opposition an independent, responsible criticism of things Southern.

This ideal of critical freedom can be seen, for example, in its comments on such subjects as minstrel-singing and antislavery novels. *Putnam's* admired the genuine folk tunes of the South and resented the degeneration of this type of music caused by what it called the ridiculous imitations of artificial minstrels.

A true southern melody is seldom sentimental, and never melancholy. And this results directly from the character and habits of the colored race. No hardships or troubles can destroy, or even check their happiness and levity. . . .

The mine from which Jim Crow and Ole Dan Tucker were dug, is not yet exhausted, and a resort to it will be alike easy and successful. Why need we groan and grumble under the inflictions of ignorant and self-conceited song-writers, when every cotton-field teems with melody, and every slave hut, throughout the Southern country, has a little list of genuine ballads, which only need to be known, in order to be received to the heart of a nation.

Putnam's editors did not consider the novel to be an appropriate medium for doctrinal proclamations. The magazine refused to classify as art the long line of antislavery novels and the opposing anti–Uncle Tom novels because those books failed to present men and manners truthfully. Moreover, such books usually failed as polemics because, in trying to prove too much, they proved nothing. *Uncle Tom's Cabin* was adjudged an exception, however, for Mrs. Stowe had created many new and well-delineated American characters and had, simultaneously, succeeded in raising the narrative itself above partisanship.

---

[18] "[Harper's] was anything but a 'journal of opinion,' except when an opinion was universally acceptable." Frank Luther Mott, *A History of American Magazines, 1850–1865* (Harvard University Press, Cambridge, Mass., 1938), p. 392. Mott also pointed out that *Putnam's* criticized *Harper's* for striving hard not to offend. *Harper's* had a large circulation in the South. See also Mott, *A History of American Magazines, 1741–1850* (D. Appleton-Century Co., Inc., New York, 1930), p. 611.

According to *Putnam's,* the great blemish of *Uncle Tom* was the intrusion of antislavery sentiment. Seven months later, in August, 1853, *Putnam's* called attention to a Southern review of *Uncle Tom's Cabin.* It praised the review for conceding the literary excellence of the novel and for correcting much of Mrs. Stowe's distortion of the slaveholder. *Putnam's* judged that the review had "vindicated Southern society with great force and intelligence."[19]

Nonfictional accounts of life in the South, whether proslavery or antislavery, were usually ignored by *Putnam's,* unless their merits in some way transcended controversy. For example, it welcomed Olmsted's studies of the South, declaring that Olmsted was neither a horror-monger nor a fanatic. "No traveler, of equal perceptive ability and intellectual power, ever made so comprehensive a statement of the aspect and character of the slave country, and so entirely free from bitterness and vituperation."[20] It also welcomed *The Life and Bondage of Frederick Douglass,* which it regarded primarily as a record of personal achievement. "Of course it is impossible to say how far the author's prejudices and remembrances of wrong, may have deepened the color of his pictures, but the general tone of them is truthful." The review pointed out that Douglass had not been indiscriminate in his denunciation and that he warred on a system rather than on individuals. Moreover, the editor's critical astuteness is suggested by his observation that Douglass tended to raise specific incidents to the level of general human truth. *Putnam's* evaluation of this book recalls Emerson's idea that nature saves men through themselves, that a Toussaint or a Douglass outweighs all the antislavery societies of the world; for *Putnam's* commented that regardless of one's stand on slavery, one was obliged to admire the force and integrity of Frederick Douglass.

At the same time, the magazine remained steadfastly literary in its treatment of the abolitionist literature of Lowell and Whittier. Lowell was a friend of Charles F. Briggs, the editor, and a contributor to

[19] "Negro Minstrelsy—Ancient and Modern," *Putnam's,* V (January, 1855), 72–79; "Anti–Uncle Tom Novels," III (May, 1854), 560; "Uncle Tomitudes," I (January, 1853), 100–101; II (August, 1853), 220.

[20] References in this and the following paragraph are to *Putnam's,* VII (February, 1856), 218; IX (March, 1867), 274–75; VI (November, 1855), 547; I (May, 1853), 547–58; IV (November, 1854), 562.

Putnam's. Nevertheless, the magazine criticized frankly his abolition work. In a review of Lowell, in May, 1853, *Putnam's* pointed out that poetry is not necessarily the handmaid of reform and that it suffers from overwork when it is used as such. "It is astonishing what bad poetry a man will write, when laboring under the conviction that he has 'a great social evil to discover and to remedy.' " Perceiving a limitation which Lowell himself confessed to Gay, editor of *The National Anti-Slavery Standard*, *Putnam's* observed that Lowell's reformatory poetry for the most part contained thoughts that were by no means new to the readers of the weekly reform newspapers. "Long before these poems were written, they had passed into the common places of reform literature and oratory. When vehemence ceases to be an outburst, and turns into a philosophical analysis of itself, it becomes flat and dull." Nevertheless, *Putnam's* praised certain poems in which the poetical survived the reformatory elements, as in *The Biglow Papers,* which it discussed at length and praised highly. *Putnam's* also strove for objectivity in evaluating Whittier. It objected to "A Sabbath Scene" because the poet had perverted the ballad form, using it "to illustrate a possible result of the fugitive slave law, and not to perpetuate an actual occurrence or a tradition, which is the true province of ballad poetry." Like the *North American,* it called Whittier the Tyrtaeus of poets and asserted that the Quaker was full of fight. But it conceded that Whittier was courteous and tender and that he wrote agreeable and graceful prose.

Putnam's evaluation of Southern authors showed a determination to remain free of regional entanglements. Simms, as a writer, was recognized for his merits and criticized for his failings.[21] In 1854, speaking of *The Yemassee,* the magazine referred to Simms as "one of the most prolific and brilliant of our romance writers." In the following November, it printed a notice of *The Scout,* which it called a vivid picture of Revolutionary days. In February, 1855, *Putnam's* responded dryly to Simms's *Southward Ho!* "Magazine readers of moderate diligence will recognize most or all of the tales and poems, some of which are very well done; but none of which, as here republished, need we examine." In 1857, reviewing *The Wigwam and the*

[21] *Ibid.,* III (January, 1854); IV (November, 1854), 562–63; V (February, 1855), 213; IX (April, 1857), 438.

Cabin, Putnam's observed: "His works have attained a distinct place in our literary history, but they can hardly be called popular or familiar." The review acknowledged Simms's ability to create stirring scenes and striking adventure, but it disliked his prolixity and weak characterization.

In respect, however, of constructive talent and affluence of production, Mr. Simms takes precedence of any other of our distinctive southern authors. Mr. Wirt and Mr. Legaré, who are usually quoted as the Pillars of Hercules of our southern literature, were both polished, and graceful, and accomplished essayists; but they displayed none of the nerve or continuity of Simms.

Three months earlier, in April, 1857, *Putnam's* had satirized a Southern convention held at Savannah for the purpose of fostering a Southern literature.[22] Feeling that the convention was more concerned with the South than with literature, *Putnam's* was derisive. In its opinion the only Southerner worthy of carrying out the task of creating a Southern literature was Simms, and he had not been chosen as a member of the convention.

At times *Putnam's* expressed appreciation of the general cultural and historical value of Southern writing even when that writing was not in a literary sense commendable—as when it welcomed, for example, the memoirs of William Pinckney, of Maryland, written by his nephew. The magazine praised Pinckney as a superior orator and a statesman of high rank. "We are pleased to see this attempt at a life of Pinckney, because our Southern friends have been comparatively regardless of the posthumous reputations of their most distinguished men." The magazine disapproved of Joseph B. Baldwin's *Party Leaders* because the book's style was too ambitious, but the editors acknowledged that Baldwin "had brought together a mass of valuable materials."[23]

If a patronizing tone sometimes crept into *Putnam's* remarks on the South, the magazine was not without a defense against charges of sectional bias. In March, 1854, it answered one such charge by calling

[22] The Savannah Convention was satirized in "Southern Literature," *ibid.*, IX (February, 1857), 207–14, and again in a review of *The Wigwam and the Cabin, ibid.*, IX (April, 1857), 438.

[23] *Ibid.*, II (December, 1853), 679; IV (November, 1854), 560–61.

attention to the fact that its present number contained four articles submitted from four slave states and that, from the beginning, every number had contained one article or more from Southern pens.[24] Despite a definite metropolitan flavor, *Putnam's* considered itself a national, not a regional, periodical. In addition to its independent, responsible criticism of things Southern, it revealed an interest in Southern culture through its stories and sketches of Southern life. The picture of Southern life which the magazine presented featured the planter aristocracy in the setting of fashionable watering places and large country estates. Its first five issues carried a story by Mrs. R. B. Hicks, of Richmond, which expressed this interest in fashionable society.[25] Emphasis upon setting was established in the title, "Virginia: In a Novel Form." The first chapter bore this caption: "Introduces an Old Virginia Family." The family dwelling was a stately, old-fashioned house with a road "bend[ing] obsequiously" before it. The estate stretched away for miles and its numerous cattle "dot[ted] the distant slopes." Here one could find "as much happiness, and charity, and eccentricity, and pride, and old-fashioned Virginia hospitality, as one need desire to find anywhere."

Putnam's portraits of the planters and their sons were frequently tinged with satire, often featuring their dilettantism and fondness for rank and title. The planter was not inclined to disarrange the books on the shelves of his library. He was a sportsman, interested in horses and game. "But on the whole, it is an axiom with him, that too much exercise, as well as too much learning, will make a man mad. He therefore detests both."[26] Personal dignity, gracious hospitality, stern politics, and the inevitable rank of colonel or judge were his identifying characteristics. The planter's son, as described by Mrs. Hicks, was "a noble, lordly, careless, dashing fellow of twenty-one," who had a "free off-hand manner and Ciceronian flow of words." He spent a good deal of money at college, and his life was described in terms of hounds, hunters, servants, house guests, juleps, and late breakfasts.

---

[24] *Ibid.*, III (March, 1854), 344.

[25] *Ibid.*, I (January–May, 1853), see especially pp. 78 ff.

[26] *Ibid.*, VII (January, 1856), 45. See "Virginia Springs," a sketch of Southern society which ran continuously from November, 1855, to January, 1856. Other references in this paragraph and the following paragraph are to *Putnam's*, I, 78–79; VII, 42–44.

The consciousness of position which marked these gentlemen was communicated to their servants, for the son's servant and groom considered themselves superior to other servants.

If these pictures of the affluent gentry savored at times of democratic resentment, it rendered more forceful by contrast *Putnam's* praise of the Southern lady. The planter's daughter in Mrs. Hicks's story was aloof, fair, and angelic. She was the idol of the young men. And her charm seemed to be enhanced by the deft shielding which she received from her family. At another time *Putnam's* described the Southern lady in a portrait that was florid and sentimental, but its praise was nevertheless eloquent and unequivocal.

Surely, the "old families" of Virginia and South Carolina are no fable. One sees in their daughters that high-born air, that easy grace, that feminine delicacy, which shows their blood is gentle; and, like oft-decanted wine, has been refined by generations. A native modesty, self-possessed, and startled only by the advances of rudeness and indelicacy, indicates an education obtained more in the sweet privacy of a rural home, than in the public academies of the cities—more in the society of relatives and familiar friends, than in the company to be met with at fashionable hotels and the world's rendezvous. I have nowhere seen young ladies whose presence was more hedged about with privacy. And yet there is no lack of natural freedom, and the play of native intellect in their manners. The laugh is gay; the word leaps from the heart; the confidence is given without a suspicion of the possibility of betrayal. It is an artlessness guarded by no premeditation. But there is, at the same time, a quick, nice sense of maidenly propriety, which, though never intrusive, still is always putting a gentle restraint upon the action of the impulses, always keeping a rein, fine as gossamer, upon the swift running of the tongue, and always guiding the burning chariot-wheels of nature's passions around all the goals of early life, with grace and safety.

In 1857 *Putnam's* published "A Slave's Story," describing the life of a Southern slave as told by the slave himself.[27] Through the story one sees the great cost of slavery, a system which was inefficient for the planter, involving him, despite good intentions, in practices that were

---

[27] "A Slave's Story," a sketch which was sent to *Putnam's* by a slaveowner in Virginia. IX (June, 1857), 614–20. The specific references in this paragraph are to pp. 615–17, 619.

contrary to the welfare of the plantation. The planters themselves were kind to the slaves, however. The mistress of one plantation gave reading and religious instruction to all young slaves and to the adults who wanted the lessons. This was an enduring policy, and two generations of slaves were taught according to their aptitudes. But the story pointed to the evils in this way of life, too, for it told of the indifference of the planters to marriage vows of the Negroes. "This utter contempt of the whites for the sacredness of marriage amongst slaves, has done more to demoralize and brutalize the slave than all the other personal wrongs he suffers." Moreover, the planters were in the habit of entrusting the management of their lands and field hands to overseers— "those dreaded and despised obstacles between slaves and their owners, who commonly have no bowels of compassion for the slave, and little care for the interests of the master." Although the harsh overseer played very little part in the account, the author emphasized what was to him a more serious evil—the constant temptation to steal. Because the slaves felt that they had a right to a fair proportion of the proceeds of their labor, they frequently stole from their masters. The poor whites, who furnished the market for the stolen goods, were likewise involved in the dishonesty. "There were, in our vicinity, plenty of poor white folks, as we contemptuously called them, whom we cordially despised, but with whom we carried on a regular traffic at our master's expense." But the western part of the state seemed to be relatively free of these evils, for the Negroes there were treated civilly by all classes of whites. They were rarely punished, their food was plentiful, and they were given considerable freedom of movement. There was the suggestion that among the farmers of western Virginia there was a closer relationship between Negro and white and that the Negro there seemed to be more a servant than a slave.

Although it presented specific criticisms of slavery, the narrative avoided stereotype notions of villainous Southerners. "A Slave's Story" left the strong impression that in some ways the slaveholder was victimized by slavery and that, to some degree, the Negro, the nonslaveholding white, and the slaveholder together, through individual failings, were responsible for the evils of the system.

The story had implications that were consistent with *Putnam's* editorial opinion about the South. *Putnam's* never wavered in its opposition to slavery, stating frankly, in May, 1856, that slavery was sustained only because it was profitable and that one should not attempt to defend it on moral grounds.[28] However, the magazine concerned itself not with abolition but with geographical restriction of slavery. In April, 1856, the editors declared that the evils of slavery should be left to the Southerner, who presumably best understood them. According to *Putnam's,* most Americans acknowledged the privilege of each state to determine its own internal affairs. *Putnam's* political editor was Parke Godwin, Bryant's associate on the *Evening Post.* Godwin was unequivocally opposed to the extension of the slave power into the territories. Editorial eyes were on the struggle for control of the territories. "The Real Question," *Putnam's* editorialized in 1856, did not relate to the South itself but "rises out of the struggle between two incompatible orders of civilization for mastery of a common field."[29] This comment came after the Kansas-Nebraska outbreak, an event which *Putnam's* regarded as representing the abandonment of the principle of compromise, a principle which alone could adjust the antagonisms growing out of the attempt to confederate "two distinct social systems." *Putnam's* view of the intersectional antagonisms was national in its perspective, and this breadth can be found, too, in Melville, Bryant, and Whitman.

[28] See review of *Liberty and Slavery* (a book by Professor Bledsoe of the University of Virginia) *Putnam's,* VII (May, 1856), 550.
[29] *Ibid.,* VII (April, 1856), 429.

· 8 ·

Melville

T HE CULTURAL conflicts that gradually divided America into two hostile regions and finally brought about the Civil War affected the mind of Herman Melville profoundly. Yet on this subject he was reluctant to express himself, either in letters or in conversation. Neither do his personal papers contain any indication of his attitude toward the South nor do the externals of his life reveal this area of his thought. Although he belonged to a politically minded family, one that was active in the Democratic party, Melville never identified himself with any political faction. When his friends rallied in an attempt to get him a government post, they found themselves handicapped, if not defeated, by his record of silence. In 1853, a fellow-townsman at Pittsfield wrote that Melville had not taken any part in politics during his residence in Pittsfield and that he had not attended the polls or made any public expression of his political views.[1] Nevertheless, Melville kept in close touch with his times. He had both relatives and friends who were actively participating in the political world, and he saw much more of

[1] Jay Leda, *The Melville Log. A Documentary Life of Herman Melville, 1819–1891* (Harcourt, Brace and Co., Inc., New York, 1951), p. 471. Hereafter cited as *Log*. Four years later, in 1857, when Melville was returning from the Holy Land, his sister Augusta concerned herself with the possibility of his getting a customhouse post in New York City. She was obliged to acknowledge that, although her family was Democratic and had done much for the party, her brother was no politician. *Ibid.*, p. 568.

America than did most Northern writers of his day. In addition to his trips through the Northeast and the West, he traveled to Washington, in 1847, when he observed the Twenty-ninth Congress in session, and again in 1861, when he shook hands with President Lincoln. During the middle fifties he lectured in Baltimore and as far south as Tennessee. But his letters remained silent about the South.[2]

This silence was not indifference, however. One must go to Melville's fiction to find his attitude toward the South, for his literary art came from the deeper levels of his mind, where he bore his tragic sense of man's incapacity in an ugly, inhospitable world. He saw the dilemma of the South as an aspect of this basic incapacity. Unlike many contemporary writers, Melville expressed this phase of his thought as an artist, and not as a propagandist. Beginning with *Mardi,* which presented through the translucent veils of its allegory an easily discernible picture of the South, he revealed an awareness of the most urgent social problem of his day and an ability to rise above regional prejudice in judging it. *Redburn, White-Jacket,* and *Moby Dick* contained a few direct, straightforward references to the South, but each book in this series contained fewer than the one preceding it. The awareness was not fading from his mind, however; it was undergoing a transposition into the minor key, a change which was concomitant with the gradual deepening of his general view of life. In *The Confidence-Man* (1857), Melville expressed symbolically, in a brief but penetrating picture of the gentleman-of-the-white-hands, the basic moral problem which confronted the South. Melville knew the injustice and inhumanity involved in the system of slavery. But unlike the New England writers of his day he was not led by this knowledge into distorting criticism of the Southerner, for he saw more deeply than they the full tragic truth which lay at the base of America's intersectional struggle.

Melville achieved a more objective view of the entire nation than did most of his contemporaries. He disliked intensely the restless chau-

---

[2] The only direct reference to the South which I have found in his letters is contained in one that he wrote to his brother Thomas after the Civil War had begun. In referring to the Confederates he used the conventional terms "rebel" and "rascal." But his concern in the letter was with the military rather than with the social or the ideological situation. *Ibid.,* p. 652.

vinism and easy optimism of the time. Writing to his brother Ganse-
voort in May, 1846, he described American excitement over the War
with Mexico in a jocose, flippant way. Moreover, one finds unmistakable traces in the letter of Melville's disappointment—and apprehension—in the direction his country was taking.[3] During the summer
and fall of 1847 he published in *Yankee Doodle* a series of comic
sketches of life at the front.[4] Entitled "The Authentic Anecdotes of
'Old Zack,' " these articles satirized Zachary Taylor, rebuking especially his eye for publicity, and ridiculed the immaturity of the popular
enthusiasm for the General. Beneath the broad humor lay the implication that perhaps Zack and his uncritical admirers were both insensitive and more than a little cavalier in their prosecution of the war.
Though Melville could not take the Mexican War so seriously as did
the nation as a whole, he never joined with the abolitionists in suggesting that the war was a sinister scheme to extend the power of the slaveholder. Melville recognized the expansive mood of the entire nation.
In *Mardi,* which he was writing in 1848, the year of the treaty with
Mexico, he warned the people of the United States, through the lips
of one of his characters, against being too grasping. "It is not freedom
to filch. . . . Neighboring nations may be free, without coming under
your banner."[5]

During this time, Melville's interest in the national scene intruded
itself into his writing. At a great cost in artistic unity, he transported a
group of Mardians from the romantic realm of Polynesia to the
America of his day. Vivenza was Melville's fictional equivalent of the
United States. In quest of an ideal, Babbalanja, Yoomy, Media, and
Taji searched Vivenza, North and South, in vain. As the travelers
approached Vivenza's shore, they saw the statue of its "titular deity."
Over the helmeted lady was chiseled in large letters: "In this repub-

[3] *Ibid.,* pp. 215–16.
[4] "The Authentic Anecdotes of 'Old Zack' " were published by Duyckinck
during the summer and fall of 1847 in *Yankee Doodle,* Vol. II. These articles
have not been republished. For additional information, see Luther Mansfield,
"Melville's Comic Articles on Zachary Taylor," *American Literature,* IX
(January, 1938), 411.
[5] This and the following references to *Mardi* may be found in *The Works of
Herman Melville* (Constable & Co., Ltd., London, 1922–24), IV, 245, 243,
224, 247–52. Hereafter cited as *Works.*

lican land all men are born free and equal." Upon closer inspection, however, they found in letters hardly visible, "Except-the-tribe-of-Hamo." After visiting the "grand council" at the capitol of Vivenza and observing the comfortable, inattentive animalism of its members, the Mardians prepared to go into the deep South. They tasted something of the pharisaical flavor of the Northern attitude toward the slaveholding states, for they were warned to expect in the South much that was repulsive to them.

The inhabitants of those southern valleys [they were told] were a fiery, and intractable race; heeding neither expostulations, nor entreaties. They were wedded to their ways. Nay, they swore, that if the northern tribes persisted in intermeddlings, they would dissolve the common alliance, and establish a distinct confederacy among themselves.

Furthermore, the Mardian visitors were assured that the North was well aware of the evils in the South and had done all it could to assuage them. The travelers had already witnessed the ardent provincialism of the North and were determined to judge the South for themselves.

"The Extreme South of Vivenza" was a caricature of the abolitionist's South. The travelers saw signs of Southern decadence even as their keel touched the Southern shore. "Though part and parcel of the shore we had left, this region seemed another land. Fewer thriving things were seen; fewer cheerful sounds were heard." They saw "prostrate palms" which were "decaying, and washed by the billows." In this land they found the Negro of the abolition pamphlet, who, toiling under the burning sun, was abused and beaten by cruel slave-drivers armed with long whips. The suffering of the Negroes inspired Yoomy, the poet of the group, to extravagant lyricism:

Oh fettered sons of fettered mothers, conceived and born in manacles . . . dragging them through life; and falling with them, clanking in the grave:—Oh, beings as ourselves, how my stiff arm shivers to avenge you! 'Twere absolution for the matricide, to strike one rivet from your chains.

Babbalanja asked one of the slaves if he were not a man, if he had no sense of right and wrong, and if he did not belie his Maker. The

Negro's reply contained the calculated emotional appeal of the abolitionist's slave.

Speak not of my Maker to me. Under the lash, I believe my masters, and account myself a brute; but in my dreams, bethink myself an angel. But I am bond; and my little ones;—their mother's milk is gall.

To this articulate reply Yoomy responded grandiosely.

"Just Oro!" he cried, "do no thunders roll,—no lightnings flash in this accursed land!"

Melville also parodied the Southern apologist. Into this scene of terror he injected Calhoun, a whip-carrying slave-driver named "Nulli."

Babbalanja advanced toward the foremost of those with the thongs,— one Nulli: a cadaverous, ghost-like man; with a low ridge of forehead; hair, steel-gray; and wondrous eyes;—bright, nimble, as the twin Corposant balls, playing about the ends of ships' royal-yards in gales.

The sun passed under a cloud; and Nulli, darting at Babbalanja those wondrous eyes, there fell upon him a baleful glare.

"Have they souls?" he asked, pointing to the serfs.

"No," said Nulli, "their ancestors may have had; but their souls have been bred out of their descendants; as the instinct of scent is killed in pointers."

Nevertheless, Nulli claimed that his serfs were happier than those of other countries, that they were fed, clothed, and cared for. He argued that since the labor of the Negro was essential to Southern agriculture, the Negro's enslavement must be both right and righteous. Furthermore, he added, his slaves had no cares, no thoughts.

"Thoughts and cares are life, and liberty, and immortality!" cried Babbalanja: "Are their souls, then blown out as candles?"

Nulli insisted that his slaves shed no tears.

"Frost never weeps," said Babbalanja; "and tears are frozen in those frigid eyes."

Angered, Nulli denied the visitors any further freedom to voice their thoughts, warning them that the South was under a constant threat of insurrection and ordering them to leave the region at once.

This was the abolitionist picture of the South with its lurid language and distortions. Melville was by no means burlesquing slavery, however; he was burlesquing the absurdities of Northern strictures against the South, as well as the Southern apologist's bland oblivion to the tragic plight of the Negro. In his satire, Melville drew upon the great bank of American sentimentalism, but his drafts were more extravagant than those of the antislavery writers. His Southerner was the blackguard who broke up the family by "unwreath[ing] the arms of sisters;" who defamed marriage by cutting "the holy unity in twain; till apart [fell] man and wife, like one bleeding body cleft;" who even violated the maternal breast by "wrench[ing] bondbabe from mother, that the nipple tear." The Mardian who voiced these charges called slavery a sin and damned irrevocably the wicked slaveholder.

Let that master thrice shrive his soul; take every sacrament; on his bended knees give up the ghost;—yet shall he die despairing; and live again, to die forever damned. . . . Methinks the great laggard Time must now march up apace, and somehow befriend these thralls.

In *Mardi,* Melville called for an end to mutual recriminations between the North and South. "Blame not, then, the North; and wisely judge the South." Though the entire party of Mardian travelers in Southern Vivenza deplored the awful evil of slavery, "no one could suggest a remedy that would not itself be a great evil." Emphasizing the accident of birth, one of the travelers said: "The soil decides the man, and, ere birth, man wills not to be born here or there." Like Cooper before him, Melville reminded his readers that slavery had been planted in Southern soil even before America had become a responsible nation. Through the lips of his Mardian, Melville pointed out that the Southerner had grown up with slavery and had been nursed and trained by Negroes. Melville understood the depth of such roots, and he knew that custom could deaden the sense of wrong. Judged in the light of private conscience, said one of his Mardian visitors, many slaveholders in Southern Vivenza "shall be found exempted from the least penalty of this sin."

One finds many remarks in Melville's fiction that undoubtedly served to caution his Northern readers against being too free in their criticism of the South. He acknowledged the barbarities of Northern attitudes toward the Negro. People stared at white Ishmael and dark Queequeg as they walked arm in arm through the streets of New Bedford. On board the schooner which carried them to Nantucket they were jeered at by the passengers, "a lubber-like assembly, who marvelled that two fellow beings should be so companionable; as though a white man were anything more dignified than a whitewashed Negro."[6] In Melville's sketch "The Happy Failure," the eccentric uncle comfortably assumed an intrinsic superiority over Old Yarpy, his Negro servant, whom he subjected to the vagaries of his mood, sometimes overworking him, sometimes cursing him, and occasionally regarding him with a condescending, sentimental kindness, as if he were a favorite pet.[7] Melville never oversimplified the American scene by equating freedom with the North and tyranny with the South. He understood the uniqueness of America's social experiment, observing in *Redburn* (1849) that America was not so much a nation as a world.[8] Having been settled by people of all nations, it was challenged by the complexity of race relations to a degree unknown elsewhere. Wellingborough Redburn learned that Liverpool, for all its former involvement in the wretched business of slave-trading, treated the visiting American Negroes more humanely than did Americans, either Northern or Southern.[9] The trip to Liverpool helped Redburn to overcome the social prejudices of his home environment. "In some things, we Americans leave to other countries the carrying out of the principle that stands at the head of our Declaration of Independence." In this connection, one thinks of an observation which Melville made in *Mardi* that freedom was social as well as political.[10]

[6] Melville, *Moby Dick, Works,* VII, 71, 74.

[7] "The Happy Failure. A Story of the River Hudson," *Harper's* (July 1, 1854). Reprinted in Melville, *Works,* XIII, 210–19.

[8] Melville, *Redburn, ibid.,* V, 216.

[9] Redburn was at first surprised by the companionship between English ladies and American Negroes. He recalled that such things had caused mob violence in America. "Being so young and inexperienced then, and unconsciously swayed in some degree by local and social prejudices, that are the marring of most men, and from which, for the mass, there seems no possible escape; at first I was surprised that a coloured man should be treated as he is in this town; but a little reflection showed that, after all, it was but recognising his claims to humanity and normal equality." *Ibid.,* pp. 259–60.

[10] Melville, *Mardi, ibid.,* IV, 244.

Melville knew that the slaveholder could be kindhearted and genial. In "The Authentic Anecdotes of 'Old Zack,' " the General's personal slave Sambo was sufficiently relaxed in the presence of his master—a Virginian and a holder of many slaves—to indulge in puns, and, on at least one occasion, to cause the tent to echo with his "hoarse and convulsive laugh."[11] In *Pierre* (1852), Melville drew a portrait of a kindly old man who, though not a Southerner, had been an owner of slaves. He was Pierre's grandfather, "the kindest of masters, . . . a forgiver of many injuries, a sweet-hearted, charitable Christian."[12] Moyar, Cranz, Kit, and Douw were his loyal and obedient slaves. They were never flogged, "a thing unknown in that patriarchal time and country." If the slaves failed in their duty, Pierre's grandfather "would refuse to say his wonted pleasant word to them; and that was very bitter to them, for . . . all of them loved grand old Pierre, as his shepherds loved old Abraham." Pierre preferred this kind of genial paterfamilias to "the greenhouse gentlemen" of his own day.

Melville maintained that at its best the Southern way of life produced a gentility and kindliness that could not be matched by the more demanding, competitive life in the North. He admired the old aristocratic Southern families. He spoke of John Randolph, that "chivalric Virginian," and quoted him as having seen more flogging aboard an American man-of-war in one voyage than had taken place on his own plantation of five hundred African slaves in ten years. Melville felt that both English and Southern officers had an advantage over the Yankee officer, which they derived from their backgrounds. They were "more accustomed to social command; hence quarterdeck authority [sat] more naturally on them."[13]

It is a thing that American man-of-war's men have often observed that the Lieutenants from the Southern States, the descendants of the Old Virginians, are much less severe, and much more gentle and gentlemanly in command, than the Northern officers, as a class.

This gentility was combined with the notion of physical prowess, for in Melville's mind the men from Kentucky, Tennessee, and the

---

[11] *Yankee Doodle,* II, 199.　　[12] Melville, *Pierre, Works,* IX, 39, 40.
[13] Melville, *White-Jacket, ibid.,* VI, 176; *Pierre, ibid.,* IX, 12.

mountain regions of Virginia were invariably tall, straight, and rugged.[14] Melville expressed admiration for those indomitable Virginians who migrated with their families to "the bloody ground" of Kentucky, pointing out that they had been courageous and self-reliant in the face of the treachery and overwhelming strength of the Indians.[15] A Southerner was aboard the *Pequod*. He was the mysterious Bulkington, whom Melville pictured with all the symbolic eloquence of his mature powers. At the Spouter Inn, Bulkington slipped silently away from the revelry of his shipmates and did not reappear until he stood at the ship's helm on that "shivering" Christmas night when the *Pequod* "thrust her vindictive bows into the cold malicious waves." Bulkington had just returned from a dangerous four-year voyage, but, driven by an inner restlessness from the security of the hearthstone, he was like a storm-tossed ship for whom the land was at once a longed-for haven and a dreaded hazard.[16]

He stood full six feet in height, with noble shoulders, and a chest like a coffer-dam. I have seldom seen such brawn in a man. His face was deeply brown and burnt, making his white teeth dazzling by the contrast; while in the deep shadows of his eyes floated some reminiscences that did not seem to give him much joy. His voice at once announced that he was a Southerner, and from his fine stature, I thought he must be one of those tall mountaineers from the Alleganian Ridge in Virginia.

Bulkington was regarded by his shipmate Ishmael with "sympathetic awe and fearfulness," for in this Virginian was the concrete embodiment of the mystery and ineffability at the heart of human nature. When Melville created Bulkington to be the South's representative to the cosmopolitan crew of the *Pequod,* his mind was as far from the current notion of a Southerner as his spirit was from the current optimistic reform zeal which marked the abolitionism of his day.

The Kansas-Nebraska Bill, enacted in 1854, ended the period of relatively relaxed tensions which followed the Compromise of 1850. With the subsequent fighting in Kansas, cultural and political antago-

---

[14] Melville, *Moby Dick, ibid.,* VII, 18; VIII, 175, 225; *The Confidence-Man, ibid.,* XII, 8, 15; "Lightening Rod Man." *ibid.,* X, 178.

[15] Melville, *The Confidence-Man, ibid.,* XII, 196–99.

[16] Melville, *Moby Dick, ibid.,* VII, 18; see also *ibid.,* VII, 132–33.

nisms flared up with hitherto unrealized intensity. Melville did not participate openly in the war of words between North and South. Nevertheless, in his fiction of the mid-fifties he wrote profoundly on the problem of slavery and its meanings for the individual and for society. "Benito Cereno," which appeared in *Putnam's* in 1855, pictured a society trapped by slavery.[17] It presented, too, a Northern attitude toward the problem. An optimistic, aggressive, yet charitable Yankee, Captain Delano, went aboard a slave-bearing ship, unaware that the ship was in the hands of rebellious slaves who had killed the slaveowner and deprived the captain of his command. The ship constituted a living demonstration of the dire consequences of slavery. In enslaving the Negroes, the whites aboard the *San Dominick* had actually victimized themselves. Don Benito, the enfeebled captain, understood the fate that had befallen him. It ranged beyond any crew or social group or region. The shadow had fallen on all mankind; for his ship was a world, and it was heavy with sins of the past.[18] On the other hand, Captain Delano, though not without misgivings, viewed the ship's condition optimistically, in terms of remedial action. In Yankee fashion, he took immediate and well-intended steps to relieve the suffering aboard the *San Dominick*. But in doing so he jeopardized his own welfare and intensified the hazards of the trapped Don Benito. Captain Delano saw far less deeply than did Don Benito. Melville's story suggests that although the Yankee's innocence saved him from destruction, it also prevented him from perceiving the complexity of the problem and from realizing that he had no solution for it.

The period of the eighteen fifties was a time of steadily darkening outlook in Melville's personal life. By 1857, the year of *The Confidence-Man,* his mood was one of bitter irony and cynicism. In this book he dealt with a motley group of travelers, including several remarkable Southerners, aboard the *Fidèle,* a Mississippi River boat en

[17] *Putnam's,* VI (October, 1855), 353–67; (November, 1855), 459–73; (December, 1855), 633–44. Printed without Melville's name. It was published in 1856 as part of *The Piazza Tales.*

[18] Delano asks: "What has cast such a shadow on you?" Benito Cereno answers: "The Negro." As has been pointed out by Chase, Winters, and others, the final exchange of comments between Don Benito and Captain Delano must be interpreted as having a broader reference than to Negro slavery alone.

route from St. Louis to New Orleans. The boat was named as ironically as the book itself, for Melville was exploring the element of distrust in human nature. The confidence man was a glib, satanic wit who masqueraded in different roles and succeeded in exposing either the foolish gullibility or the falseness of the passengers aboard the ship. Though the irony of Melville's mood makes it hazardous to draw conclusions from the sardonic human comedy of this book, *The Confidence-Man* reveals some important aspects of Melville's attitude toward Southern character and customs.

One of the idealists aboard the *Fidèle* was a young Methodist minister, "a tall, muscular, martial-looking man, a Tennessean by birth," who in the Mexican War had been chaplain to a volunteer rifle regiment.[19] The clergyman was angered by the insolence of a one-legged cynic who attempted to discredit a crippled Negro beggar. The minister's support was misplaced, however, because the beggar was merely the confidence man in disguise, and Melville suggested that the minister's faith in mankind was insupportable. But what is important here is that Melville's Southern clergyman, who was conscientious and charitable, offered a sharp contrast to the Southern clergy pictured by such men as Whittier and Lowell.

Charles A. Noble, another Southerner aboard the *Fidèle,* did not come out so attractively in Melville's bitter portrait of mankind. The confidence man, under the pose of garrulous "Francis Goodman," shared a bottle of wine in the ship's bar with this convivial gentleman from Alabama. Noble knew his Shakespeare and discussed him readily and at length; he liked conviviality and fellowship; he appeared to enjoy his wine and cigars; and he regarded Puritans as "sourly conceited old Malvolios."[20] Melville's Alabamian was subtle and sensitive enough to realize that Polonius' advice to Laertes was prudent utilitarianism. Noble wished to appear generous and was contemptuous of a philosophy that excluded Christ's admonition to sell all and give to the poor. Nevertheless, when Goodman asked him for a loan of fifty dollars, he immediately became suspicious of his drinking companion. The request for a loan was supposedly the test of Noble's gen-

[19] Melville, *The Confidence-Man, Works,* XII, 15.
[20] *Ibid.,* 227.

uineness, and he was found wanting. Thus it turned out that the pleasant, social-minded gentleman from Alabama was at heart distrustful
of his comrade.

Applying this incident to the question of Melville's regard for the
South and his attitude toward Southern character, one must keep in
mind that falseness was ascribed to Noble as a representative of mankind in general and was in no way associated with the particulars of
Southern culture. As with Melville's picture of the Southern clergyman aboard the *Fidèle,* his treatment of Noble was free of the sectional bias and the distortions of propaganda which typified Northern
antislavery portraits of Southern gentlemen. Certainly Melville was
not ridiculing the conviviality of the Southerner. Melville's own de-
light in sharing gin and cigars with friends indicates that affability
rated high in his roster of desirable characteristics. The relish with
which he described the fellowship of the "Paradise of Bachelors" is
a further demonstration of his taste for sociableness. It should be
recalled, too, that the genial atmosphere of the bachelors' quarters
suggested to him the legendary "Ol' Virginny."[21] To return to Noble
aboard the *Fidèle,* one cannot help concluding that, although the
Southerner bore the stain of human depravity, he was nevertheless a
congenial companion for sharing wine and conversation.

That the legend of Southern hospitality mingled in Melville's mind
with other, less congenial, considerations of Southern character is
suggested by the gentleman-of-the-white-hands, a passenger aboard
the *Fidèle.* This immaculate gentleman was a tall, portly Southerner
"dressed with a strangely festive finish and elegance."

The inner side of his coatskirts was of white satin, which might have
looked especially inappropriate, had it not seemed less a bit of mere
tailoring than something of an emblem, as it were; an involuntary
emblem, let us say, that what seemed so good about him was not all
outside; no, the fine covering had a still finer lining. Upon one hand he
wore a white kid glove, but the other hand, which was ungloved, looked
hardly less white.

This was the Southern gentleman par excellence. Kindly and generous, he lived in a world of sumptuous hospitality. He was on his way

[21] Melville, "The Paradise of Bachelors," *Works,* XIII, 232.

to a plantation wedding party for his niece. But the irony of this portrait was deep. Who protected this immaculate gentleman from the grime of the world? Melville reminded the reader that the *Fidèle*, like all steamboats, was covered with streaks of soot, especially on the railings.

It was a marvel how, under such circumstances, these hands retained their spotlessness. But, if you watched them awhile, you noticed that they avoided touching anything; you noticed, in short, that a certain negro body-servant, whose hands nature had dyed black, perhaps with the same purpose that millers wear white, these negro servant's hands did most of his master's handling for him; having to do with dirt on his account, but not to his prejudices.

Melville's ships were usually worlds in miniature carrying mankind on its journey through life. The *Fidèle* was no exception. This passenger, Melville observed, "knew how to keep his hands clean." He was "one whose very good luck it was to be a very good man." The servitude of the Negro made possible his life of luxury and ease. The moral culpability of the slaveholder was a question obliquely raised: [22]

But if, with the same undefiledness of consequence to himself, a gentleman could also sin by deputy, how shocking would that be! But it is not permitted to be; and even if it were, no judicious moralist would make proclamation of it.

When the confidence man asked this spotless gentleman for a donation to the fund for Seminole widows and orphans, a spurious charity of his own creation, the gentleman contributed willingly but apologized urbanely for not giving a larger sum. He professed that to him charity was more of a luxury than an effort and that his steward was obliged at times to caution him against being too liberal. But Melville said that the steward was a humorist. This comment, although made parenthetically, was not unintrusive, for its implications were disturbing. Charity could be seen as an incongruity in such a one as the spotless gentleman, whose entire way of life was based upon the selfish utilization of the Negro.

This vignette was a brief, symbolical representation of Melville's

[22] Melville, *The Confidence-Man, ibid.*, XII, 46, 48.

evaluation of the master-slave relationship. Nature herself seemed to have joined in man's conspiracy to exploit the Negro on behalf of the privileged planter. Whiteness was for Melville a mysterious, awe-inspiring phenomenon. All nations, he said in *Moby Dick*, have recognized a certain pre-eminence in whiteness, "giving the white man ideal mastership over every dusky tribe."[23] Consider, too, the thoughts which passed through Captain Delano's mind when, aboard the *San Dominick*, he struggled against his instinctive fear. Could a white man ever join in mutual complicity with a Negro? He thought the Negro stupid, the white man shrewd. He thought it not unlikely that "a man with some evil design would . . . speak well of that stupidity which was blind to his depravity."[24] Later in the story Melville spoke of "the docility arising from the unaspiring contentment of a limited mind" and concluded that nature had endowed the Negro with a temperament which fitted him ideally for the avocation of servant. Since, however, Babo was actually holding his master in subjection, there was irony in this observation, too, although more dramatic and less philosophical than that of the spotless gentleman. In the latter anecdote Melville left no doubt that he considered the planter's way of life to be based upon intimidation of a less fortunate group.

Melville's bitterness in *The Confidence-Man* had its roots in idealism, an idealism which seemed to him incongruous in view of man's total ineptitude in a bleak world. He recognized the moral implications underlying the immaculate gentleman's way of life. He knew what the system had done to its "Pips" and "Black Guineas" and "Rose-waters." And his treatment of them showed well the twofold aspect of his derision: his grim view of reality reacting, like acid, upon his native idealism. Bewildered in a white man's world, little Pip pathetically prayed to the great white God to have mercy on the little black boy.[25] Der Black Guinea readily admitted that a "Free Dog"— that is, a Negro without a "Massa"—had no protection. Crippled and unwanted by the planters, he slept on the streets of St. Louis, under the protection of the heavens. Understandably he dreaded winter.[26]

[23] Melville, *Moby Dick, ibid.*, VII, 234.
[24] Melville, "Benito Cereno," *ibid.*, X, 108, 120.
[25] Melville, *Moby Dick, ibid.*, VII, 221.
[26] Melville, *The Confidence-Man, ibid.*, XII, 10–11.

"Den dis poor old darkie shakes werry bad . . . Oh, sar . . . don't speak of der winter," he added, with a reminiscent shiver, shuffling off into the thickest of the crowd, like a half-frozen black sheep nudging itself a cozy berth in the heart of the white flock.

It is true, of course, that Der Black Guinea was only a masquerade of the confidence man, and his name was intended to fit his role as beggar. Nevertheless, Melville obviously put him into a realistic con-- text, if only to make the hoax more convincing to the gullible passengers. There was nothing unusual about this manner of living precariously along the banks of the river, sleeping in nooks and corners of St. Louis. Aboard the United States man-of-war the *Neversink,* for his own personal amusement Captain Claret often called two Negroes to appear before him in a head-bumping contest. Melville dealt with the incident sardonically. Underneath the drollery of the sport was the pathetic plight of the two Negroes. Their mannerisms, their conversation, even their bizarre names showed their vulnerability. They were not only the victims of the insensitivity of the white man, but they had also naïvely and uncritically adopted some of his false values. When May-Day, a full-blooded Negro, called his mulatto opponent, Rose-water, a "nigger," the latter asserted proudly, by way of refutation, that he was not a nigger but a bastard son of a rich planter by a Negro maid.[27] That Fleece, the cook aboard the *Pequod,* could so easily be intimidated by the third-rate intelligence of Stubb was another testimony to Melville's realization that the "freed" Negro was painfully unprepared for life in a competitive, commercial world. Fleece admitted ingenuously that he was born "'Hind de hatchway, in ferry-boat, goin' ober de Roanoke.'"[28] Melville's exuberance as a writer often caused him to caricature his people, as he was no doubt doing with his Negroes. But the element of exaggeration here sprang from his recognition of the appalling social cost of slavery. He knew that this social cost extended beyond the Southern plantation, that the Negroes of his generation in America were a completely disenfranchised folk.

There are other indications of Melville's awareness of the cruelty involved in slavery. White-Jacket, for example, commented on the

[27] Melville, *White-Jacket, ibid.,* VI, 345.
[28] Melville, *Moby Dick, ibid.,* VIII, 17.

kind treatment the ship's purser gave to his slave and mentioned that this kindness, "under circumstances peculiarly calculated to stir up the resentment of a slave-owner, still more augmented my estimation of the Purser's good heart."[29] On the voyage out, Redburn was ordered to clean the chicken coops and the pig pens aboard the *Highlander*. "Miserable dog's life is this of the sea! commanded like a slave, and set to work like an ass! vulgar and brutal men lording it over me, as if I were an African in Alabama."[30] In Liverpool he viewed the bronze statuary of Lord Nelson dying in the arms of Victory. His mind again turned to the South, for around the pedestal of the statue were four naked figures in chains.

These woe-begone figures of captives were emblematic of Nelson's principal victories; but I never could look at their swarthy limbs and manacles without being involuntarily reminded of four African slaves in the marketplace.

And my thoughts would revert to Virginia and Carolina; and also to the historical fact that the African slave-trade once constituted the principal commerce of Liverpool; and that the prosperity of the town was once supposed to have been indissolubly linked to its prosecution.

Redburn had learned about life aboard a slave-trader from a fellow-seaman who, "with a diabolical relish," had told of the unbelievably inhuman treatment of the slaves in "the middle passage."

As early as 1848 Melville was aware that the Southern planter was not comfortable in his ascendancy. He had pictured "Nulli" trying in vain to preserve South Vivenza by forceful suppression of freedom. Mohi had surmised, however, that "these South Savannahs may yet prove battle-fields."[31] During the sectional struggle that marked the decade of the fifties, Melville could see the unmistakable tightening of tension. In 1857, he told of one of the *Fidèle*'s passengers who had crossed the Alleghenies in a misanthropic flight from the human scene. Melville must have put much of his own personal point of view into the brusque speech of this passenger, whom he called the "Missouri Bachelor." Sedgwick called him the one honest man aboard the *Fidèle*; Thompson advanced the theory that the "undeceived," such as

[29] Melville, *White-Jacket, ibid.,* VI, 478.
[30] Melville, *Redburn, ibid.,* V, 84, 198.
[31] Melville, *Mardi, ibid.,* IV, 250.

the peg-legged cynic and the bachelor, expressed Melville's personal view.[32] At any rate, there was something of Bartleby, the scrivener, in the question which the bachelor asked of the confidence man: "Who is your master, pray; or are you owned by a company? ... Come from Maine or Georgia, you come from a slave-state, and a slave-pen, where the best breeds are to be bought up at any price from a livelihood to the Presidency." He was contemptuous of abolitionism, which, he said, "but express[ed] the fellow-feeling of slave for slave." But the full extent of the bachelor's bitterness was revealed when he declared that the moderate man was "the invaluable understrapper of the wicked man. You, the moderate man, may be used for wrong, but are useless for right."[33] The bachelor had renounced mankind and was in search of machines to supplant him. Like Bartleby and Jimmy Rose, the bachelor was a voluntary exile from the servile state of man. Melville knew no solution for the social evils the South was heir to. His pessimism no doubt darkened as he watched the nation move irrevocably toward a war which he could not have believed to be a remedy for her social ills.

[32] William Ellery Sedgwick, *Herman Melville: The Tragedy of Mind* (Harvard University Press, Cambridge, Mass., 1944), p. 189; Lawrence Thompson, *Melville's Quarrel with God* (Princeton University Press, Princeton, N.J., 1952), pp. 297–328.

[33] Melville, *The Confidence-Man, Works,* XII, 148–50.

· 9 ·

Bryant

Because Bryant's reputation as a man of letters has fallen far below that of many of his contemporaries, there is a tendency to forget that he occupied a position of great prominence in America one hundred years ago. Renowned as a poet—to which was added his long and conscientious career as an editor, lecturer, and traveler—he became during the middle years of the century a public figure whose prestige and influence were unsurpassed in America. When the Civil War began, Bryant had been editor of the *New York Evening Post* for over thirty years. He attempted to make the paper metropolitan in the truest sense, for the horizons of this well-traveled editor were broad. Faithful to his ideals of freedom of thought and freedom of speech, he welcomed letters and other communications from all sections of the country. Bryant was an eminently fair-minded editor who read the newspaper exchanges regularly and often quoted at length from Southern journals. It is to be noted, too, that in an atmosphere of growing tension, he strove with commendable success to rise above regional prejudices. Bryant was one of the few Northerners of his generation who viewed the South and its cultural conflicts from a point of view that was national in its scope. In Bryant's verse there is nothing about the South or slavery until after the Civil War,[1] but in his journalism he dealt with these subjects. To watch the mind of Bryant the jour-

[1] "The Death of Slavery," *Atlantic Monthly*, XVIII (July, 1866), pp. 120–21.

nalist during this period is to understand in small measure the complexity of the antagonisms which finally led to the Civil War.

Bryant was the only major Northern writer of the period who had an extensive firsthand knowledge of the South. Before the Civil War he made three trips to the South, traveling through Kentucky, Virginia, and Maryland, in 1832; through Virginia, the Carolinas, Georgia, and Florida, in 1843; and, six years later, to Charleston by coastal steamer, then to Savannah by railroad, and, finally on to Cuba. Furthermore, Bryant had the advantage of learning Southern attitudes directly from Southern friends, especially from the novelist William Gilmore Simms. Simms, who delighted in the society of literary men, sought out Bryant. The two men took walking tours in the Berkshires and along the Palisades and entertained one another in their homes. When Bryant made his Southern tour in 1843, his reception along the route was assured by Simms, who had written ahead to influential friends.[2]

This was Bryant's most extensive trip through the South. It was well reported to his readers in a series of letters, which appeared in the *Post* as they were written and, in 1850, in Putnam's edition of the *Letters of a Traveller; or, Notes of Things Seen in Europe and America*.[3] Parke Godwin, Bryant's son-in-law, said that Bryant did not criticize Southern slavery because he regarded himself as a guest and therefore under an obligation of gratitude. But Godwin attributed to Bryant stronger and more explicit antislavery sentiments than he actually felt at this time.[4] It is true that Bryant had always been opposed to slavery; but he recognized the right of a state to maintain slavery under the Constitution. His opposition to slavery expressed itself con-

---

[2] *The Letters of William Gilmore Simms,* coll. and ed. Mary C. Simms Oliphant, A. T. Odell, and T. C. Duncan Eaves (University of South Carolina Press, Columbia, S.C., 1952), I, 112, 179, 306–307 note, 345–46, 355, 358, 384, 431. Hereafter cited as *Letters of Simms.* For Simms's letters of introduction for Bryant, see pp. 341–44.

[3] Bryant's letters were published in the *New York Evening Post* under the following dates: Mar. 14, Apr. 1, Apr. 12, May 4, May 10, May 24, May 30, 1843; Apr. 6, Apr. 9, 1849. However, for convenience all references are to the George P. Putnam edition of the *Letters* (New York, 1851). See pp. 71–88, 90–94, 100–110, 126–27, 341.

[4] Parke Godwin, *A Biography of William Cullen Bryant* (D. Appleton & Co., Inc., New York, 1883), I, 408.

sistently in his tireless support of the free-soil principle and was related therefore not primarily to the South itself but to the territories. His letters home contained no suggestion of restrained disapproval or judgment withheld because of politeness. They were uncritical and affable in tone. The cordiality of Southern manners suited Bryant's taste, and the genial hospitality which he received along the way must have tempered his critical acumen.

Bryant wrote admiringly of Southern cities and pictured Richmond, Charleston, Savannah, and Augusta for his readers in an article that praised these cities for their wide streets, beautiful squares, spacious houses, rolling lawns, and shade trees. The people whom he met pleased him with their genteel and polished manners; he readily admitted that in point of manners they were superior to the Northerners. Richmond had the added charm of its association with the past. On the Capitol grounds overlooking the city was Houdon's statue of George Washington, a figure which constituted a center of reference for the picture of Richmond which Bryant presented to his readers. Richmond was proud of its great Virginians, and Bryant caught this spirit in his letters.

If Bryant presented the Southern town without backstreets and shanties, his picture of the Southern countryside was more varied and therefore more accurate. To be sure, *Post* readers were told of the large plantation with its main dwelling surrounded by smaller buildings and, farther out, the Negro village. They could envisage a South with areas of large plantations, but these were islands among a vast undeveloped wilderness; and it was this wilderness, rather than the plantation itself, which dominated Bryant's picture of the Southern country. Even between Washington and Richmond, Bryant was struck by the solitude of the country dwellings. South of Richmond the occasional patches of cleared land and the crude cabins were not enough to relieve the monotony of the pine forests. In east Florida Bryant's coach forded little streams whose waters, reflecting the crimson of the bay root, reminded him of the butcheries committed there by the Indians. The Indian War had recently ended, and Bryant witnessed the increased pioneer movement into Florida. From his coach he saw small groups of Negroes and whites working together in the occasional plots of cleared ground.

There were other suggestions of frontier conditions, too, in his letters to the *Post*. The woods abounded in wild game, and the Southerner was a good man with a rifle. Bryant described a hunter bringing home in his canoe a deer, which he had killed in the deep forests along the St. John's River. Bryant also wrote about the popular sport of alligator-hunting and the speech ways of many Southerners. He told of a "sallow-complexioned man from Burke county, Georgia, who spoke a kind of Negro dialect." And he quoted the wife of a "South Carolina cracker": "Coon and collards is pretty good fixins, but 'gator and turnips I can't go, no how." He described the rough manners of the tobacco-chewing, hard-spitting natives who "had never been disciplined by the fear of woman into any hypocritical concealment of their talent, or unmanly reserve in its exhibition." Donald Davidson observed, in his introduction to Simms's *Letters,* that the Northern critics of the South have never realized adequately the frontier nature of the prewar South.[5] But Bryant's letters to his paper described the South in the aspect of its newness, and alert readers of the *Post* could see to what extent the South was a region being tamed and domesticated by the combined efforts of Negroes and whites.

In one of his letters Bryant asserted, affecting an air of achievement, that he had "passed three weeks in the interior of South Carolina." On his way to see the Barnwell and Orangeburg districts and to visit Simms at Woodlands, he had traveled more than seventy miles from Charleston by a train whose route crossed what appeared to be endless tracts of pine forests, broken only by occasional patches which settlers had cleared and on which they had erected small log houses. But in the more productive lands near the streams and marshes were the large plantations where much of the world's cotton was grown.

On these large plantations, however, there were gentility and ease for the planter and his family, as Bryant knew from his visit with Simms at Woodlands. Bryant's description of this home was included in *Homes of American Authors.*[6] Woodlands was "a spacious country dwelling," comfortable, but without "pretensions to architectural elegance." Clustered around the main dwelling were numerous smaller

---

[5] Oliphant *et al., Letters of Simms,* pp. xxxviii, xl.

[6] *Homes of American Authors,* by various writers (Putnams, New York,

buildings. On the edge of the large clearing lived the Negroes who, according to Bryant, led an easy life and were treated indulgently. Simms, the son-in-law of the planter, spent half of each year on the plantation, "its pleasant winter, and portions of its spring and autumn." His was the life of the cultured aristocrat. He wrote until early afternoon in his "well-chosen library." Then he participated in outdoor recreations, played host to his house guests, or pursued his favorite pastime, landscape gardening. Bryant observed that "the grounds adjoining his residence afford agreeable evidence of his good taste." He praised his friend as a man of personal integrity and charm. "His manners, like the expression of his countenance, are singularly frank and ingenuous, his temper generous and sincere, his domestic affections strong, his friendships faithful and lasting, and his life blameless." At Woodlands Bryant had the opportunity of seeing Southern life at its best. Later, when sectional animosity made such geniality virtually impossible, the memory of Simms at Woodlands must have strengthened his determination to remain above the personal vindictiveness that marked the exchange of words between North and South.[7]

Bryant's letters to the *Post* spoke easily and uncritically about the place of the Negro in the South. In 1843, Bryant was not self-conscious about the questions of race relations and social strata. It was perhaps too early for Americans to be generally aware that slavery was but one aspect of racial relations, a problem about which they were at this time amazingly naïve. *Post* readers were given many casual vignettes of Negroes in the South. From a window of his train, Bryant watched Negro workers building enormous fires of resinous wood from the pine forests, for they "like a good fire at almost any season of the year." Changing trains one night, he and the other travelers were helped by the Negroes, one lighting their path with a

---

1853; also published by D. Appleton & Co., New York, 1854). The following quotations are taken from the 1854 edition, pp. 257–59. For Bryant's impressions of the large plantations which he visited in 1849, see *Letters,* pp. 345, 350.

[7] Max L. Griffin, "Bryant and the South," *Tulane Studies in English,* I (1949), 53–80. Griffin tells of Bryant's friendship with Simms, Hayne, and Thompson. He points out that Hayne and Thompson, both Confederates, were the only *literary* editors whom Bryant hired for his *Post*.

blazing pine torch, others crowding in behind with the travelers' baggage. In Savannah the Negroes lived in an atmosphere of concord and piety, attending their own attractive, well-maintained church, which had been built by the community—the whites furnishing the material, the Negroes the labor. In St. Augustine, Bryant observed that the Negroes were neatly dressed and well treated. On a Carolina plantation, he listened to banjos, ballads, and jokes of the Negroes and witnessed their dances and a husking festival. What caught his attention was the singing and dancing Negro. In work or play, the Negro was presented in the letters to the *Post* as a docile occupant of his peculiar niche in the social structure. Of the labor on the South Carolina plantation, Bryant observed:

It is, of course, the desire of the master that his slaves shall be laborious; on the other hand it is the determination of the slave to lead as easy a life as he can. The master has power of punishment on his side; the slave, on his, has invincible inclination, and a thousand expedients learned by long practice. The result is a compromise in which each party yields something, and a good-natured though imperfect and slovenly obedience on one side, is purchased by good treatment on the other.

Yet there were brief moments, despite the geniality of the letters, that revealed the plight of the slave, for example, when Bryant quoted some of the Negro folk songs—"Johnny come down de hollow, de nigger-trade got me, de speculator bought me, I'm sold for silver dollars"—or when the letters told of young Negro boys in a Richmond tobacco mill who sang in unison as they worked. The singing was encouraged, Bryant's guide was quoted as saying, because the boys worked better when they sang. Bryant did not dwell upon the irony implicit in the guide's remarks, nor upon the days when, as he was told, not a single note was sung. But on his way to the tobacco factory, he had peered through the window of the church in which Patrick Henry had called vehemently for liberty or death. Thus the contradictory elements in Southern life, the slave in a society established in the name of personal freedom, could be found in his letters; but they were not juxtaposed so as to suggest a contradiction or to imply criticism. The only personal response to the tobacco factory which Bryant expressed was, "the sight . . . amused me, though the narcotic fumes made me cough."

When Bryant returned to the South six years later, in 1849, the nation had annexed Texas, had fought Mexico, and in other ways had threatened his free-soil ideals. This demonstration of political power by the slaveholder had naturally stiffened his opposition. But he refused to consider the slave power and the South as identical. The letters he again sent to his paper were silent about the former and were still essentially uncritical of the latter, though they dealt with one of the conflicts that resulted from the Southern social structure.[8] Telling of the newly established cotton mills along the Savannah River, the letters spoke of the difficulty of utilizing the vast labor potential of the so-called poor whites; for, he was told, these people regarded manual labor as disgraceful and refused to work in the same mill with Negroes. The letters described the white girls from the backwoods of South Carolina and Georgia who came to the mills barefooted, sullen, and shy, seeking relief from their wretched poverty—a poverty, Bryant was told, which was largely the result of the idleness of the backwoods whites. By importing trained operators from New England to act as instructors, the proprietors had been able to train workers for their mills. In this nascent industrialism, Bryant saw the promise of condensing the scattered, "half-wild inhabitants" of the Southern pine barrens and thus helping to make available to them "the institutions of civilized life."

Bryant's direct experience with the South was a great advantage to him in the political and ideological struggle that preceded the Civil War. It saved him from the common Northern error of oversimplifying the Southern socioeconomic problem. Southern culture, he knew, was not so homogeneous as most Northerners assumed. He knew the demands of its frontier, its labor problems, and its inevitable social stratification. This knowledge gave him objectivity and restraint— attributes which were rare and precious in the current political struggles. Bryant had seen the admirable qualities of Southern character, and, although he perceived the complexity of the slave economy, he was confident that eventually the South would free itself of slavery.

[8] Bryant, *Letters*, pp. 346–49.

This optimism blended with his state-rights sympathies to confirm him in his free-soil ideal. Bryant was content with the policy of limiting slavery geographically, and in support of this ideal he was unrelenting. It became one of the major editorial policies of the *Post*.

Those who had read the *Post* steadily over the years of Bryant's editorship would have found the amicable tone of his letters from the South perfectly consistent with the paper's general presentation of things Southern. Perhaps they would have recalled that, with the beginning of nullification in the South and organized antislavery in the North, Bryant had consistently played down in the *Post* the divisive forces inherent in these issues. The *Post* had held, for example, that the tariff question was one of party, not of region, and that Maine, New Hampshire, and Missouri, just as surely as South Carolina and Alabama, had suffered by the legislation against free trade. Firm in its low-tariff position, the *Post* had urged that "the grievances of the South" be redressed. It had been careful to comment, too, that South Carolina's revolt did not represent the whole South. "If South Carolina has grown restive and shown a rebellious spirit, the other southern states, on the contrary, have preserved a noble degree of equanimity."[9] In 1833, the *Post* expressed fear that political opportunists in the South would serve their personal ends by exaggerating the power of incipient abolitionism. "The quarrel between the north and the south looked too likely to be forgotten—the old jealousies were passing away, and new matter of animosity must be furnished to keep it alive. The doings of the emancipators have therefore been spread with great parade before the public." The *Post* regarded abolitionism, too, as a source of "the bitterest enmity" between the sections. "The slaveholder grows jealous of the interference of those to whom the laws have given no right to meddle in the matter, and is naturally led to watch his slaves with greater strictness, and to subject them to a severer discipline." When it discussed the place of the Negro in Amer-

[9] In this footnote and in most of the following, the references to the *Post* are for obvious reasons illustrative only. During the period covered in this study, the *Post* did not number its pages. Although references are thus identified by date only, they can be easily located because they are for the most part taken from the editorial section, p. 2 of the usually four-page paper. Jan. 7, June 17, July 15, 16, Sept. 9, 28, 1831; Jan. 4, 8, 9, 14, 17, 21, May 1, 1833.

ican society, the *Post* directed the attention of its readers not to the
South but to the North, where it pointed to many examples of
prejudice.[10]

On many incidental issues, too, the *Post* presented its readers with
a consistently sympathetic view of the South. During the slave upris-
ing in Virginia, in the late summer of 1831, the *Post* apprehensively
reported all rumors and whatever facts were available and declared
that the men of the North must stand ready to rescue their Southern
neighbors. When Georgia—in defiance of a "writ of error" issued by
the United States Supreme Court—executed a Cherokee Indian for
murder, the *Post* went to considerable lengths to defend the state's
action on legal grounds and to rebuke those editors who called the
governor and his chief magistrate traitors.[11] Writing of the Cincinnati
riots during the summer of 1836, Bryant reported the alarming decision of the townsmen to silence, by violence if necessary, the expression of unpopular opinions. Seeking to discourage purely sectional
alignments, he pointed out that the hostilities against the abolitionists
were caused by overly anxious merchants, who numbered Southern
slaveholders among their customers, and that there were thousands of
Southerners who supported the principle of free speech and agreed
with those Northerners who disapproved of the use of force against
the abolitionists.[12] At another time, a *Post* editorial scolded Northerners who were inclined to imagine that judgment, temperance, and industry were qualities peculiar to themselves and presumed that the
Southerners were "hot and rash, loose in their morals, and thoughtless
and improvident in their general conduct."[13]

With the help of John Bigelow, who joined him in 1848, Bryant
continued his coverage of the South. He and Bigelow published the

[10] Apr. 25, May 14, Aug. 15, 16, 1833.

[11] Aug. 27, Sept. 8, 13, 20, 21, Nov. 12, 1831. The *Post* also defended the
state of Georgia in its policies regarding the Cherokee Indians within its borders
and in its treatment of certain missionaries who lived among the Cherokees.
Jan. 11, Mar. 21, June 18, Sept. 23, Oct. 8, 1831; May 18, 24, 25, 1836.

[12] Aug. 8, 9, 1836. In ascribing certain editorials specifically to Bryant himself, I have followed the "List of Bryant's editorials in the *Evening Post* partly
in Godwin's hand and partly in that of a secretary." Bryant-Godwin Collection,
New York Public Library.

[13] Nov. 14, 1831.

speeches, usually in full, of prominent Southerners. They followed political and social trends by reporting faithfully the newspaper exchanges and by opening their pages to letters from Southern readers.[14] Running through this manifold of Southern items in the *Post* were three basic themes: the distinction between the slave power and Southern society as a whole; the success of the slave power in national politics; and the effect of slavery on the moral fiber of Southern society. These themes were logical outgrowths of Bryant's fidelity to the free-soil ideal. The first two themes were given full development from the earliest signs of restlessness on the part of the slaveholders. The third was left almost completely undeveloped until rather late in the decade of the fifties, although traces of it could be found earlier in Bryant's concern for the inevitable interference of slavery in the development of free labor.

Social and political differences within the South were given particular emphasis during periods of increased agitation. When Texas was the storm center, for example, the *Post* printed news items and comments to show that many Southerners were indifferent and some were even opposed to the annexation. When the Free-Soil party was organized, the *Post* frequently printed articles by Southern sympathizers, reporting such items as the formation of Free-Soil chapters in various Southern cities. During the disunion agitation that preceded the Compromise Bill of 1850, the *Post,* mindful of its duty to its readers, quoted large portions of the fiery addresses of Southern leaders and the desperate resolutions of its legislatures as well as all available signs of Union sentiment in the South. Despite the fervent protestations of Southern spokesmen to the contrary, it was the firm opinion of the editors that most Southerners were determined to keep the states together. During the vitriolic exchange of views over the Kansas-Nebraska Bill, the *Post* pointedly reminded its readers that the South

[14] The editors drew from a wide range of Southern papers, quoting news items and editorials from such papers as the *Washington Union* and the *Washington National Intelligencer,* the one being the organ of the Southern Democrats, the other of the Southern Whigs. The *Post* frequently mentioned and often quoted from the *Baltimore Patriot,* the *Richmond Enquirer,* the *Richmond Republican,* the *Wheeling Times,* the *Charleston Mercury,* the *Macon Journal,* the *Alexandria Sentinel,* and the *New Orleans Picayune.*

was not, as its spokesmen affirmed, unanimously in favor of the bill. The temper of the times made antislavery sentiment in the South less and less articulate.[15]

To maintain free-soil principles in the face of the territorial expansion of slavery, the *Post*'s strategy lay in continually pointing out to its readers the frightening effectiveness of Southern political power. It pictured the slaveholders as a group of determined men lashing the timid and granting trivial favors to the venal until they had bullied and intrigued their way into political control of the entire nation. By controlling the national conventions, the slave power had put the men of its choice into the President's chair; it had dominated both houses of Congress, packing the committees in order to control legislation. The *Post* charged that its own party, the Democratic, had fallen from its original principles until it had become the harlot of the slave interests. Bryant left the Democrats, temporarily, to support the short-lived Free-Soil party, and, permanently, to help form the Republican party. But from within the Democratic party as well as from without, he struggled to prevent it from becoming "an association formed for the aggrandizement of a class." In November, 1858, asserting that the slave power had triumphed in a way to astonish the world, the *Post* reviewed the events of the decade and named what it called the offensive doses the North had been forced to swallow—the Fugitive Slave Law, the repeal of the Missouri Compromise, the "Kansas frauds and bloodsheds," the Dred Scott decision.[16]

In attacking the slaveholder, toward whom he was resolutely hostile, Bryant's reference was almost completely to slave power in the political arena. When on rare occasions his paper dealt with the planter at home, it described him as resembling an English lord or a German baron whose domestic position may have been contrary to democratic tastes, aloof and aristocratic, but was not wicked and tyrannical. The *Post* never suggested that Southern character was by nature vicious, nor did it paint emotional images of cowering slaves

---

[15] Examples of the positions stated in this paragraph may be found in the following issues: June 22, July 26, 1844; Aug. 11, 17, 21, 26, 30, 1848; Jan. 5, 26, Feb. 14, 21, Mar. 4, 7, 20, 1850; Jan. 17, 24, 25, 26, 31, Feb. 9, 13, 14, 27, Mar. 4, 17, 1854; Apr. 10, 28, Sept. 8, Nov. 12, 1858; Sept. 9, 14, 1859.

[16] July 14, 1848; Jan. 12, 17, 1850; Nov. 15, 1858; July 6, 1859.

and sneering drivers. Even in political battles the *Post* usually avoided personal vilification, attacking the slaveholders as a group. In referring to those Southerners who were not represented by the planter and his political puppet, the newspaper often used such descriptive terms as "sensible, diligent, and patriotic." Consistently it held to the position that the fuming partisans in Washington never expressed the desires of thousands of "quiet constituents"—the majority of Southerners— whose welfare was placed in jeopardy by an institution which both competed with their labor and degraded it.[17]

Bryant's natural optimism of spirit led him to hope that slavery would gradually give way of its own innate weakness before the advance of free labor. He welcomed to his paper any news that might indicate signs of this breakdown. The *Post* reported signs of conflict within the South itself—such items, for example, as the report that a Mississippi steamship line was replacing its white workers with slaves to prevent agitation for wage increases. It quoted a correspondent from the South who said that "thousands . . . of poor and intelligent Southerners" were held down because of "the prevailing idea at the south, of the degradation of labor." Census reports were analyzed to show that a free society was more dynamic than a slave society. Understanding the diversity of Southern life, Bryant and his editors watched the western borders of the South for signs of antislavery sentiment. Such traces of this sentiment had usually been found in the western country, or at least in the mountain regions of the South, where the leveling effects of its particular frontier had weakened the influence of the planter aristocracy. The *Post* quoted the *Wheeling Times* as stating that slavery had impoverished the inhabitants of the South, reduced its population, and retarded the development of its natural resources.[18]

Antislavery activity in the North, however, rarely received coverage in the *Post*. Although it always had insisted on the right of the abolitionist to speak, the *Post* was not in accord with the incendiary rhetoric of the abolitionist nor with his frequent falsification of life in the South. One of the few times the *Post* acknowledged antislavery sentiment in the North followed the passage of the Fugitive Slave Law,

[17] July 19, Aug. 21, 1848.
[18] July 19, 1848; Mar. 11, Apr. 10, 26, 1854.

which it despised and for which it reviled Daniel Webster.[19] Another acknowledgment of Northern feeling followed the publication of *Uncle Tom's Cabin,* which the *Post* defended against the attacks of the *Times* (London).[20] To demonstrate Mrs. Stowe's fidelity to Southern life, it cited true stories about the South. From the *Journal of Commerce* it quoted an account of Simon Harrison, a pious, intelligent, long-suffering slave whose character and deeds were no less credible than those of Uncle Tom. The *Post* refused to concede anything essentially improbable about the planter Legree, for, it held, he treated Tom as cruel men sometimes treat their cattle. To bolster its defense of the book as a whole, it quoted a news story from the Philadelphia *Sun* which told of the cruel mistreatment of a Negro named Fleming by a heartless Southern community. "As to the dealers in slaves, if they are coarse, brutal, and unfeeling, it is not Mrs. Stowe's fault. She simply describes them as she finds them, and as they are believed to be by people of the south, as well as the north." Yet within two weeks of this defense of Mrs. Stowe, the *Post* reprinted an item from the *New Orleans Christian Advocate* about a free Negro who had returned to the South. The people of the North, the Negro was quoted as saying, "charged me like a white man and treated me like a nigger and that way o' doing ain't fair."[21]

As the sections scrambled for new territory in the West and the increased representation in Congress which it would bring, cultural differences were magnified. Bryant was surprisingly successful in keeping his attention focused on the issue of free-soil; time and time again he made clear that his hostility to the South was caused by the determination of Southern leaders to make the spread of slavery a political program. When Bryant introduced Lincoln to a New York audience in February, 1860, he emphasized the role of the western settler in the struggle against the spread of slavery into the territories. He praised those who were "not ashamed to till their acres with their own hands, and who would be ashamed to subsist by the labor of the

[19] Mar. 9, 11, 1850.

[20] Commenting on the unprecedented popularity of Mrs. Stowe's novel, the *Post* observed: "There are but two causes to which we can look for the extinction of slavery, first the interest of the planters, and, secondly, the power of public opinion." This was in September 18, 1852.

[21] Aug. 30, 1852.

slave." His ideal was unchanged—geographical restriction, not the abolition, of slavery. "These children of the West, my friends, form a living bulwark against the advances of Slavery."[22] As late as November, 1858, the *Post* had reminded its readers of "the binding social influences upon North and South." It spoke of the common heritage of geography, politics, and history, the allegiances of family, travel, and trade; "these obvious designs of Providence, these wise schemes of our fathers" would finally prove too strong for regional prejudices and the schemes of petty politicians.

The effects of mounting tension were inevitably expressed in the *Post*. Late in the decade, denunciations of Southern manners and customs began to appear in its pages. In April, 1858, the *Post* scorned the "tobacco chewing chivalry" of Virginia, and during the following year it began to adopt the legend "of the young Virginia bloods, who shoot each other for the sport of the thing, or for what they call honor." A report of a slave auction, an innovation for the *Post,* emphasized both the roughness of Southern manners and the casual, insensitive way in which slaves were handled. There were miscellaneous expressions of animosity, such as articles reporting the excesses of revivalism in the South, satirizing Southern pride in its local writers, and asserting the inferiority of Southern schools to those of the North.[23] The *Post* misjudged the self-confidence of the South, assuming that the slaveholder, despite his bluff, recognized the relative weakness of the South and its dependence upon the North for its prosperity.[24] But even more serious in reflecting the widening breach were the accounts of crimes and violent mob action which the *Post* began to print. It reported, for example, a street shooting and some incidents of the burning of Negroes at the stake. This sort of violence,

[22] "Introduction by William Cullen Bryant, the Eminent Poet" (privately printed, New York, 1915). It had originally appeared in the *New York Tribune* (Feb. 28, 1860).

[23] Apr. 10, 1858; Mar. 9, July 13, 22, Aug. 5, 1859; Jan. 9, 18, 19, Feb. 8, Apr. 11, 1860.

[24] "For our part, we have never been for a moment misled by the warlike manifestos of the South; we have always supposed that the Union was of as much advantage to them as it was to us; and we have given its leaders too much credit for discernment, to imagine that they would throw away the certain advantages of it for the precarious benefits of the state of uproar that might follow its overthrow." Dec. 3, 1858.

it admitted, was never contemplated in Southern training. "Nevertheless it is perfectly fair to say that such high-handed villainies appear more in harmony with Southern institutions than with those of the North."[25]

The long political war, climaxed by the heated battle which preceded the success of the Republican party, had understandably taken its toll. In 1860, Bryant flatly claimed that the North was superior to the South in population, capital, energy, trade, and "whatever else imparts power to nations." He regarded the secession movement as proof of the inherent weakness of the South. "It is envious of the greater advancement of the North, and dreads, constantly, lest the North should use those advantages to its detriment." In support of this theory Bryant quoted De Tocqueville, who had observed, some thirty years earlier, "a deep-seated uneasiness and ill-defined agitation" in the South, which he had accounted for by the principle that the weak usually distrust the strong. Bryant called for resolute opposition to the secession movement. However, he was thinking in terms of political and what today is called "cold-war" opposition, for he was reluctant, as Godwin pointed out, to recognize the imminence of armed battle.[26]

Despite the intensity of his denunciation, however, Bryant still tried to keep alive among *Post* readers a sense of social and political difference within the South. He pointed to the election of Lincoln as sure indication that "a large proportion" of Southerners were sympathetic with "their brethren of the North." The secession movement he presented as the effort of "the vanquished faction, working upon the

[25] July 25, 1859. Until this time, the *Post* had occasionally reported instances of crime in the South, as it had elsewhere in the nation, but it had not associated these crimes with regional characteristics. However, an exception to this practice occurred during the heightened tension which preceded the Compromise of 1850. In meeting an attack of the *Richmond Republican* upon New York for the extent of its juvenile deliquency, the *Post* simply denied that crime in its own city exceeded that of New Orleans, Vicksburg, Natchez, Memphis, or St. Louis. Instead of pointing to corruption in the South, however, it raised its defense to a theoretical level, asserting that the evils of the South "proceed[ed] inevitably from the very structure of its institutions" and adding that therefore the South, unlike the North, was unnaturally sensitive to criticism. Jan. 21, 1850.

[26] Feb. 5, 18, 1861. Since the early fall of 1858, Bryant had been without the help of his colleague Bigelow. The references in the two remaining paragraphs are to the issues of Nov. 7, 1860; Jan. 14, 29, Feb. 18, 1861.

prejudices and fears of a large part of the community." Quoting newly appointed Secretary of State Seward in his promise to help "amend the Constitution so as to guaranty slavery from future interpositions of Congress," the *Post* expressed hope that the moderate men of the South would heed the "liberal tone" of Seward's remarks and make their voices heard in opposition to their leaders. Until the actual outbreak of the Civil War, Bryant and his editors misjudged the mind of the nonslaveholding South in its fidelity to slavery.

Bryant's perception of America's tragedy was deepened by his firsthand knowledge of the South. Unlike many of his contemporaries in the North, he understood that in reality the fight was not against a cloak-and-dagger villain fashioned in the likeness of Simon Legree. It was perhaps this knowledge of the variety of Southern life and character that inflamed his rancor against Southern leadership, for he saw it as a betrayal not only of America but also of the South. In January, 1861, Bryant editorialized: "A majority of the people of the slaveholding states originally became allies of Jeffersonian republicanism, not because it promised federal guarantees to slavery, but because it respected state rights, and thus based their safety upon principle, and not upon favor." In his attacks upon Southern leadership, Bryant matched the current fashions of invective. "Mr. Davis and his confederates are no more like Washington and his compeers than a chimpanzee stealing an African baby is like Columbus discovering a new continent. We . . . wonder that the ghosts of those illustrious men [do] not cry shame from their graves." This was in February, 1861. Soon all eyes would turn toward Fort Sumter, and a long time would pass before Americans could allow themselves the luxury of such distinctions as Bryant and his editors had striven to maintain in ante bellum America.

· 10 ·

Whitman

W|ALT WHITMAN was among the many admirers of Bryant. Writing in the *Brooklyn Daily Times* in 1858, he referred to Bryant as "one of the most lovable characters in the country." He had long regarded Bryant as America's foremost poet and one of the world's great poets. But what is more to the point here, he admired Bryant as a journalist, praising particularly his qualities of fairness and courtesy. Looking back over his life in Brooklyn and New York before the Civil War, Whitman recalled that he and Bryant had often chatted together and had taken "rambles, miles long, till dark, out toward Bedford or Flatbush."[1] They shared a genuine interest in the South, and their political views were remarkably similar. They were united in their free-soil principles, their respect for state-rights, and their ardent support of union. Both recognized the tremendous potential of the West and realized that the crucial fight would be over slavery in the territories.

[1] Emory Holloway and Vernolian Schwarz (eds.), *I Sit and Look Out, Editorials from the Brooklyn Daily Times* (Columbia University Press, New York, 1932), pp. 66–67. Hereafter cited as *I Sit and Look Out*. Cleveland Rogers and John Black (eds.), *The Gathering of the Forces* (G. P. Putnam's Sons, New York, 1920), II, 261; Emory Holloway and Ralph Adimari (eds.), *New York Dissected* (Rufus Rockwell Wilson, New York, 1936), p. 132. That Whitman continued to admire Bryant can be seen in Horace Traubel, *With Walt Whitman in Camden* (Small, Maynard, New York, 1906–14), I, 56; II, 3, 533; see also Whitman, *Prose Works* (David McKay, Philadelphia, n.d.), pp. 113–14.

Both men had a strong affection for the South and learned a good deal about it through personal travels. Both kept in touch with the South through the newspaper exchanges, Whitman somewhat less systematically and industriously than Bryant. As hostilities between the North and South increased, both men emphasized more and more the distinction within the South itself between the slaveholding power on the one hand and the mass of nonslaveholding citizens on the other.

Whitman was more outspoken than Bryant in his denunciation of the abolitionists. He considered them carping extremists who needlessly strained the bonds of union.[2] As late as 1857 Whitman felt that, in its practice, slavery was "not at all without its redeeming points, and also that there [were] just as great reforms needed" in the North as in the Southern states.[3] He stated unequivocally that outsiders could not interfere in the government of individual states.[4] Whitman recognized the sovereignty of the state and labored not for abolition but for geographical restriction of slavery. He shared Bryant's optimism in feeling that eventually slavery would give way before the power of freedom.[5] Both he and Bryant came into conflict with the Democratic party because of their free-soil ideals—Bryant finally left the party, and Whitman lost his job as editor of the *Brooklyn Daily Eagle* because he would not compromise with the conservative element of the party. Yet Whitman's involvement was not so completely political as was Bryant's. Whitman became disillusioned with party machinery and turned his efforts to nonpolitical writing. His influence in the ante bellum period was insignificant compared to that of Bryant, but for this reason he was in many respects freer than Bryant in the ideological war. He responded with a poet's heart, without the burden of political commitment. His writings which bear upon the current cultural struggle have a timelessness about them that Bryant's

[2] Rogers and Black (eds.), *The Gathering of the Forces,* I, 191–92, 198–99, 226.

[3] Holloway and Schwarz (eds.), *I Sit and Look Out,* p. 87.

[4] See, for example, his article of Apr. 22, 1847, *Brooklyn Daily Eagle,* "New States: Shall They Be Slave or Free?" in Emory Holloway (ed.), *The Uncollected Poetry and Prose of Walt Whitman* (Peter Smith, New York, 1932), I, 160–62. Hereafter cited as *Uncollected Poetry and Prose.*

[5] See particularly his "American Workingmen, Versus Slavery," originally published in the *Brooklyn Daily Eagle,* Sept. 1, 1847, and reprinted in Holloway (ed.), *Uncollected Poetry and Prose,* I, 171–74.

lack. One can find no deeper dismay at the failings of American political and social life than that expressed by Whitman in the "Eighteenth Presidency" and no more penetrating treatment of the problem of American culture than in *Democratic Vistas*.

Whitman's early training in the newspaper offices of Brooklyn and New York is of importance in considering the formation of his attitude toward the South. The proprietor of the *Long Island Patriot*, for whom Whitman worked as a boy of twelve, was a genial Southerner named Samuel E. Clements, who frequently took the boy for rides through the streets of Brooklyn and opened to him his personal library. Clements' printer, William Hartshorne, had a storyteller's enthusiasm for the patriotism of the American Revolutionaries and recounted for the young printer's devil many tales of their devotion to the cause of freedom and independence.[6] As Whitman matured in the environment of the metropolitan newspaper office, his feeling of involvement in the life of America became more pronounced. The recently opened Erie Canal increased his awareness of the new West. He observed the accelerated commercial activity of the nation's largest and most rapidly growing port as it bulged with supplies from the interior. He watched, too, the flow of immigrants from Europe and the excitement of the westward movement as many of them joined in the push for new land in the territories. His perception of the dignity of these people and the awareness of the untold opportunities for them in America's vast interior created in him a profound respect for America's destiny and a determination that the new territories be kept free for these workers. Whitman's horizons were most certainly nationwide. His home was America, for he identified himself with his "New World," accepting its problems as his own.

Whitman's mind was characteristically free from critical selectiveness, and his response to the life of America was all-inclusive. He regarded the South as an integral part of the New World. This great caresser of life resented agitation and was disappointed in the American flair for catchy but caustic epithets that inflamed the passions and strained national unity.[7] Embracing the South as he did the North

[6] See Emory Holloway's introduction to *Uncollected Poetry and Prose*, I, xxviii; see also *ibid.*, II, 246–47.

[7] Rogers and Black (eds.), *The Gathering of the Forces*, I, 191–92, 226.

and the West, his catalogues included the overseer, the slave, the planter, the rich man's son, the old mulatto nurse, the backwoodsmen, and the boatmen of the South. He knew that the chanter must somehow strike up for them no less than for the rest of America.

Whitman's affection for the South had a mysterious quality to it, and scholars have been puzzled by the place of the South in his biography. Certainly, his few weeks in New Orleans have taken on an importance in his biography which is out of proportion to actual chronology. He journeyed to New Orleans in 1848, at a time when his poetic powers were developing fast. Very likely, he associated the South in some way with the awakening of his poetic powers. This association could account, at least in part, for the peculiar tenderness with which he spoke of the South, one time saying, "I call myself a Southerner" and, after the Civil War, predicting that the South would yet outstrip the North.[8]

During the late thirties and early forties, when he was establishing himself as a poet, Whitman wrote a few lines in opposition to slavery.[9] But his scorn was directed primarily at Northern "doughfaces," whom he derisively called "terrific screamers of freedom." In his opinion, the spineless Northern sycophants of slavery, together with the abolitionists, were doing more to balk freedom in America than were the planters themselves. Whitman assumed that the slaveholder was sincere in his theoretical justification of slavery and accorded him the respect owed to sincerity. He spoke of "the dashing Southern lords," accrediting them with being at least "manlier foes" of freedom. He called Virginia the "mother of greatness" and told her to "blush not for being also the mother of slaves." "Hot-headed Carolina," he said, could well curl her lip at the spectacle of Northern screamers and "doughfaces."

Reflecting the ardent patriotism of his early period, Whitman defended the South against foreign attacks. One of his editorials in the New York Aurora, 1842, described a lithographed picture which

[8] Clifton Joseph Furness (ed.), *Walt Whitman's Workshop: A Collection of Unpublished Manuscripts* (Harvard University Press, Cambridge, Mass., 1928), p. 225.

[9] "Dough-Face Song" and "Wounded in the House of Friends," reprinted in *Prose Works* (David McKay, Philadelphia, n.d.), pp. 339, 373.

showed a scene of miserable poverty in the family of an English laborer and, by contrast, a picture of cheerfulness and well-being among the slaves of a Southern plantation. Whitman concluded that the Britishers ought to mind their own problems and not censure the South for slavery. The conditions of some of the workers in England, he added, were far worse than those of the slaves in the South.[10] Five years later, Whitman observed in the *Eagle* that "thousands and millions of *slaves* exist in [England] to whose lot the condition of the South Carolinian negro is paradise."[11]

Many of Whitman's national heroes were Southerners. He had a lifelong admiration for Andrew Jackson, whom he regarded as "a man of the people worth more than hundreds of political leaders." In 1846, Whitman recalled for readers of the *Eagle* that Jackson had toured Brooklyn years earlier in an open barouche, "his snow-white hair brushed stiffly up from his forehead, and his piercing eyes quite glancing through his spectacles." He praised the selflessness, the "unalloyed patriotism" of Jackson and described him as a "massive, yet most sweet and plain character!" Whitman spoke frequently of Washington and Jefferson, acknowledging their solicitude for the people. During the Mexican War he praised Jefferson Davis for efficiency, leadership, and bravery. He admired Henry Clay, a "splendid politician," and praised him as a man of lofty carriage, completeness, suaveness, and sincerity. Writing for the *Aurora* in 1842, Whitman spoke in romantic terms of Clay's lack of caution: "His forte is a bold dashing kind of warfare. He resembles some fire brained political Murat, riding gallantly into the midst of the enemy." Four years later, on behalf of the *Eagle,* he wished Clay well. "For Henry Clay is a noble souled fellow—barring his politics. And even with them, he is the truest, heartiest man the Whigs ever had! 'Luck' to him we say again—in everything but the Presidency!"

Even Calhoun, who was cursed by nearly every Northern writer of

---

[10] Joseph J. Rubin and Charles H. Brown (eds.), *Walt Whitman of the New York Aurora: Editor at Twenty-two* (Bald Eagle Press, State College, Pa., 1950), pp. 126–27. Hereafter cited as *Walt Whitman of the New York Aurora.*

[11] For this and the two following paragraphs, see Rogers and Black (eds.), *The Gathering of the Forces,* I, 42–43, 199, 203–208; II, 178–79, 181, 191–92, 196–97; Holloway (ed.), *Uncollected Poetry and Prose,* I, 173; *Walt Whitman of the New York Aurora,* p. 93.

his day, received deferential treatment from Whitman. Though objecting strenuously to nullification, Whitman praised Calhoun for being "a bold honest *morally* heroic man! . . . We like him, though he runs directly in the teeth of what we think was his first duty as a Senator of the United States."

This pride of southern chivalry is a great man—one of the leading spirits of our national legislature. We have always admired, and do admire Calhoun. We admire his spirit, his vigor, his fiery breath, and his brilliant eloquence. We admire his very faults—his devotion to his native south, and his ardent advocacy of her interests beyond all else.

Whitman's support of Calhoun was consistent with his attitude toward the Mexican War, which he regarded as an opportunity to extend the boundaries of democracy. When his free-soil principles forced him to oppose Calhoun, he still avoided personal strictures, believing the South Carolinian to be sincere and conceding his abilities and powers.

He admitted that the North was not matching the South in leadership. Before the Compromise of 1850, when Webster still enjoyed the approbation of most New England writers, Whitman reviled him, attributing his eloquence to the brandy bottle, his position to the Whig brokers. "Overrated more than any other public man ever prominent in America, his political rank has never been bestowed by the people." It was Whitman's belief that, unlike the Southern statesmen, Webster was not a man of principle. Like Emerson, Whitman placed the secret of Southern political power in dynamic Southern individuals. Throughout all the vindictiveness that marked the latter part of the fifties, he continued to express his respect for the frankness and sincerity of the Southern personality. Writing for the *Brooklyn Times*, 1857, he said: "We like the refreshing openness of the Southern character. You know where to find such men—you see what they are after, and prepare to meet them and answer them." A year later he was quite willing to admit that the Southerner, "whatever may be said about him, has an open, aboveboard, independent way of carrying himself and giving out his opinions, quite different from the deferential, secretive, civilized Northerners." And, he added, this quality explained why "leading Southerners get the Presidency so often, and though they are the few, somehow come to subordinate the many."[12]

The tradition of Southern hospitality received little recognition from the New England writers, though Melville and Bryant paid tribute to it. Whitman, who at the time had never been away from Long Island and Manhattan, dealt with Southern hospitality quite specifically in *Franklin Evans; or the Inebriate,* which he wrote in 1842 as a temperance tract and thought well enough of to publish serially four years later in the *Eagle.*[13] Franklin Evans traveled to one of the Southern counties of Virginia. There he met the planters of the neighborhood, roamed about their plantations and chatted with the slaves, "from whose liveliness and cheerful good-humor, [he] derived no small share of mirth." "The Virginians are proverbially hospitable and friendly to strangers." Quite casually, Evans met a congenial planter named Bourne, who proved to be a generous host and affable companion. A native of France, Bourne came to America in search of quiet, bought a plantation and slaves, and settled down to a life of the country gentleman. Before leaving France, he had been indoctrinated with the ideals and schemes of the Revolution, accepting them completely and "afterward [taking] every occasion to instill them into the mind of his son." But he found no contradiction between these ideals and his way of life as a planter. After observing life in the South, he

became convinced of the fallacy of many of those assertions which are brought against slavery in the south. He beheld, it is true, a large number of men and women in bondage; but he could not shut his eyes to the fact, that they would be far more unhappy, if possessed of freedom. He saw them well taken care of—with shelter and food, and every necessary means of comfort: and he wondered in his own mind, as he remembered what misery he had seen in his travels through various countries of Europe, that the philanthropists of the Old World should wish to interfere with the systems of the New—when the merely nominal oppression

[12] Rogers and Black (eds.), *Gathering of the Forces,* II, 181–82; Holloway and Schwarz (eds.), *I Sit and Look Out,* pp. 88, 95.

[13] See Emory Holloway's introduction to Whitman's *Franklin Evans, or the Inebriate: A Tale of the Times by Walter Whitman* (Random House, New York, 1929). The following quotations from *Franklin Evans* refer to this edition, pp. 168–69, 172–76.

of the latter is overbalanced, so many hundred times, by the stern reality of starvation and despotism in the former.

Evans took up residence with Bourne at the plantation and became thoroughly familiar with its affairs. Bourne was a benevolent patriarch, and life on his plantation was generally happy for slaves and whites alike. But Whitman was not unaware that the nature of the Southern labor system created certain problems in human relations. The difficulty of balancing justice and order on a plantation was implied in his description of a "trial" which Bourne was obliged to hold in his parlor. The irony of the passage is transparent. One of the slave girls, whom Whitman called a "Creole," rejecting the improper advances of the overseer, scuffled with him and knocked him unconscious.

Mr. Bourne was preplexed in no small degree as to the decision he should give. [The slave girl] had evidently had more of his good will, as she had of the justice of the dispute; but the planter feared the danger of making a precedent by letting her off triumphantly. He could not bring his conscience to chastise her, and yet something was necessary in the way of punishment. So, leaning partly to justice and partly to expedience, he put on a severe face, lectured the girl upon the enormity of her offence, added a few words and threats—which the grumbling overseer thought smacked far too much of being done merely for effect—and then signified his desire to hear no more upon the subject.

The overseer, whose pride "had been wounded too deeply for forgiveness," remained something of a sinister figure, lending suspense to the story. It must be noted, however, that the overseer was not a Southerner—he was from the North—and that his wickedness was balanced by the virtues of prudence and industry. Furthermore, Whitman did not ascribe his vices to occupation, but to human nature. Nevertheless, the incident suggested that the problem of controlling such vices was complicated by the plantation system.

The slave was a girl of refinement and training, having once been the favorite slave of a lady who had given her a good education. What is more, her physical charms were awe-inspiring. "She was of that luscious and fascinating appearance often seen in the south, where

a slight tinge of the deep color, large, soft voluptuous eyes, and beauti-
fully cut lips, set off a form of faultless proportions." Indeed, Franklin
Evans could no more withstand her overpowering beauty than could
the overseer. During a drinking bout he declared to his friend Bourne
his infatuation for the dark-eyed "Creole." Thereupon his host freed
her from servitude, assigned Evans and the girl an apartment in his
plantation home, and, handily being a justice of the peace, joined
the two in wedlock. Hospitality could ask nothing more. But the dis-
enchantment soon set in, for Evans began to feel revulsion from the
marriage. When he turned his attentions to a smart, sophisticated
widow from the North—a relative of the overseer—the "Creole"
became the woman spurned, reverted to savage instincts, killed the
widow, and, finally, in prison, ended her own life.

Despite the apparently sympathetic treatment of the Southerner in
this novel, Whitman mingled the evils of alcohol with certain other
evils that seemed to arise from slavery. In addition to the problems
which arose from the relationship of overseer to slave, there were
those that resulted from the combined leisure and means of the
planter—a combination that was especially suspect in America of the
mid-nineteenth century. It was a deadly environment for anyone with
Evans's propensities for indulgence. Moreover, its demoralizing consequences extended to the comely slave girl whose misfortune it was to
attract the attentions of the gentleman of the manor house. Even at
best the situation would be offensive to the sensibilities of the age, for
if the planter was truly kind and obliging, as Bourne was, the deference
paid to morality would still bring the inevitable social concomitants
of miscegenation. After the nightmarish consequences of their drinking bout, Bourne and Evans parted good friends, the host unruffled
in his geniality.

In 1848, Whitman traveled South to join the staff of the *New
Orleans Crescent*. Although the notes he jotted down while en route
were few and rather inconsequential, in reading them now, one feels
a sense of new vistas being opened for this young poet who would
soon strike up for the New World. Crossing the Alleghenies by coach
and sailing down the Ohio and Mississippi, Whitman missed the
heart of the plantation areas. His comparison of Kentucky and Ohio

along the river was similar to the observations of William Leggett, which Whittier had reported just a year earlier in the *Era*.[14] Leggett had pointed to the prosperity of free Ohio and contrasted it to the squalor of Kentucky. Whitman made less of the difference than did Leggett. "At the stopping places on the northern shore," Whitman noted, "there seems to be more thrift and activity. The shore, each way, is much of it barren of interest. . . . Here and there, already, is a comfortable house; and, at intervals, there are tracts of well-tilled land, particularly on the Ohio line." Whitman stopped at Blenner-hassett Island on his trip down the Ohio and was hospitably entertained by a farmer there. In Louisville, he found further proof of Southern hospitality. "Louisville has many noble and hospitable citizens, whose family circles make a 'happy time' for him who gets on visiting terms with them."[15]

Returning North by river boat, Whitman again missed the larger plantation areas of the interior which Bryant had visited, and he has left no statement of his personal reaction to the plantation or to the Southern city. But he had not gone forth from fish-shaped Paumonok with his eyes or his heart closed, as the poetry which he would soon write showed so clearly. Whitman was storing up images for his catalogues, images that had the flavor and content of personal observation. He was gathering ideas, too, for his continued support of free-soil principles. Like Bryant, Whitman had learned that the South was a complex structure and that the canvas on which the abolitionists painted was too narrow and insubstantial for the true South.

Whitman's attitude toward Southern character seems to have been formed primarily from his respect for Southern political leaders. The series of "Sketches," which he wrote for the *Crescent* while he was in New Orleans, presented a motley and mundane group of characters, but they were not, for the most part, necessarily Southern; and he did not discuss the Southern personality in the abstract. Along the "Side-walks and Levees" of New Orleans, there were Peter Funk, Esq., a

---

[14] *The National Era,* I, No. 9 (Mar. 4, 1847).

[15] "Excerpts from a Traveller's Note Book—[No. 3]," published in the *New Orleans Daily Crescent* (Mar. 10, 1848), reprinted by Holloway (ed.), *Uncollected Poetry and Prose,* I, 24, 90, 188.

"by-bidder in a Mock Auction"; Miss Dusky Grisette, "a young 'lady' who took her stand nightly opposite the St. Charles Hotel . . . [sold] her flowers 'by retail,' her charms 'by wholesale' "; John J. Jinglebrain, a sleek gentleman whose precise source of income was never mentioned; Patrick McDray, a stout, jolly fellow, "somewhat pitted by the small pox," who hauled cotton bales; and Timothy Goujon, the oyster vendor.[16] Whitman responded to the color and variety of New Orleans, and his "Sketches" had an earthy quality about them that none of his previous writing had shown.

Whitman sketched some of the frequenters of Southern hotels—the young gentleman in a shiny black coat, with a large diamond breast-pin and a massive gold chain, who played cards and spent his summers at Saratoga; an older gentleman with gold-mounted cane who drank brandy toddies and shared stories with other raconteurs; the neatly-dressed young man who discoursed confidently on the New York theater but who had probably never been north of Baton Rouge, Whitman thought. Of particular interest to Whitman, however, was a gray-haired farmer with "a hickory stick and a hickory soul." This simple countryman subscribed to the *Union* and *National Intelligencer,* for his son was a senator and it thrilled him to see his name in print. "The cultivation of potatoes and turnips . . . the sale of the little field of corn, brought money to send the son to college. Intense energy, application to study, determination and industry" had done the rest, said Whitman. Here was a portrait of success that would have been out of place in the abolitionist gallery of squalid, slothful Southern farmers.

The one cruel man in the gallery of Southerners that Whitman sketched for the *New Orleans Crescent* was a frontier figure, a romanticized "tough guy" named Daggerdraw Bowieknife, Esq. Daggerdraw had moved to a village in Mississippi from one of the Carolinas. "There are parts of Mississippi where a man may graduate into public favor, through the merits of gunpowder, with a rapidity that is astonishing." Daggerdraw had the abundance of swagger and self-confidence that was required for this kind of career. "Never did a man

---

[16] For references in this and in the two following paragraphs, see *ibid.,* I, 193–95, 199–216.

stand more upon a point of honor than he did: he would cavil upon the hundredth part of a hair if he thought a bit of a fight was to be got out of his antagonist: and upon the most trifling misunderstanding in the world, he would attack you in a street fight." When Daggerdraw moved to Texas, where he became a political figure, he was "followed by the ghosts of no less than six hale, hearty, men, at least that were such before his 'bloody-minded' shooting irons made daylight shine through them." Here was Emerson's fighting Southerner presented in caricature. Daggerdraw had a wild, restless eye, and the stamp of a cruel heart "legibly fixed in the very lineaments of [his] face." But pugnacity and daring were united in this man with the Southern tradition of courtesy. He was not bad-looking, said Whitman, and what is more, he was "gentle enough in his dress and address."

The tone of this sketch suggests that Whitman was playing with popular notions. Emerson had noted the chivalric manners and fighting temper of the Southern gentleman, as other serious observers had done. But the mythologizing power of the popular imagination was busy investing a type of Southerner with an exaggerated mingling of elegance and contentiousness, which was an uncritical combination suggesting those other contradictory creations of the popular imagination—the gentle, but sword-bearing knight, the high-principled, though pistol-packing cowboy. Whitman, in Daggerdraw Bowieknife, only partly anticipated this pattern, a pattern which time and the romanticizing force of retrospect established more fully for a later generation. Whitman's own attitude toward this Southern type was primarily critical, matching his implied disparagement of a public with whom this kind of merit could find favor. Whitman did not fail to perceive something "repulsive" in the brow of this colorful figure, and there was also the sobering intrusion of his comment that Daggerdraw would be pursued by the ghosts of the men he had slain.

But Whitman did not reflect sentiment or popular notions about the South in the few vignettes which he sketched for *Leaves of Grass*. Without the myopia of the ranting abolitionist, Whitman's poetic eye had seen the South and his pen re-created in simple strokes:[17]

[17] References in this and in the following paragraph are to *Leaves of Grass*

The camp of the Georgia wagoners just after dark, the supper-fires and
the cooking and eating by whites and negroes,
Thirty or forty great wagons, the mules, cattle, horses, feeding from
troughs,
The shadows, gleams, up under the leaves of the old sycamore trees,
the flames with the black smoke from the pitch-pine curling and rising;
Southern fishermen fishing, the sounds and inlets of North Carolina's
coast, the shad-fishery and the herring-fishery, the large sweep-seines,
the windlasses on shore work'd by horses, the clearing, curing, and
packing houses;
Deep in the forest in piney woods turpentine dropping from the incisions
in the trees, there are the turpentine works,
There are the negroes at work in good health, the ground in all directions
is cover'd with pine straw;
In Tennessee and Kentucky slaves busy in the coalings, at the forge, by
the furnace-blaze, or at the corn-shucking.
In Virginia, the planter's son returning after a long absence, joyfully
welcom'd and kiss'd by the aged mulatto nurse,
On rivers boatmen safely moor'd at nightfall in their boats under shelter
of high banks,
Some of the younger men dance to the sound of the banjo or fiddle,
others sit on the gunwale smoking and talking.

In these skillfully drawn word pictures, Whitman suggests that both
Negro and white "belong," for they seem to be living in accord with
themselves and with nature. The one reference to plantation life—
the planter's son and the aged mulatto nurse—strengthens the idea
of the adhesiveness of Southern society. In "Song of Myself," he spoke
of the planter as "nonchalant and hospitable." There was no social
ferment, no large discontent in Whitman's South. The wilderness
dominated almost to the exclusion of the town life and the ordered
nature of the plantation.

In lower latitudes in warmer air in the Carolinas the large black bus-
sard floating slowly high beyond the tree tops,
Below, the red cedar festoon'd with tylandria, the pines and cypresses
growing out of the white sand that spreads far and flat,

(Small, Maynard Co., Boston, 1900), "Our Old Feuillage," pp. 139–40; "Song
of Myself," pp. 42, 59, 60.

Rude boats descending the big Pedee, climbing plants, parasites with
    color'd flowers and berries enveloping huge trees,
The waving drapery on the live-oak trailing long and low, noiselessly
    waved by the wind

.   .   .   .

Late in the afternoon the mocking-bird, the American mimic, singing
    in the Great Dismal Swamp,
There are the greenish waters, the resinous odor, the plenteous moss,
    the cypress-tree, and the juniper-tree. . . .

Uniting man and nature, Whitman succeeded in communicating
through the suggestive power of names the quality of "placeness."
Over his inventory of things real, however, he cast an illusive but
evocative haze of remoteness and fancy that could have come only
from a heart that loved the South.

    Whitman's affection for the South placed conflicting emotional
demands upon him, for he hated slavery. This poet of freedom, of
"en masse," could only have been offended by the fact of slavery in
America. Whitman had the power to unite himself in sympathy with
the underprivileged and the suffering slave. He did not need to ask
the wounded fugitive how he felt; he himself became the wounded
fugitive. The Fugitive Slave Act of 1850 hurt Whitman to a degree
impossible in a less sensitive person. "My hurts turn livid upon me
as I lean on a cane and observe." The pain and sense of enforced
passivity in these lines suggested Whitman's later poem, penned on
the eve of the Civil War, "I Sit and Look Out." Whereas much of
the poetry dealing with the escaped slave played on the surface, using
vivid terms and overworked sentiments to substitute for imaginative
insight, Whitman, in a few sincere lines, brought the reader and the
fugitive together in sympathy and understanding. This poet could
say: "I was the man. I suffered. I was there." And with him, one feels
personal participation in the sufferings of the nation because of its
slavery.

    Whitman was disappointed with the co-operative attitude of the
North in returning fugitive slaves. "The next worst thing to having
such enormous outrages put into laws and acquiesced in by the people
without any alarm, is to have them practically carried out.—Nations

sink by stages, first one thing and then another."[18] Whitman's response to the Fugitive Slave Law was similar to Dana's, for he acknowledged that certain states had a legal claim to their slaves under the Constitution. It was the particular form of the law that he despised. The law, he thought, was careless of the human rights of the Negro, for it dispensed with many "of the wise checks and delays which we have found it necessary to plant along the road of our judicature." And he feared the consequences of allowing certain privileged persons to decide "at their pleasure . . . which man among us has the right to his liberty and which has not." Whitman pointed to the contradictory moods of the people who could welcome a political refugee from Europe "with banners flying and the sound of trumpets and drums."

But if some poor Cudjo dodges this way, with the marshal of the United States on his track, and the police to aid in the hunt, that's a different affair. An abolitionist or two may bandy words with the court; but in the main we join against the man and the few who stand up for him.

That Whitman penetrated imaginatively the plight of the "poor Cudjo" can be seen in the powerful simplicity of these lines.

The runaway slave came to my house and stopt outside,
I heard his motions crackling the twigs of the woodpile,
Through the swung half-door of the kitchen I saw him limpsy and weak,
And went where he sat on a log and led him in and assured him,
And brought water and fill'd a tub for his own sweated body and bruis'd
    feet
And gave him a room that enter'd from my own, and gave him some
    coarse clean clothes,
And remember perfectly well his revolving eyes and his awkwardness,
And remember putting plasters on the galls of his neck and ankles;
He staid with me a week before he was recuperated and pass'd north,
I had him sit next me at table, my fire-lock lean'd in the corner.

Here is concrete imagery set down without the intrusion of sentiment. Elsewhere in the same poem he spoke of the fugitive as a martyr. Whitman was writing the "Song of Myself"; he was the hounded

---

[18] References in this paragraph are to C. J. Furness (ed.), *Walt Whitman's Workshop*, pp. 77, 80–81, 108; "Song of Myself," *Leaves of Grass*, pp. 36, 59–60.

slave wincing at the bite of the dog, clutching the rails of the fence; he felt the "hell and despair" upon him.

The hatred of slavery did not pose for Whitman as it had for Lowell the problem of whether to give his talent to poetry or to social wrongs. Knowing the South and loving all mankind, he could write poetically of the South without sacrificing his integrity as a social thinker. His respect for the worth of the individual was ever present, and consequently the Southerners whom he pictured in *Leaves of Grass* were invested with a human dignity whether they were free-men or slaves. They had a lifelikeness about them that the Southerners of Lowell, or Longfellow, or Whittier lacked.

The negro holds firmly the reigns of his four horses, the block swags
    underneath on its tied-over chain,
The negro that drives the long dray of the stone-yard, steady and tall
    he stands pois'd on one leg on the string-piece,
His blue shirt exposes his ample neck and breast and loosens over his
    hip-band,
His glance is calm and commanding, he tosses the slouch of his hat
    away from his forehead,
The sun falls on his crispy hair and mustache, falls on the black of his
    polish'd and perfect limbs.

And Whitman imparted the tragic grotesquerie of placing such a human being on the auction block. "How much for the man?" he asked in his "Anti-Slavery Notes."[19]

He is of value
For him the earth lay preparing billions of years without one animal
    or plant
For him the things of the air, the earth and the sea
He is not only himself
He is the father of other men who shall be fathers in their turn

.   .   .   .

In his appointed day he becomes a God

.   .   .   .

He is the one loved—
He is the master.

[19] *Walt Whitman's Workshop*, p. 83.

One of the catalogues of "Song of Myself" contained an eloquent juxtaposition of subjects:

The quadroon girl is sold at the auction-stand, the drunkard nods by the bar-room stove,

. . . .

As the woolly-pates hoe in the sugar field, the overseer views them from his saddle.

The criticism in these lines points primarily to the insensitivity of man and not to the wickedness of the Southerner per se, though of course there is the added implication that the Southern institution of slavery exhibited man's callousness more flagrantly than did other social systems.

Whitman was aware of slavery's threat to the workingman. In September, 1847, he wrote an editorial for the *Eagle* entitled "The American Workman, Versus Slavery." Here, as always, Whitman's intention was not the abolition but the geographical restriction of slavery. His concern was for freedom of labor in the territories. The lands to the west, he felt, must be open to the "millions of mechanics, farmers, and operatives of our country." He saw that the welfare of America depended upon these workingmen, and not upon "the few thousand rich, 'polished', and aristocratic owners of slaves at the south."[20] In the *Eagle* he had continually maintained that the South was not keeping pace with the progress of the North and West, once contrasting its "meagre leanness" to the "stalwart . . . free young West." He was opposing slavery because it jeopardized the future of labor.

We wish not at all to sneer at the south; but leaving out of view the educated and refined gentry, and coming to the "common people" of the whites, everybody knows what a miserable, ignorant, and shiftless set of beings they are. Slavery is a good thing enough, (viewed partially,) to the rich—the one out of thousands; but it is destructive to the dignity and independence of all who work, and to labor itself. . . . It is of no use to reason abstractly on this fact—farther than to say that the price of

[20] For references in this paragraph, see Holloway (ed.), *Uncollected Poetry and Prose,* I, 161, 171–74; Rogers and Black (eds.), *The Gathering of the Forces,* I, 25.

a northern American freeman, poor though he be, will not comfortably stand such degradation.

During the eighteen fifties, however, such events as the Fugitive Slave Law and the Kansas-Nebraska feuds strained his attachment to the South.[21] This strain he relieved in part by insisting more and more upon a distinction between the freedom-loving citizens of the South and the aristocracy of the planter. He had recognized this difference in 1847 while still writing for the *Eagle,* at which time he had objected to Calhoun's suggesting that the Southerner and the slaveholder were one.

He speaks as though the people of the slave-holding states were all slaveholders. This is any thing but true. In every slaveholding State, we believe, except perhaps South Carolina, a majority of the white freemen are nonslaveholders.

However, Whitman agreed with Bryant that the slave power controlled the legislative bodies, that the so-called "voice" of the South was in reality that of the aggressive slaveholders. The common people, he felt, had lost their representation. Like Bryant, he misjudged the loyalties of these nonslaveholding Southerners. Dismayed by this threat to his dream of New World democracy, he jotted down notes for a proposed oration to be addressed "to the young men of America, North, South, East, and West." "How much longer do you intend to submit to the espionage and terrorism of the three hundred and fifty thousand owners of slaves?" And looking to the slaveholders themselves, he asked if there were no men among them who were tired of serving their false ideals, who might therefore respond to the logic of freedom. In Whitman's mind the division in America was not essentially regional but social and economic—the age-old division of class.

He believed, too, that reform must come from within the individual state. The national government could not interfere in the internal affairs of the state; if the individual state was false to its heritage, the nation at large "must wait, no matter how long." "A cornerstone

[21] For references in this and in the following paragraph, see Rogers and Black (eds.), *The Gathering of the Forces,* I, 203; Furness (ed.), *Walt Whitman's Workshop,* pp. 96–98, 102–103, 107–10.

of the organic compacts of America is that a State is perfect mistress of itself. If that is taken away . . . this Union is dissolved." His attention, like Bryant's, was therefore focused on the West, where he believed the future of America lay. He wanted the new West closed not to the Southerner, but to "the aristocracy of the South—the men who work only with other men's hands." Whitman looked to the "American young men, the offspring of these States," to defeat the slave power and its politicians.

Along with Thoreau and Emerson, he understood that the primary evil in America was materialism. "The current that bears us, is one broadly deeply materialistic and infidel. It is the very worst kind of infidelity because it suspects not itself but proceeds complacently onward and abounds."[22] As he searched for "the real America," he began to feel the whole nation was "one vast plantation." He steadily refused to assign the blame for slavery and its complications to the South alone. Contrary to many of his New England contemporaries, he had never attacked the South for the real or imagined abuses of slavery. Instead he pointed to the contradiction between slaveholding and the expressed theories of democracy, to the conflict between slave labor and free labor, and to the inevitable consequences of opening the territories to slavery. In 1856, as in 1842, he attacked those who held the extreme views toward slavery. But his attention was necessarily directed more and more toward the aggressive proslavery forces of the South and their Northern supporters: the "melodramatic blusterers" and "braggarts" of the South, and "the swarms of dough-faces, office-vermin, and kept-editors" of the North. These men were "ignorant of principles and the true glory of a man."

America was moving down the path to war, and Whitman feared the horror and brutalities it would bring. Prophetically, during the middle fifties, he saw "in dim outline" that "if the hot rebellious rise we call the south" refused to recognize the inevitable drift of America toward broader freedoms, and "dare[d] to lift the knife to plunge it at the breast" of Union, on her head would be "the red blood of civil war." And he saw in his mind's eye the "prisoners in war clothes, with wretched blankets . . . faint and sick in hospitals." Prophetically, too,

[22] For references in this and the following paragraph, see Furness (ed.), *Walt Whitman's Workshop*, pp. 74–75, 81–83, 92–95, 226.

he called for a leader, a heroic, tanned, bearded-faced American worker from the West who would "walk into the Presidency, dressed in a clean suit of working attire" and save the country from the professional politicians. During the war, Whitman remained as close to the center of things as was permitted a noncombatant. In May of 1863, after seeing a procession of prisoners, he said: "We talk brave and get excited and indignant over the 'rebels' and drink perdition to them—but I realized how all anger sinks into nothing in sight of these young men." This caresser of life, whose ambition it was to absorb as much of the nation's life as was possible for one heart, wrote the most poignant lyrics of the battle front and, at the death of Lincoln, sang the nation's greatest dirge.

· 11 ·

Conclusion

T HE ROMANTIC idealism which is part of the American character has often caused us to deny instinctively to ourselves as a nation the open-eyed, realistic acceptance of limitations which we willingly accept for ourselves as individuals. This paradox has been of value to us in countless ways; yet it repeatedly involves us in grave difficulties, both at home and abroad. At every period in America's history we had need for disinterested, measured evaluations of ourselves. Our most conspicuous failure in self-assessment occurred one hundred years ago. It was a significant part of the greatest crisis this nation has ever known. Today we are manifesting a concern for sober scrutiny, as an expression of a newly achieved maturity, to understand ourselves more thoroughly and more honestly than ever before. In this effort our attention steadily and earnestly returns to the Civil War and its causes. We are impressed by its decisive place in our history and moved by the thought that only about three generations ago our people suffered the heartbreak of fratricidal war.

Looking back to the writers of that generation—those who made up the "American Renaissance"—one is curious about their reaction to, their part in, the crucial events of their day. The image of the South assembled from the numerous and often scattered comments of Whittier, Lowell, Longfellow, Emerson, and Thoreau is essentially the same image of evil which was portrayed by Garrison and Phillips in their fight against slavery. These men of letters, for the most part, did not know the South. Having no conception of the fullness and variety of Southern culture, their attitudes toward the South were in reality attitudes toward slavery. Their emotional and imaginative attitudes arose from the awesome gap between their ideas of what life ought to be and their view of life in the South as colored by abolitionism. Since benevolent slavery seemed to these writers a contradiction in terms, their eyes could see only the abuses of slavery. Instances of cruelty, privation, and wickedness were equated with slavery, and the totality of these extreme instances in turn was, for them, the South.

The powerful literary potentials of America's tragic experience were left unrealized in the writings of these men. Subordinating the poets to the agitators, they dissipated much of their poetic powers. Their failure in sympathy was paradoxical, indeed, in the light of their social consciousness and their expressed concern for slavery. They caricatured both slaveholder and slave, without really knowing either. The Southerner was a whip-bearing villain, the Negro an earth-bound angel. These writers lacked the magic of the seemingly contradictory mixture of involvement and detachment which enabled the Greek mind, for example, to glean from equally tragic situations profound and powerful utterances on man in an inhospitable world. It is only now in the twentieth century that the South is finding its rightful place in American literature. Today, at long last, in such books as William Faulkner's *Light in August,* the penetrating, clarifying force of literary vision illuminates the human factors which were always present in the Southern tragedy and have ultimate meaning for man.

As for New York writers before the Civil War, their closeness to the South tended to discourage them from forming an image of a supposedly homogeneous culture which might otherwise have been for them equivalent to the South. Moreover, they had the benefit of a metropolitan atmosphere which undoubtedly helped them to see America's cultural conflict from a national, rather than a regional, point of view. Bryant acquired an extensive knowledge of the South not only from travel and association with Southern friends but also from years of reading the exchanges of Southern papers. His opposition to the South, like that of Walt Whitman, involved the application of the natural-rights philosophy of freedom as a standard of judgment and an assertion of the preference of free labor to slave labor. His firm and continued avowal of state-rights determined, however, that his efforts would be directed not to abolition but to a geographical restriction of slavery. Bryant kept his work as poet and his work as journalist distinct; in the one he refused to treat of the South, in the other he presented a remarkably fair and thorough picture.

Melville and Whitman were profoundly involved in the problem of slavery. They were not able to separate the artist from the propagandist. But their dismay was profound, and it pervaded their thoughts as artists. Melville distrusted reformers; Whitman disliked agitation and hated the American flair for invective. Melville was able to caricature the abolitionist's picture of the South and at the same time to satirize the Southern apologist. His perception of evil, like Hawthorne's in its somberness, enabled him to make the most penetrating evaluation of Southern culture. His derision reflected his grim realization of mankind's total incapacities and servitudes of which, he knew, slavery was but one expression. Whitman saw the South as an integral part of the New World, and his catalogues knew no regional boundaries. But his was probably the most painful conflict of all, for he had from first to last a love for the South and also a distressing awareness of the slave's suffering. It is significant that of all the literary men it was he who was drawn to the center of the struggle by the depth of his sympathy.

From the writings of these three men, a picture of the ante bellum South emerges: in Bryant, comprehensively, with due regard for complexity and difference within the South itself; in Melville, evaluatively; and in Whitman, sympathetically. Yet it is clear that although the New York writers understood the problem of the South more accurately and more deeply than did their contemporaries in New England, nevertheless, as literary men, they talked of it less. There can be little doubt that the image projected by the New England group was more vivid, less complex, and therefore more acceptable to the popular mind. It has endured through the years with surprising tenacity. One can scarcely measure the influence of this image upon successive generations of Northerners in their view of the ante bellum South.

Index

Putnam's Magazine: critical independence of, 122–123; commented on Southern folk tunes and minstrel-singing, 123; on antislavery and proslavery novels, 123; review of *The Life and Bondage of Frederick Douglass*, 124; praised Olmsted's studies of South, 124; judged abolition literature by literary standards, 124; on Whittier and Lowell, 125; reviewed Simms, 125, 126; reviewed Baldwin, 126; portraits of planters, 127, 128; serialized story of Virginia society, 127, 128; "A Slave's Story," 129; advocated geographical restriction of slavery, 130; published "Benito Cereno," 140

Quakers and Quakerism: 18–20, 34; *see also* Society of Friends

Randolph, John: 95, 138
Redburn (Melville): 132, 137
Republican Party: 4, 158, 162
Richmond, Virginia: in Kennedy's *Swallow Barn*, 90; its Negroes described by Paulding, 112, 114, 115; pictured by Bryant, 150, 153; mentioned, 58, 127
Roger, N. P.: abolitionist, 63
Roman Republic: South compared to, 26
Rourke, Constance: 9

"Sabbath Scene, A" (Whittier): 25, 125
St. Augustine, Florida: 153
St. John's College, Annapolis, Maryland: 106
St. Louis, Missouri: visited by Emerson, 52; described in Irving's *Astoria*, 118, 119; in *The Confidence-Man*, 145; mentioned, 44, 140
Savannah, Georgia: 149, 150
Scarlet Letter, The (Hawthorne): 101
Scudder, Horace E.: *James Russell Lowell, a Biography*, 39n

Secession: 4, 82, 83, 162
Sectionalism: spirit of, strengthened by Garrison and Phillips: 17
Sedgwick, William Ellery: *Herman Melville: The Tragedy of Mind*, 147
Seward, William Henry: 12, 163
Shadrach: Boston Negro, 76
Shenandoah Valley: 120, 121
Shubrick, William Branford: Southern friend of Cooper, 118
Simms, William Gilmore: reviewed by *New England Magazine*, 91; reviewed by *North American Review*, 100, 101; reviewed by *Putnam's Magazine*, 125, 126; and Bryant, 149–152 *passim*
Sims, fugitive slave: Thoreau on, 66; Longfellow's reaction to return to slavery of, 74; Dana's defense of, 76
Slaveholder: number of, viii; attacked by Garrison, 7–17 *passim*; described by Whittier, 20, 21, 34; Lowell's notion of, 45, 46; Emerson on, 51, 52, 57, 58; attacked by Helper, 80–82; Thoreau on, 70; Dana's view of, 76, 77; as presented in *North American Review*, 90, 91, 96–100 *passim*; in *New England Magazine*, 91; Paulding on, 112, 113; portrayed in *Putnam's Magazine*, 127, 128; Bryant on, 151, 152, 158, 159; Whitman on, 167, 176, 180, 181
Slavery: its beginnings in America, ix; viewed as sin in New England, 4, 8, 9; Garrison on, 5–10 *passim*; Phillips on, 11–17 *passim*; Whittier on essence of, 20; Whittier on slavery as sin, 19–22 *passim*; *The Narrative of James Williams*, 23; Whittier's pictures of its effects on children, 28; Lowell's opposition to, 38, 39, 50; Lowell praised Olmsted's discussion of, 48, 49; Emerson's "Vision of Slavery," 51, 52; described by Emerson, 54, 55, 57; Thoreau on, 63; Alcott perceives complexity of, 65; viewed by Thoreau as moral question, 69, 70; Long-